£15.95
£12.00
CW01623453

MAYO

DISRAELI'S VICEROY

George Pottinger

MICHAEL RUSSELL

In Memory of Don

© George Pottinger 1990

First published in Great Britain 1990
by Michael Russell (Publishing) Ltd,
The Chantry, Wilton, Salisbury, Wiltshire
Typeset at The Spartan Press Limited,
Lymington, Hampshire
Printed and bound in Great Britain
by Biddles Ltd, Guildford and King's Lynn

All rights reserved
ISBN 0 85955 164 4

Contents

	Map	8
	Author's Note	9
1	Evangelical Elegance	11
2	At the Court of the Czar	18
3	Minister and Master	27
4	En Voyage	42
5	Brave Men before Agamemnon	52
6	His Excellency	65
7	The Public Good	80
8	Two Blades of Grass	90
9	'Heaven's Light Our Guide'	101
10	Sepoys and Sabres	112
11	Petty Wars and Princes	123
12	The Afghan Amir	135
13	Masterly Activity	146
14	The Fiscal Can of Worms	158
15	A Bubble in the Native Mind	170
16	The Convict Settlement	181
	Epilogue	190
	Notes	200
	Bibliography	212
	Index	217

The Order of the Day being read for taking into consideration Her Majesty's most Gracious Message of Friday last, respecting an Annuity to the Countess of Mayo;

The said Message was read by the Clerk. After short Debate, It was moved by The Lord Sundridge, That 'an humble Address be presented to Her Majesty, to return Her Majesty the Thanks of this House for Her most Gracious Message, informing this House, "That Her Majesty taking into consideration the distinguished services performed by the late Richard Southwell Earl of Mayo, Her Majesty's Viceroy and Governor-General of India, and the loss of his life in Her service, and in the discharge of public duty, and being desirous, in recognition of such services and in view of the circumstances of his death, to confer some signal mark of Her favour upon his widow, Blanche Julia Countess of Mayo, recommends it to the House of Lords to concur in enabling Her Majesty to make provision for securing to the Countess of Mayo a pension of one thousand pounds per annum for the term of her natural life;" and to assure Her Majesty that this House will cheerfully concur in such measures as may be necessary for securing to Blanche Julia Countess of Mayo a pension of one thousand pounds per annum for the term of her natural life.'

The same was agreed to, nemine dissentiente.

Ordered, That the said Address be presented to Her Majesty by the Lord with White Staves.

HOUSE OF LORDS PROCEEDINGS
22 July 1872

'The People of India, Proud and Indignant, raise this statue.'

Inscription on the statue of the Earl of Mayo,
in the Maidan, Calcutta (since removed).

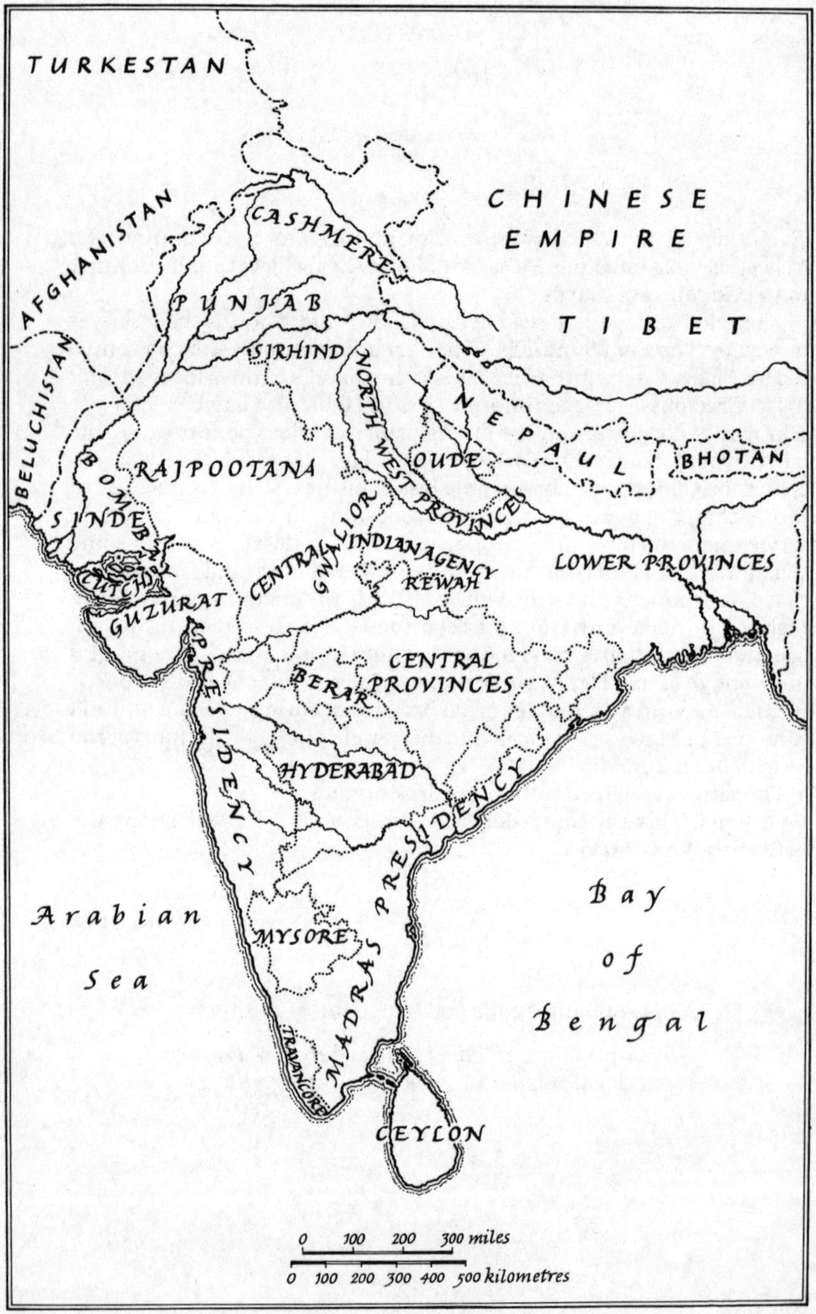

TURKESTAN
AFGHANISTAN
CASHMERE
CHINESE EMPIRE
TIBET
PUNJAB
SIRHIND
BELUCHISTAN
NORTH WEST PROVINCES
NEPAUL
OUDE
BHOTAN
RAJPOOTANA
BOMBAY
SINDE
CUTCH
GUZURAT
CENTRAL INDIAN AGENCY
GWALIOR
REWAH
LOWER PROVINCES
CENTRAL PROVINCES
BERAR
PRESIDENCY
HYDERABAD
MADRAS PRESIDENCY
MYSORE
TRAVANCORE
CEYLON
Arabian Sea
Bay of Bengal
0 100 200 300 miles
0 100 200 300 400 500 kilometres

Author's Note

A minor Irish peer, whose appointment as Viceroy and Governor-General of India was greeted with derision and who was assassinated before he had finished his term of office, may at first glance seem an unlikely subject for a new biography.

Sir William Hunter brought out a *Life of the Earl of Mayo* in 1875, three years after his murder. The worthy Hunter, however, is best known for his statistical survey and his compilation of the *Imperial Gazetteer of India*, and his 'Life' falls into the category described by Lytton Strachey as 'the two fat volumes with which it is our custom to commemorate the dead ... as familiar as the cortège of the undertaker'. An abbreviated version of Hunter's work is included in the Rulers of India series, but since then there has been no separate assessment of Mayo, though he appears fitfully in histories of the period. More recently, Mark Bence-Jones in *The Viceroys of India* writes about him briefly, but with enthusiasm, and concludes that 'there never *could* be another Viceroy like Mayo'. Therein lies the invitation to examine the career of an Irish Paddy, as he often called himself, who in a short time carved out his place in the roll of the great Governors-General – Hastings, Dalhousie, and, later, Curzon.

It is a story full of surprises. Brought up on a modest country estate, as a young man Mayo wrote a shrewd account of his experiences at the Court of the Czar at St Petersburg, before he became a Member of Parliament and eventually Chief Secretary for Ireland – for two short periods and latterly during the Fenian rebellion. He was also a popular Master of the Kildare Hunt, and this provides a glimpse of the gusto and panache which were his hallmark.

But why did Disraeli recommend him to Queen Victoria for the most powerful of all proconsular posts? How did he comport himself as Viceroy, presiding over his own Cabinet, winning the confidence of the native princes, and attacking the problems that constantly arose with Afghanistan and the other states along the frontiers of Hindustan? How did he play the Great Game with Russia? How are the mysterious circumstances of his murder to be explained?

In attempting to answer these questions, to assess the gifts that Mayo brought to Government House and to evaluate his highly individual domestic and foreign policy, full use has been made of official documents, and, in particular, his personal papers. The core of this book is derived from the almost daily letters he exchanged with the Duke of Argyll, Secretary of State for India. Not that they contradict the Minutes of the Governor-General in Council or the formal Despatches; they afford a gloss, an indication of Mayo's inner thoughts, doubts, and ambitions. As the image emerges, it becomes clear that he exemplifies more than modest merit struggling with the hazards to which he was exposed – in Smollett's phrase 'from his own want of experience, as well as from the selfishness, envy, malice and base indifference of mankind'. He had a genuine imperial vision, recognising that British rule could be justified only if it made the whole country more prosperous, and could be secured only by a temperate but positive foreign policy.

To set Mayo in perspective in the long history of the Raj, his merits and demerits are compared with those of his immediate predecessor, Lawrence, and his successor, Northbrook, and tested against the comments of his principal civilian and military advisers – those formidable figures the Stracheys, Richard Temple, Henry Durand, William Mansfield, and Napier of Magdala, whose private papers and memoirs make up a rich quarry.

Many have helped me, including the staff of the Cambridge University Library which houses the bulk of the Mayo papers; Sir Oliver Millar, the Surveyor of The Queen's Pictures; Dr R.J. Bingle and his colleagues at the India Office Library; the staff of the National Portrait Gallery, the National Library of Ireland, the National Gallery of Ireland, and the Public Record Office, Northern Ireland. To them, and to individuals too numerous to mention, it is a pleasure to offer my grateful thanks.

I

Evangelical Elegance

On 21 February 1822 there was born in Dublin to Robert and Anne Charlotte Bourke a son, Richard Southwell. The first of the latest generation of Bourkes, young Richard came from a lineage as long as can be found in the blood-stained quartering of Irish history and latterly respectable.

Bourke, Burke, or Burgh are all variations of de Burgh, and the de Burghs were a very old family indeed. Some would trace their pedigree back to Charlemagne, but it will suffice to say that de Burgh was a Norman name, and that one of the tribe who accompanied his half-brother William the Conqueror to Hastings scooped up the earldom of Cornwall as a reward. His son, in the Christian manner of the times, had his eyes put out for an ineffective rebellion. One grandson, Hubert de Burgh, appears in Shakespeare's *King John* where he shrinks from blinding the young Prince Arthur. Another grandson William Fitzadelm was with more certainty despatched to Ireland by Henry II to receive the homage of the native kings of Connaught and Meath. In 1175 he published the Bull confirming the English monarch as ruler of Ireland, and two years later he succeeded Strongbow as governor of the island.

In the next two hundred years, under the nominal but distant authority of the crown, the expatriate English nobles applied themselves zealously to the business of pillage, rapine, and the carving out of large estates. Fitzadelm's son Richard, by now the 'Great Lord of Connaught' exemplifies the next stage. He married a descendant of Red-hand, the old Connaught king, and settled down to become more Irish than the indigenous population. As Hallam put it, the English intermarried with the Irish, adopted their dress, language, and customs, and in effect became 'chieftains rather than peers'.[1]

For the next two centuries the Bourkes, or de Burghs, lived and died with customary savagery; in addition to the normal forms of extinction in battle, two were hanged, one suffered from a bout of fratricide, and one was pressed to death. Gradually, however, two distinct branches emerged with the sons of Sir William Burke who died in 1324, the more tenacious branch becoming Earls of Clanricarde, and the other producing the eventually extinct Viscounts of Mayo. The most colourful figure of the period is undoubtedly Graine-ni-Mhaile (Granny O'Malley), celebrated in legend as a pirate queen who spoke impertinently on equal terms with the English Queen Elizabeth. More credibly, she was a friend of Sir Philip Sidney, whose widow later married a Clanricarde Burke. The Clanricardes were royalist under the Stuart kings, suffering exile on occasion, and persevering with support for James II. The ninth Earl, captured at the Battle of Aughrim, was attainted for treason and outlawed, but later exculpated. Meanwhile even if not spectacularly, the Mayo branch prospered. In 1689 John Bourke of Monycrower prudently transferred his allegiance to the Protestant religion, and so escaped the embargo on Catholics holding land. The Bourkes began to take their place as substantial country gentlemen who looked after their estates, expanding them when opportunity offered, and not neglecting to make good marriages.

The trend is continued by a later John Bourke of Kill and Monycrower, who in 1725 married the heiress of Joseph Deane, the influential Lord Chief Baron of Exchequer in Ireland. The patent as Earl of Mayo crowned the ambitious John's career. Making the most of his connections, he served as a Member of Parliament, was made a member of the Irish Privy Council, and took the name of his constituency when he was created Baron Naas in 1776. Promotion to Viscount Mayo of Monycrower followed in 1781, and the earldom four years later. Joseph Bourke, the third Earl of Mayo, was appointed Protestant Bishop of Tuam (in the fifteenth century an ancestor John Burke had held the same see as a Roman Catholic). Other clerics – the Bishop of Waterford and the Dean of Ossory – now begin to appear in the family roll.

The fourth Earl of Mayo, the future Viceroy's great-uncle, was a genial but undistinguished Irishman whose most memorable activity was to make an artificial lake by flooding ten acres of his estate at Palmerstown. His principal public office was as

Colonel of the Kildare Militia, and he would now be forgotten but for the charming lines written by his relation by marriage William Mackworth Praed to accompany his portrait. They suggest an agreeable perverseness.

> A courtier of the nobler sort,
> A Christian of the purer school;
> Tory, when Whigs are great at Court,
> And Protestant when Papists rule.
>
> Prompt to support the Monarch's crown,
> As prompt to dry the poor man's tears;
> Yet fearing not the Premier's frown,
> And seeking not the rabble's cheers.
>
> Still ready – favoured or disgraced –
> To do the right, to speak the true.
> The Artist who these features traced
> A better Subject never knew.

The ancestral picture can be quickly completed. The fourth Earl's second son, Richard Bourke, Bishop of Waterford and Lismore, married Mary, the daughter of the Archbishop of Dublin. In 1820, their eldest son Robert, the future fifth Earl, married Anne Charlotte Jocelyn, a granddaughter of the Earl of Roden, and the good Bishop then took himself to his official residence at Waterford, leaving his own house at Hayes to his son and daughter-in-law. There, two years later, the Richard who was to become Viceroy of India was born.

Richard derived no arrogance from ancestors stretching back to the Norman Conquest, and he never boasted of a noble lineage. But he thought of himself as a genuine Irishman, albeit originating across the water. 'I come of a family that cast in their lot with the Irish people,' he told the House of Commons, and his Parliamentary reputation was rooted in his concern for Irish affairs. Years later, when he made a pious visit to the forlorn plain of Chilianwalla, he had an Irish cross erected to commemorate those who had fallen in battle with the Sikhs, and the same cruciform marked the grave in Johnstown where, by his own wish, he was buried.

Hayes, where Richard was brought up, was an unpretentious estate in Meath, twenty miles from Dublin and nine miles inland from Drogheda, with a peacefully rural setting. Hayes looked across the valley of the Boyne from Dean Hill, from whose summit twelve counties could be seen. The mountains of Down to the north and Wicklow to the south marked the distant horizons, and nearby features, the ancient Slane Abbey and Tara Hill, were redolent of the country's history. The house itself was a modest building, as befitted the son of a second son, but the grounds, beech walks and walled garden provided an atmosphere of undisturbed domestic peace.

At a distance of a century and a half the impression remains of a self-contained, self-reliant family, almost completely insulated from extraneous events, with few intrusions from the outer world except for the father's attendance at assizes. The elder Bourke could not afford to send his large brood of eight children away for schooling, and a succession of governesses and tutors undertook their early education. Bourke, who had spent two years at Oxford, took a keen interest in his children's progress and joined them in their eager activities, cricket, riding, and all the house-bound entertainments which Georgian and Victorian families had to devise for themselves.

Either the rudimentary instruction which the Bourkes received was sounder than might be supposed, or the genetic strain was strong, for five of Richard's younger brothers made their way with rewarding careers. John Jocelyn served in the Crimea and the Indian Mutiny, and became Deputy Adjutant General. Robert, a barrister who married the daughter of the Marquess of Dalhousie, was a Member of Parliament and Under-Secretary of State at the Foreign Office. George Winfield entered holy orders and married the daughter of the Archbishop of Canterbury. Charles Fowler was Richard's private secretary in his last spell as Chief Secretary for Ireland, and became Inspector-General of Prisons in Ireland. Edward Roden, a soldier, was Richard's Military Secretary while he was Viceroy and later achieved high office in the Madras Presidency.

Richard developed an impressive physique; he was an extrovert, ebullient, and as the eldest of a clutch of brothers tended to take the lead in their outdoor pursuits. His learning was not profound, and like most boys not subject to school discipline he was inclined to study the matters which he found most interesting, rather than follow a conventional curriculum. He had no great creative ability, and there is no record of his confessing to inflated ambitions. It was his mother who quickened his sensibility. Mrs Bourke from all accounts was a saintly person, devoting herself to her family and the welfare of those on the estate and of her less fortunate neighbours, even running her own dispensary for the poor. From her must have come his sense of obligation to others and his extraordinary conscientiousness in the performance of routine tasks. He was fortunate in his parents.

A feature of the Bourke household was its strong evangelical connection. Richard's forbears had been bishops, his grandmother was an Archbishop's daughter, and his mother's kinsman the Earl of Roden was a prominent philanthropist; with such a provenance it was predictable that he himself acquired something of a religious outlook. It would be a mistake to attach too much importance to this, but in an age when most of the leading officials and generals whom he subsequently met in India believed that God was the senior officer in the British Army, there is no reason to question his strong personal faith. At Hayes, as he listened to his father's Sunday evening lectures to his tenants and the discussions with the evangelical leaders who frequented the house, he learned that religion was not merely a question of accepting an establishment doctrine, or memorising the catechism. In Ireland, as later in India, it was the root of the matter.

In 1838 the Bourke finances were sufficient for the family to embark on an extensive European tour, most likely at the prompting of Mrs Bourke, anxious that her children should see something of the world outside the rustic confines of Meath. In the autumn of that year all the Bourkes, from grandmother Jocelyn to Edward, then only three years old, moved to Paris and rented a house in the Champs Elysées. It was perhaps not as amusing as Richard had hoped, with a French teacher and a dancing-master insisting on a rigorous programme, and it apparently took some time for the Bourkes to acquire more civilised habits, since there was an extensive bill for 'barrack damages' when the family left for Switzerland.

Geneva was the next base, and expeditions to Chamonix, a tour of the Bernese Oberland and mountaineering were more acceptable to Richard and his brothers than the niceties of French irregular verbs. In the autumn the family took up residence in Florence, and there were routine pilgrimages to wonder at Brunelleschi's great Duomo, admire Ghiberti's gates, and inspect Giotto's frescoes. Mrs Bourke was also active in securing invitations to the best Italian houses, and there was plenty of entertainment from the English colony. There Richard was able to put to use the teaching of his dancing-master. An earlier escapade at a bal masqué in Paris had caused some parental concern, but Richard, then as later, conducted himself with propriety. It has to be admitted that throughout his career he was somewhat deficient in vice, perhaps lacking a worldly mentor, but it was a more polished young squire who returned to Hayes in May 1840.

No one brought up on an Irish country estate could be long out of the saddle, and Richard, now eighteen, set up his own hunter from the small allowance which his father gave him. He was a big, and eventually a heavy, man, but from the start a good and fearless rider. Later he was to earn the respect of Irish sportsmen for his exploits with the Kildare Hunt, and much of his instant popularity when he arrived in India arose from the recognition that he enjoyed nothing more than a 'gallop at a pig'. He wrote home that it was 'the only sport in this country that is congenial to the feelings of an old fox hunter'.[2]

In December 1840 he was commissioned as a captain in the Kildare Militia. This was more a social appointment than a military one – his great-uncle was the commanding officer, and the duties were not onerous. Later, however, his lack of army experience did not deter him from setting about such formidable warriors as Sir William Mansfield, Sir Henry Durand, and Lord Napier, when he turned a very critical eye on the shortcomings of the military establishment in India.

In 1841 he enrolled at Trinity College, Dublin. This was the conventional step for someone who did not aspire to Oxford, and he did not take the requirements of academic discipline – such as they were – very seriously. He did not reside in college, and with the help of a sympathetic tutor he eventually took an unexceptionable degree. But by then there was a more important influence on his life.

While still an undergraduate, Richard had begun to spend much of his time at Palmerstown, his great-uncle's property. Palmerstown was on a grander scale than Hayes. The estate amounted to some five hundred acres, with a rambling old house whose irregular extensions bore witness to a succession of occupants. It was elegantly furnished, and the Earl's eclectic taste could be seen in the Reynoldses and other paintings that lined the walls. But for Richard it had other attractions. The Countess of Mayo was not only the châtelaine; she was also extremely active socially, running her own salon. Unattached young men, especially young men as personable and well-behaved as Richard, were always welcome at such gatherings, and she took her great-nephew under her personal protection. Her patronage extended beyond Palmerstown, for she and her twin sister, who had married a West Indian fortune, had the entrée to fashionable London society, particularly to the Conservative houses. Lady Mayo was also a lady-in-waiting at Court, and with her sponsorship Richard was not short of invitations.

Another kinswoman, Lady de Clifford, a very political hostess and a celebrated whist player, made it known that she was pleased to see him at her assemblies at Carlton Terrace. Lady Jersey's house in Berkeley Square, the scene of many historic entertainments, was open to him, and young Bourke was soon earning a reputation as something of a blade. In a contemporary letter he appears as a 'very young man, with a fine bearing; one of the best waltzers in town, and a great deal made of'.[3] He was easy-going, popular, and if not outstanding for any particular gift, charming to everyone. Although he mixed in Conservative circles, and was in time to become a Conservative Minister, at this stage one would look in vain for evidence that he had any preoccupation with politics. It would have been no surprise if he had been recruited as an ADC, or appointed as personal assistant to a Colonial Governor or one of Her Majesty's Ambassadors. Instead, in May 1845 he set off for Russia.

2

At the Court of the Czar

'Another Tourist throws himself on the kindness of the already way-worn public. Another Author seeks to gain for himself and his adventures a small share of the attention that the world has so often kindly bestowed on literary wanderers.'[1] With such seemly diffidence Richard Bourke prefaced the account of his Russian travels, entitled *St Petersburg and Moscow: A Visit to the Court of the Czar*. The book, which was published in 1846, the year after his return, had some success, partly because he was an unexpected author and partly from the nature of its subject. As he claimed in his conclusion, a treatise on Russia which was written in a dispassionate manner was at least a novelty, since contemporary writers had 'given utterance to the deepest flattery, or to the most unmeasured abuse'.[2]

It was the abuse of the Czar's government in a remarkable book by the Marquis de Custine which sharpened Bourke's interest in undertaking the journey to Muscovy. *La Russie en 1839*, first published in Paris in 1843, was twice reprinted in the next three years, while translations appeared in England and other European countries at the same time. Astolphe de Custine was born a French aristocrat in 1790, and his father and grandfather were both guillotined during the Reign of Terror. In 1839 Custine, already an experienced traveller with a reputation as a writer and a monarchist, went to Russia hoping to find 'arguments against representative government', but came back 'a partisan of constitutions'. As General Bedell Smith has pointed out, he was, in a reverse sense, the first of the fellow travellers to make public confession of his disillusionment.[3]

Custine is witty and perceptive, but he overeggs the pudding and his diatribe against the evils of Russian despotism is too unrelieved. Bourke admitted that Custine's book had caused a great sensation and he conceded that he would go down to posterity as a clever and observant traveller. But in his strictures on the Czar's court, Custine had gone too far; he had breached the laws of hospitality; he was biased and often inaccurate. Bourke dismisses Custine with a flourish: 'He avows himself to be a radical in Russia, and a faded aristocrat in France; an unfortunate line in hermaphrodite politics, as absurd as it is impossible, as affected as it is Quixotic.'[4]

St Petersburg and Moscow, however, is not in the same class as the Frenchman's work with its 'sparkling malice'. William Hunter, in his biography of the future Earl of Mayo, which otherwise recognises few faults in his subject, is severe on Bourke's journal, saying that judged by the three essentials of simple words, clear structure and well-ordered ideas, it falls short in many ways. (Perhaps Hunter felt that this was the one field where his hero did not outshine him.) It is very much a young man's book, and refreshingly free from self-importance; yet there are moments when he does not know when to stop, being carried away on wings of high-flown Victorian rhetoric. His first sight of Moscow, for example, moves him to a very purplish passage, beginning 'Reft from the conquering Tartars, the cross was on her towers first firmly planted above the humbled crescent . . .' Fortunately there is not too much of this, and a few pages later he is likening the new palace being built within the Kremlin to a Manchester cotton factory, adding 'How the Russian committee of taste could have induced themselves to set up an eye-sore of such gigantic proportions on so holy a spot, can only be conceived by those who have mused on the edifices of Trafalgar Square'.[5]

If Bourke had relied on his architectural appreciation, his journal would have been quickly consigned to oblivion. Much more interesting are the style of his approach and his reactions to Russian society. The style is a very personal one. There is no suggestion of his enlisting help in its compilation, and this unassisted work has a place of its own among Bourke's writings. When looking at his later speeches in Parliament, or official despatches, minutes, or correspondence from India, it is never certain how much the presentation, the content, or the original idea came from a loyal dragoman and how much was contributed by Bourke himself as Chief Secretary for Ireland or Viceroy. Even today, senior civil servants will confess that with only a little practice they can catch the Minister's favourite nuances and submit a draft which he will readily approve – and which will be accepted elsewhere as his own. But *St Petersburg and Moscow* was Bourke's, penned by himself and no one else. The remarkable thing is that though his account is more sketchy than Custine's, and does not delve as deeply into its subject, and though his language is more temperate, except in one important respect he comes to much the same conclusions.

Bourke soon detected an 'absence of animation, and of all appearance of business' in those walking the streets of St Petersburg, which he contrasted with the 'busy hive of London, where occupation is imprinted on the features and movements of every person one meets'.[6] He noted how the press was under police surveillance, with a demi-official Gazette which contained 'most of the ingredients of a journal, except news – a commodity exceedingly scarce in Russia'.[7] Class distinctions, the gulf between peer and peasant, were, he thought, wider than in any other country except, he ruefully admitted, in Ireland. This he attributed to the lack of a middle class, 'that cement of the social state, those cramping irons of the constitutional edifice'. Custine makes the identical point: 'Where can one find that middle class which forms the might of States and without which a people is only a herd led by a few skilfully trained bloodhounds?'[8]

There are occasional waspish touches. Commenting that the priests in Moscow churches did a good trade selling wax candles to pilgrims, who left them lit before the picture of their favourite saint, Bourke noticed that the saint did not always profit from their light, since the priestly custodians, 'justly arguing that one or two candles are sufficient for the few wants of his or her holiness, put away the remainder of the votive papers, and they are presently worked up into fresh candles, to suit the pious needs of the next comer'.[9] He was not impressed by the monasteries, observing that Russian monks 'lead as lazy a life as their brethren in other countries, and few works of any literary merit ever emerge from the Russian cloisters'. A priest who showed him over the churches of the Seminoff earned the comment that his vows of abstinence from flesh extended to ablution. As for the harlequin extravagance of the Church of St Basil in Moscow, Bourke thought it resembled a gaudy ornament done in sugar by an insane confectioner, rather than a real place of Christian worship. Custine, who does not spare the Russian clergy, thought St Basil a 'masterpiece of caprice'.[10]

At the opera Bourke was astonished that the performance was held up for an hour till the City Governor had taken his seat, and that the second act was delayed for almost as long to suit the convenience of Prince Frederick. While recognising that travellers should leave their patriotic prejudices at home, he could not help thinking that 'were we in the Strand instead of the great Place of the city of Moscow, the probabilities are that the interior decorations of the theatre would, before three quarters of an hour had elapsed, have adorned the streets outside', and that the Governor, Prince and performers would have fled to escape the wrath of the audience. 'Be that as it may,' he went on, 'no rebellious tongues, among the small audience here, dared to express even impatience, and they sat as silently and quietly doing nothing, as if they had been in a conventicle.'[11] Custine, too, was struck by the Russians' 'extraordinary obsequiousness'.

Bourke cast a critical eye over the droshky races, and found that the horses were in poor condition and 'seemed to have had quite enough of it' when they had trotted their mile and a half. The racing was poor, and the uninterested crowd did not stir to applaud the winner. 'But on no occasion or in no assembly in Russia, a popular cry either of acclamation or displeasure is ever raised, so universally does the spirit of submission and a passiveness amounting almost to fatalism, hang over the people.'[12] Bourke compared the reaction of 'his own inflammable people' at the races, when the success of a favourite produced a volley of hats and sticks and 'such a hurrah as is never heard out of the Emerald Isle'.

Briefly, Bourke, and his young friend Lord Eliot, had sailed to Hamburg, then driven to Lubeck before taking the longer sea voyage to St Petersburg, where the British Embassy staff saw that they were admitted to the highest Russian circles. There were concerts, balls at which Bourke danced the polka and the mazurka, and receptions. He was presented to the Grand Duke Michael, and invited by the Czarina to a concert at her palace of Sniaminsky in the Park of Peterhof. There he was charmed by his hostess and greatly impressed by the dignified bearing of the Czar, though he had doubts regarding the autocratic nature of his rule. Custine was much more critical of the Czar's unbridled power, noting sarcastically that 'a fly that buzzed unnecessarily during a chapel service humiliated His Imperial Majesty'.

Bourke had first been presented to Czar Nicholas when asked to witness army manoeuvres near St Petersburg. Some fifty-six thousand troops went through their paces for four hours in the Imperial presence, and Bourke recorded that 'although I bore the uniform of the Kildare Militia bravely through the day, and I hope supported the renown of that ancient and distinguished corps, I cannot say that I am much of a soldier, so do not pretend to give any opinion concerning the military perfections of the great army that we saw at the camp of Crasnoe Seloe'.[13]

The appearance of the small regiment of four hundred Circassians, however, provoked him to reflection. They were evidently people of considerable rank among their own tribes, and were more properly regarded as hostages than as soldiers of the Imperial army. Bourke noted that the war in the Caucasus was decidedly unpopular in Russia. Little was known in Europe of the actual state of things in that distant region, but Bourke's information was that the Russians had over the years incurred heavy casualties and drained the exchequer in a vain attempt to subdue the tribesmen.

> It has now become a useless war of extermination, for were the Caucasus to become a part of Russia tomorrow, it would add little to her importance or power; it is certainly the high road to Persia, and Circassia once quieted, the Black Eagle might wave triumphant as it has done once lately, on real oriental soil. But tottering as the Persian Empire is, I hardly think that she can so soon fall an unresisting prey to her ancient enemy, and there are too many powerful interests involved in her integrity to allow of her becoming a tributary of Russia.

Bourke went on to conclude that while the Circassians held their hills there was little danger of their passes being made a path to eastern conquest, and he hoped the Russians would realise 'the impossibility of gaining a province, the inhabitants of which inherit with a perfect knowledge of their own peculiar mode of warfare, an ancient and inveterate hatred of that power whose armies had failed in every attempt and had only succeeded in desolating the country'.[14]

A little cumbrous, but the message is clear. There can be no doubt that when, twenty-four years later, Bourke, now Earl of Mayo and Viceroy, came to play his cards in the continuing Great Game with Russia, he remembered his original impression of the difficulties the Russians had met, and would meet, in pursuing an aggressive expansionist policy. Here Bourke and Custine part company.

Custine was much more pessimistic. The Russians, he thought, 'mean to seize by armed force the countries accessible to them, and thence to oppress the rest of the world by terror. The extension of power they dream of is in no way either intelligent or moral; and if God grants it to them, it will be for the woe of the world.'[15] Oddly, these two contradictory views expressed by Bourke and Custine both have some validity. In the short term, meaning in his lifetime, Bourke was right. The Russians did not come sweeping down across the Oxus to threaten British India – the nightmare that haunted the India Office – and his foreign policy while he was Viceroy was vindicated. But, strategically, Custine has the edge. It is hard to believe that his comment was written as long ago as 1843, and he reinforced it with a dreadfully accurate prophecy. 'Russia sees Europe as a prey which our dissensions will sooner or later deliver up to her; she foments anarchy among us in the hope of profiting by a corruption she promotes because it is favourable to her views.'[16]

An Irishman, coming from a country where seventy per cent of the rural population were labourers or smallholders with five acres or less, Bourke could not fail to notice the primitive state of Russian agriculture.

> I often saw a man sallying forth to his day's work, carrying his plough in one hand, and leading a little shaggy pony that was to draw it, with the other. This tool would startle a Lothian farmer, being little more than a strong forked stick, one point of which is shod with iron, and scratches the ground as the pony pulls it along, while the other is held in the man's hand. The whole turn out is very like representations I have seen in old pictures of the progress of domestic arts in the time of the Saxon Heptarchy.

His practical eye noted that the Russians evidently did not think that straight ploughing improved fertility, since they wandered about scoring the ground as their fancy took.[17]

A visit to the Academy of Arts at St Petersburg provoked the comment that 'the Muses have not yet reached Russia in a body'. In Bourke's view the Russians' national disposition was to imitate; they had to be taught everything and had been 'rarely known to originate useful invention or design a great work'.[18] Literature, he observed without quoting his authority, was not on the increase, most of the books in circulation being either translations or imports, and only 780 volumes in Russian were published in the last year. Neither Bourke nor Custine, who also refers to the Russians' 'imitative mind', could foresee the flowering of Russian culture that was to come.

Russian commerce came in for pungent criticism from Bourke, monopoly and excessive protection being identified as among the main defects. He found to his amazement that while the import of unwrought foreign iron was prohibited, in manufactured form it was allowed entry free of duty, although the foundries of St Petersburg could do the work adequately. 'But the real secret of the unhealthy state of the commercial interest in Russia is the incompetency of the rulers to legislate properly in this important branch of political economy . . . . As long as the government of the country is entirely in the hands of men selected mostly from the highest class of nobles, a really enlightened commercial Minister will in vain be hoped for.'[19]

It is noteworthy that Bourke, a young sprig of the minor Irish aristocracy without any business experience of his own, should have taken so early the point about the need for a practical commercial policy. Compare, for instance, the egregious Hunter's reaction to a talk many years later with the Viceroy after dinner at Simla. Writing home to his wife on 1 October 1869, Hunter said: 'His [Mayo's] conversation was exactly that of an intelligent and highly educated merchant, who had a landed estate to manage in addition to his trading concerns. He discoursed of corn, coals, factories and, above all, the people of the land, and his great scheme for securing them against famine.'[20]

Two further quotations will suffice to give the full flavour of Bourke's account. First, the retention of slavery – although the Czar had no slaves, twenty million of his subjects still bowed to the iron rod – greatly distressed him. He recounts many conversations on this topic, and the most promising reaction he could find was that while manumission might be desirable, and even practised in isolated instances, it was generally impracticable. His conclusion is in heavy Victorian terms.

Until the children of the soil be free, Russia may vainly hope to possess the preponderance in the scale of nations that her vast territory entitles her to. She may conquer the effeminate Persian, or by the aid of her enormous armies keep enslaved Poland in subjection; she may march her hosts of serfs to extend her already too wide domain, or to starve the gallant Circassian into amenity to her power; but never will the nations of Europe feel that the clutch of the Black Eagle is to be feared, that her armies when met by equal numbers are to be dreaded . . . till the slave is free, and until thraldom is banished from the land.'[21]

Or, as Custine put it, the Russians were 'intoxicated with slavery'.

Few would care to have their earliest works quoted indefinitely against them – though that is a risk the author takes when he agrees to publication – but Bourke remained consistent in his realistic appreciation of Russia's internal problems.

In the more generous passages of his book Bourke was content to take refuge in the generalisation that everything in Russia was incongruous, the social edifice being yet unbuilt and the materials for its erection lying in splendid confusion on desert ground, but he regarded one practice, the use of the knout, with particular abhorrence. The knout was still in lethal use, even though the Russians boasted that no capital punishment was authorised in their criminal code. He gives this example:

The slave who shot Prince Gargarin some years ago suffered this terrible death. He was made a soldier for the purpose, as this is in a degree a military punishment. He was forced to walk up and down between ranks of men while the heavy whip of leather tore away the flesh at every stroke; at the hundred and twentieth lash he fell; his sentence was a thousand lashes; he was asked whether he would have the rest of it then, or wait for another day; he said he would have it then – knowing that to defer it would only prolong his agony. He was then set up, and received a few more blows till he fell again; they put him up a third time, when he fainted and was carried away insensible. He died the next day from the mortification of his wounds.

Bourke observes that although a grave crime had been committed this did not excuse the form of execution, and his comment on the issue of capital punishment as a deterrent is ingenuous but humane. To his mind, the use of the knout hardened the people to the sight of brutality and disposed them towards further crime, whereas a less inhuman mode of execution would 'increase the respect of the naturally wicked towards the laws, without decreasing the fear of death as a punishment.'[22]

Hunter in his biography claims that these words are memorable when it is borne in mind how Bourke's (Mayo's) assassin received the same delays of the courts, the same safeguards of evidence, and the same penalty, as if the murdered man had been the humblest among the millions of subjects and feudatories over whom the Viceroy ruled.

3
Minister and Master

When Richard Bourke went home to complete his Russian manuscript, with its account of the poverty of the Muscovite peasants, he found distress in his native Meath, as elsewhere in Ireland. For these were the years of the famine. The cause of the 'Great Hunger' was the failure of the potato crop – the sole food of one third of the people – totally or partially from 1845 to 1851. There had been localised outbreaks of famine earlier in the century, but in the autumn of 1845 potato blight reduced the whole country's crop to rotting pulp. Blight was general in 1846, and by the beginning of 1847 Ireland was in the grip of a disaster on an unprecedented scale. The famine brought epidemics in its wake, typhus, scurvy, hunger oedema, relapsing fever and cholera, and between 1841 and 1851 the population of Ireland fell by about one fifth to 6.5 million. In the same period – the figures are notoriously unreliable – deaths from starvation and disease were put at 1.3 million and another 1.4 million emigrated, mostly to America.

The British Government, though accused of hesitancy, inefficiency, and callousness towards the sufferings across the Irish Sea, showed some initial generosity. A relief organisation was set up, public works were started, and considerable funds were advanced from the Exchequer. But it was not enough, and after 1847, when the care of the destitute was transferred to the Poor Law, Westminster earned its obloquy.

Prime Minister Peel had begun his Parliamentary career as Member for Cashel, Tipperary and served for six years as Chief Secretary for Ireland, a period marked by his animosity towards Daniel O'Connell. In the autumn of 1845 he moved away from a protectionist policy when he decided that grain must be freely imported to feed the millions of Irish who had depended on the potato for their subsistence. That meant that the Corn Laws must be repealed. Although he first told the Cabinet of his decision on 31 October 1845, it was not till 25 June 1846 that the Repeal Bill was passed. But the protectionist Tories were not appeased. Led by Bentinck and inspired by Disraeli, on the very day that the Lords passed the Repeal measure they combined with the Whigs to defeat Peel on the Irish Coercion Bill. The Prime Minister resigned and Lord John Russell assumed office as head of a Whig Government.

In the months when the vindictive debates on the Corn Laws engrossed Parliament and the public, opponents of repeal tried to minimise the extent of the Irish famine, but Peel was still active. In November 1845 he appointed a Scientific Commission to see what could be done to save the potato. (Unfortunately its diagnosis was faulty and its report ineffective.) As a more practical step, without Cabinet approval he authorised the purchase of £100,000 worth of maize from America and appointed a Relief Commission to supervise distribution. In March 1846 he secured the passage of four bills to provide employment – and cash for starving Irishmen to buy food – on road and harbour improvements. He encouraged voluntary relief committees and set up special food depots to prevent profiteering. Even the *Freeman's Journal*, a newspaper sympathetic to O'Connell's Repealers, said of Peel:

'No man died of famine during his administration, and it is a boast of which he might well be proud.'[1]

Lord John Russell, a dedicated laissez-faire man, did not accept that he had an obligation to feed the people. Instead, his view was that the extent of the state's commitment was to keep down prices. He believed that, while the Government might provide employment, it was up to private enterprise to make food available and that Irish property should pay for Irish relief. In keeping with this policy, Peel's Relief Commission was abolished. In March 1847, however, Russell had to authorise the distribution of food, but by restricting eligibility to those with less than a quarter of an acre he aggravated the basic problem as many gave up their smallholdings rather than starve. Later in 1847 he transferred the care of the destitute to the Poor Law, though well aware that the most distressed areas were bankrupt and that local rates to support the Poor Law enactments were, for all practicable purposes, uncollectable. Worst of all, no attempt was made to teach the growing of alternative crops, or, even more basically, to amend the system under which land was held in Ireland.

Landowners did their best to temper the calamity in their own districts. That keen sportsman, the young Lord Clonmell, said to his agent 'I am fond of hunting, but I will part with hunters, hounds and servants rather than let my tenants want.'[2] Landlords, as well as such bodies as the Society of Friends and the British Relief Association, established soup kitchens. (Regrettably, some Anglican clergymen became notorious for 'Souperism', insisting on spiritual conversion in return for temporal diet.) Soup kitchens were also, eventually, organised under Government auspices, and by the end of 1847 they were feeding three million people a day. In this unhappy scene Bourke played a full part, as both his great-uncle and his father looked on him as their right-hand man. Though Palmerstown and Hayes were not by any means as badly affected as the more impoverished west and south west, Bourke was busy, spending full days in the saddle seeking out the worst-hit cases. He was also instrumental in bringing what there was of local craftwork, knitting and sewing, to market, even arranging sales in London, and – a familiar response of the upper classes to charitable appeals – in mounting amateur theatricals and concerts, for which subscriptions were exacted from all within reach.

Looking ahead to Bourke's later career in Hindustan, it could be argued that in these years at Hayes he was required to adopt a role not unlike that of a District Officer in the Indian Civil Service. He was involved with local hardship, he took his share of county and committee work during the famine, and certainly he did not forget what he had seen of the miseries attendant on the 'Great Hunger'. He may also have reflected, then or later, on a couple of paradoxes.

First, there was the strange occurrence that Ireland, even at the height of the famine, exported wheat, barley and oats worth, on average, about £100,000 a month. (Later he learned that Indian famines did not prevent rice being shipped overseas.) He may also have remembered Peel's purchase of maize from America when, soon after his arrival in India in 1869, he warned the Secretary of State in London that imports might be necessary to cope with growing famine in the north west provinces.

The second paradox is that while tens of thousands were

starving the *haut monde* carried on their fashionable round as though they had not heard of the famine. Richard Monckton Milnes, Florence Nightingale's friend, attended a party in County Meath given by the Marquess of Headfort where lively charades were performed. At Lord Bessborough's seat in Kilkenny his guests hunted all day, and Monckton Milnes wrote a prologue for the play by Sheridan which they acted at night.[3] In Dublin Castle there was a full round of levees and other official ceremonies, and Bessborough, the Lord Lieutenant, complained to the Prime Minister that it was not the duties of his office that 'knocked him up', but 'balls and drawing rooms'.[4] In 1849 Lord John Russell and Lord Clarendon (now Lord Lieutenant) decided that Dublin should not be denied the ultimate placebo of a royal visit, and at the beginning of August Her Majesty and her consort, accompanied by four of their children, were received by her loyal subjects with more enthusiasm, and in the circumstances less sense of outrage, than might have been expected. Twenty years later, one of Bourke's early problems as Viceroy was to arrange for the reception in India of the Queen's second son, the Duke of Edinburgh, at a time when famine was thought to be imminent.

Just when it might seem that Bourke's time was fully occupied with his famine work, with local relief meetings, with running the small farm that his father had made over to him, and – when opportunity offered – with the odd day riding to hounds, his career took another course. According to Hunter, the possibility of his entering Parliament for an English borough had earlier been discussed in London, but had come to nothing. His father, who had been active scrutinising the names on the register of voters, a very necessary part of Victorian electioneering, came to the view that his son might win one of the two seats for the County Kildare constituency.

The candidates nominated in August 1847 were the Marquess of Kildare (Whig), Mr Bourke (Tory), and Mr O'Neill Daunt and Mr John O'Connell (Repealer). The election of the noble marquess was a certainty, and the contest for the second seat lay between Bourke and O'Neill Daunt. Contemporary press reports suggest that the election was very much a parish pump affair, national issues such as the Corn Laws being ignored in favour of earth-shaking questions like the administration of the town funds of Naas. Bourke's address, when he came to make it, was bland enough to avoid offending any of the supporters whom his father had enlisted. Naturally, he was opposed to the repeal of the Union, but he favoured giving compensation to tenants for improvements and amending the Poor Law. In an ingenuous defence of the revenues of the Established Church, he argued that while the Church's adherents were not a majority in the country, it was still the Church of the property-owners. The landlords paid the tax, and tenants would be no better off if it were abolished.

On 18 August, along with the Marquess of Kildare, Bourke was declared elected, though his success was less due to his political stance than to his personal popularity. He had been energetic during the worst of the famine, he was admired as a sportsman, and he was well connected. At the time, no more was expected, but he did not immediately set Westminster alight. Indeed for the next two years he was no more than lobby-fodder, voting loyally with his chiefs and serving on Committees of the House, as required. It was not until 6 February 1849 that he broke his Parliamentary silence to speak, regretfully as he explained, in favour of continuing the suspension of Habeas Corpus in Ireland for another period. His intervention, which recognised that 'a maniac, an anarchical, and a traitorous spirit' was now abroad among his fellow countrymen, had one great merit in a maiden speech – it was short.[5]

One reason for Bourke's silence was that Parliament, as reports from Dublin suggested that the forces of rebellion were gathering, was not sympathetic to Irish declamations. In July 1846 the Young Ireland party, led by William Smith O'Brien, had seceded from the Repeal Association, and in January 1847 formed a new militant body called the Irish Confederation. Revolution was in the air throughout Europe, with the rising in France in February 1848 that led to the flight of Louis Philippe; insurrections in Sicily and Vienna; and at home the suspected menace of the Chartists. On 15 March 1848 Smith O'Brien called for the formation of an armed National Guard. The British Government reacted by sending massive troop reinforcements to Dublin and in April the Treason Felony Bill, which made speaking against the Crown punishable by transportation, was rushed through Parliament. The Habeas Corpus Act was suspended for a year. In July Smith O'Brien tried to raise the country, but he had misjudged the feelings of his fellow Irishmen, more concerned with food than constitutional reform, and the rebellion petered out after the farcical skirmish with the police at Widow McCormack's house at Ballingary. In England resentment against the Irish became more vocal. *The Times*, which had already said that the aftermath of the recent attempt at insurrection was 'not a good atmosphere for compassion for Ireland', thundered that 'In no other country have men talked treason until they are hoarse, and then gone about begging for sympathy from their oppressors . . . As a matter of state economy, some relief will be given to Ireland, in case she needs it, but we warn her that such relief will not be carried to the extent, or dealt forth, after the measure of former years.'[6] The famine, and emigration, were unabated, leaving their legacy of hatred for the English.

Richard Bourke's distraction from Parliamentary oratory had another, more personal, explanation. He was courting a young lady he had met in London society – the Honourable Blanche Julia Wyndham, third daughter of Lord Leconfield. Socially and financially her family was in a different class from the Bourkes, and her father could be forgiven for looking on his daughter's suitor as an unwelcome Irish thruster. But when it came to marriage settlements great-uncle Mayo came to the rescue and the wedding was celebrated on 31 October 1848. Six months later the generous old Mayo died; Mr Bourke of Hayes became the fifth Earl; and Richard took the courtesy title of Lord Naas (pronounced to rhyme with 'chase'). Leconfield had no subsequent doubts regarding his son-in-law and eventually gave him a London town house in Eccleston Square.

Lord Naas's marriage can be disposed of briefly – not because it was unimportant, but because, like many of the happiest unions, there is little to say about it. He seldom wrote to his wife, for the most satisfactory of reasons that they were hardly ever apart for long enough to make a letter necessary. In India she was a lively and popular Vicereine, and though many of her predecessors at Government House had provoked envious, or scandalous, comment, no one spoke ill of her. When she went home for a short period in 1870 her husband wrote ruefully: 'We have never been separated before for any length of time. I hope you will dislike it.'[7] Seven children were born of the marriage, of whom six, four sons and two daughters, survived infancy. His heir, Dermot Robert Wyndham Bourke, was born on 2 July 1851.

During the next three years Naas's interventions in the Commons were neither frequent nor memorable. He spoke twelve times and, with two exceptions, his speeches were all on Irish topics. In June 1850, for example, he spoke on the iniquity of taxing home-distilled spirits while still in bond.[8] In February 1852 he made a brisk attack on collusion between the Government and the editor of the disreputable Irish newspaper *World*, causing some amusement by his claim that on the House's decision rested 'the scale of public morality'.[9] The Whigs had no difficulty in defeating his motion. In 1851, however, he had engaged the reluctant attention of the House with a detailed, well-documented account of the problems of the Irish milling trade.

In March 1852 the Tories were back in power and Lord Derby invited Naas to be Chief Secretary for Ireland. He was surprised; he was only thirty years old and the press promptly dubbed him the 'Boy Secretary' (a title held in the past by Peel and Derby himself). It is not clear why he was preferred, but Derby's Cabinet included more untried men than usual, and Naas may have been chosen *faute de mieux*. Having accepted the portfolio, he had – in the custom of the time – to offer himself for re-election. He went back to Kildare, but local feelings had changed since he first won the seat and the franchise had been extended. His prospects were at best doubtful, and it was thought prudent to find another, safer, seat for him at Coleraine, which he held for the next five years. In 1857 he moved to Cockermouth, where his connection with the Wyndhams ensured his election, and he represented the constituency till he left for India as Governor-General designate in 1868.

The Tories remained in office for only nine months, to December 1852, and by the time Naas had learned something of ministerial mystique he was back in opposition. He had, however, brought forward a few domestic bills and, as always, shown himself concerned about the intractable problem of tenants' rights. The Whigs were in power till 1858, and Naas gradually made his name among the Tories as their leading spokesman on Irish affairs. He had another spell as Chief Secretary, only marginally longer than his first term, from February 1858 till June 1859, while Derby was again Prime Minister, and then followed seven more years in opposition.

In his first nineteen years in Parliament, from 1847 to 1866, Naas tasted office briefly and was latterly regarded by his party as a 'sound' man who could be relied on to make run-of-the-mill interventions on the whole range of Irish business, from education to the prison system, agriculture and the registration acts. But not even his closest friends would say that he was a dominant figure in the House. After the abortive rising in 1848 the political scene in Ireland was, on the surface, fairly tranquil; there had been a modest improvement in the economy, and Westminster was now apathetic towards Irish debates. Naas was never an orator who would bring Members crowding into the Chamber to hear him, and when Irish business was called he had, for the most part, to speak to empty benches.

He had other private worries. He was anxious for news of his brother John, on active service in the Crimea with the Connaught Rangers. His young family was growing and making more demands on his time. He had taken over his great-uncle's place at Palmerstown. His father, on succeeding to the earldom, took only a short time to decide that he would rather keep Hayes as his residence, and Naas moved to the grander house at Palmerstown. But he also found time to combine his duties as father, landlord, and Member of Parliament with one of his most abiding interests – hunting.

On 4 May 1857 Naas took over the Mastership of the Kildare Hunt from Lord Clonmell, with Baron de Robeck as Treasurer and Robert Kennedy as Secretary. First, he had to deal with the hunt finances, which were in a poor state. Against estimated expenditure of £1,650 he could count on only £900 from subscriptions and £250 of field money, leaving a deficit of £500. These are not enormous sums, but anyone who has been responsible for club, or society, funds knows how much tact is required to raise subscriptions, and how much tenacity to see that they are paid. Naas attacked this problem with his usual vigour, and by the end of his first year he had got the subscriptions up to £1,450, and the field money to £358, changing the deficit to a surplus of £150. The improvement was maintained, and during his Mastership the hunt was never in debt.

Sometimes engagements at Westminster coincided with the meet, and Naas was a familiar figure at Kildare station, where he would change from his hunting clothes and start for the boat from Kingston. When he became Master the Kildare country was feeling the full effects of the damage done to the coverts by a succession of severe winters. Kennedy wrote that Naas 'infected all men in Kildare with his most wondrous enthusiasm, and all set to work with most willing hands, so that in five years when he resigned he handed over the country in the most perfect state, practically a six days a week country'.[10] (It had been feared that Kildare would have to be content with two days' hunting a week for a long time to come.) Though a 'Parliament man', and so subject to some local suspicion, he visited every covert during the summer, and many twice.

On 26 November 1859 the Kildare Hunt enjoyed the most famous run then recorded. The celebrated Laragh run lasted for eighteen miles without a check, and – eyewitness reports are not consistent – it seems that only a dozen of the hundred and fifty who started were in at the finish. When news of the run, which had strayed well into Meath country, reached the Kildare Street Club in Dublin, it was not too well received by the Meath hunting men. It is also alleged that when someone asked why the fox had not gone to ground during an eighteen-mile point, the answer was that it was a Meath fox, who thought it was the Meath Hounds that were hunting him. 'He knew, therefore, that his life was safe and that there was no need to get to ground. He made a bad mistake and paid the penalty.'[11]

Much to his regret, Naas took only a minor part in the Laragh run. Having hurt his back, he drove to the meet in an old double-seated buggy, went on in advance, and put a couple of hounds into a covert. The pack then took up their pursuit over the memorable course. Naas was, however, fully engaged in two other great runs, still preserved in legend, from Baltiboys and Baltinglass. When he resigned at the end of the spring season in 1862, he handed over a prosperous hunt to his friend Baron de Robeck. Robert Kennedy wrote that 'by far the best sport ever known in Kildare was during Naas's mastership'.[12]

When the Tories came back to form the Government in the summer of 1866, Naas had established a preemptive right to the Chief Secretaryship, which he now took over for the third time. As this period covered the Fenian rising, some account of its origins is required.

The root cause was the famine of the forties. It was not only the deaths from hunger or the imperative necessity of emigration which by themselves nurtured the rebellious spirit. It was also the attitude of many of the English towards Ireland. Charles Trevelyan, the Treasury official most concerned with the Government's relief programme at the time of the famine, had written in unmistakably Malthusian terms that the overpopulation of Ireland, 'being altogether beyond the power of man, the cure had been applied by the direct stroke of an all-wise Providence in a manner as unexpected and unthought of as it is likely to be effectual'.[13] His verdict was that 'the great evil' was not the famine itself, but 'the selfish, perverse and turbulent character of the people'.[14] This is an extreme view, but a strong undercurrent of anti-Irish feeling persisted, and is reflected, for example, in the pages of *Punch*. Meanwhile the apparent calm of the fifties in Irish relations was about to be broken.

The attempted rising in 1848 had been a fiasco, but some of those who had emigrated, and some of the Young Irelanders who had contemplated rebellion, were intent on further subversion, with financial support from across the Atlantic.

One such Young Irelander, James Stephen, who had fled to France in 1848 and had come into contact with the Carbonari, the revolutionary French-Italian secret society, came back to Ireland and on St Patrick's Day, 17 March 1858, he founded the Irish Revolutionary Brotherhood, later called the Irish Republican Brotherhood – the I.R.B. – whose members swore to keep 'inviolable secrecy' and strive for an independent Republic. In New York on the same day, another Young Irelander, John O'Mahony, founded an Irish-American secret society named the Fenian Brotherhood, called after the legendary band of warriors, the Fianna. Recruitment in Ireland, which had been slow over the intervening years, received a fillip following the end of the American Civil War with the return of hundreds of Irish veterans from the American armies. On 11 November 1865, in the midst of rumours that a rising was imminent,

Stephen, who had been an indecisive leader, was arrested, only to escape and make his way to Paris and New York. Thomas J. Kelly took over as leader of the I.R.B. and in 1867 planned a raid on the British army depot at Chester Castle. It was unsuccessful and Kelly, with his colleague Timothy Deasy, was arrested in Manchester. A week later they were rescued from a police van and escaped to America, but one of the police guards was shot and three of Kelly's accomplices – William Allen, Michael Larkin and Michael O'Brien – were arrested, convicted, and hanged on 23 November.

Three weeks later, on 13 December 1867, the Fenians attempted to free prisoners from Clerkenwell gaol by blowing a hole in the prison wall. Twelve people were killed at once, eighteen died of injuries, and 120 others were wounded. British public opinion was aghast and the Fenians were denounced as terrorists. One Fenian, Michael Barrett, was executed – in the last public hanging in England – for his part in the Clerkenwell explosion, but in Ireland Larkin and O'Brien were hailed as the 'Manchester Martyrs'. Two others who were charged with them managed to escape the death penalty; one got a free pardon, but the other, Edward O'Meagher, managed to exclaim 'God save Ireland' from the dock before his sentence was commuted. This became the title of the I.R.B. marching song.

On the other side of the Atlantic the Fenians were no more successful. In the summer of 1866 two groups attempted to invade Canada from Buffalo and Vermont, but were easily defeated. In Ireland a significant feature was the opposition of the Catholic Church to Fenianism. In 1861 Archbishop Cullen excommunicated members of the I.R.B. and in 1867 Bishop Moriarty of Kerry called for divine intervention against the Fenians. 'Oh, God's heaviest curse, his withering, blighting blasting curse on them . . .'[15] The Church held that four conditions had to be met before rebellion could be justified – the government had to be extremely oppressive; the rebellion must be a last resort, after all other courses had been tried; there must be a reasonable prospect that the rebellion would not make matters worse; and the rising must command a popular majority. (It is interesting that in India the Muslim doctors engaged in a similar argument, albeit on different grounds, when considering whether the Wahabi rebels could be supported.)

Against this background, Naas's Parliamentary performance became more decisive. On 2 August 1866, moving the second reading of the bill to continue the suspension of Habeas Corpus, he asserted that the Fenian conspiracy was entirely of a rebellious character, whose only object was the annihilation of British power in Ireland and the establishment of a republic. He quoted a speech made by Stephen in Boston on 10 July, in which he promised to return to Ireland and looked forward to 'the final battle between England and Ireland, even on Irish soil this very year'. He rejected the claim that laws passed by Parliament had provoked Fenianism. Debates in the House in recent years, he said, had been concerned with the Established Church and land tenure, and the Fenians were not concerned with these issues.[16] It was an impressive speech.

In February 1867, asking the House to renew the suspension of Habeas Corpus, he gave an up-to-date account of Fenian activities, and emphasised three points. First, the real leaders and the principal organisers were not in Ireland. Second, his policy, which he was very ready to defend, was not to make indiscriminate arrests, but to apprehend the most prominent Fenian sympathisers.[17] Lastly, he praised the Catholic Church for trying, often at personal risk, to dissuade their flocks from joining the rebels, and for good measure he commended Bishop Moriarty's curse (noted above). The emergency had, if nothing else, improved his delivery from the front bench.

On 6 March he gave the House a further assurance which was badly needed. Telegrams from Dublin, he freely admitted, told of insurrection round the city, and at Castlemartyr. There was, however, no occasion for panic; he was confident that the military authorities were fully prepared.[18] On 23 May, nettled at the charge that the Government had deliberately let the rebellion simmer till it could be put down by force, he gave a long list of instances of speedy action. For example, 'M'Cafferty and Flood, both of whom have since been convicted, were arrested on board a collier at the entrance to the Liffey, in consequence of information received by a telegram from Whitehaven.' He had not 'allowed a person to be at large for a moment whom he had reason to think was deeply engaged in the movement'.[18] On 14 February 1868, Naas, now Earl of Mayo in succession to his father who died on 12 August 1867, moving for yet another suspension of Habeas Corpus, argued that 'no Irish resident of character, position, and intelligence' had become an active Fenian leader, and that of 265 persons arrested, 95, including some of the principal men detained, had recently been in America. He pointed out that the Fenians were now more active in England, where Habeas Corpus was still operative.[20]

Mayo's most substantial speech as a Minister, one which he thought sufficiently important to have published as a separate pamphlet, was made on 10 March 1868, in reply to the motion by Mr Maguire, the Member for Cork, to appoint a committee of the whole House to consider the 'state of Ireland'.[21] In this debate he again inveighed against American support for the Fenians, and skilfully contrasted the ideals and character of the 1848 rebels with the disreputable nature of the present conspiracy. He next dealt with three separate charges against the Government. To the claim that the English oppressed the Irish for their own ends, he reminded the House that all the higher Irish posts in the administration and the judiciary were held by native Irishmen. The franchise had been extended and at the local level the Irish had their own elected representatives. This may be thought to be routine establishment stuff, but it was put across with some conviction.

He was on much weaker ground when he harked back to the Normans in an attempt to refute the allegation that the English invaders had confiscated the land and property of the original Irish inhabitants, who had been reduced to peasant status. Then, to answer the more immediate criticism that material progress had been deliberately retarded, he produced – as Ministers do – a deluge of statistics to show improvements in the economy, instancing the greater acreage under the plough, a peculiar test of rising prosperity in the increase in spirit consumption (up 13% from 1866 to 1867), and, more convincingly, a much heavier tonnage of vessels using the port of Dublin.

He had positive proposals to offer for the future. Among them, he proposed the creation of a third, Roman Catholic, university to complement Trinity College and the Queen's University. On the vexed question of land tenure, he referred to the bill he had unsuccessfully promoted the previous year to register tenants' improvements, as a first step. He now promised to bring forward a very similar measure, and – the last resort of Governments who do not really know what to do – he gave notice that a 'solemn inquiry into the whole state of the relations between landlord and tenant' would be instituted. On the second great issue of the day, Church disestablishment, he remained as obstinately defiant as he had been since he was first elected. 'If the Irish Church was abolished tomorrow, I do not believe that we should have a single Fenian the less in the country.' He opposed any change, arguing that the Roman Catholic farmer or labourer did not pay a shilling towards the Church.

It is a matter of history that events took a different shape from that envisaged in Mayo's speech. For the opposition, Gladstone, who had given notice in March that he was now in favour of disestablishing the Irish Church, fought the general election in November specifically on this issue and was returned with a substantial majority. 'My first mission is to pacify Ireland' he told the Queen,[22] and the symbolic Church Act of 1869, which severed the legal connection between Church and State, followed. Gladstone had also promised the 1868 electorate land reform, and a bill which gave tenants compensation for improvements and for eviction, in fact extending the 'Ulster custom', was introduced on 15 February 1870. (This particular Act was largely ineffective, mainly because despite the new panoply of protection the landlord could still increase the rent.)

In sum, it would appear that Mayo's third term as Chief Secretary had ended in failure. But there is much to be said in mitigation. Unlike some of his colleagues, he did not regard Ministerial office as a mere extension of his social activities. At the bread and butter level, he had mastered the work of his department, earning the respect of his legal draughtsmen for his rigorous attention to detail, and introducing more than thirty bills while he kept his place on the front bench. (His principal speeches filled more than 524 columns of Hansard.) He spoke on Irish problems from first-hand knowledge – Disraeli never visited Ireland – and he was more liberal in his outlook than the rest of the Cabinet. But both by upbringing and conviction he was primarily a Conservative, and as such he was willing to react to events rather than anxious to impose theories of his own. He was not an intellectual, and whatever view is taken of the creed expounded in his 10 March speech, there is little sign of the vision or the impetus he displayed from the moment he disembarked at Calcutta. But it is relevant that he was not the first, or the last, 'geographical Minister' to find that he had not sufficient clout in Cabinet to enlist support for the more radical policy his country needed.

His control of the Fenian conspiracy was a different matter, and it is fair conclusion that it was his determined attitude in the emergency that prompted his friend Disraeli, who had taken over the leadership of the Tories in May 1868, to see that here was someone eminently suited for the highest proconsular rank. (Disraeli said as much when addressing the electors at Buckinghamshire in November 1868.) Disraeli was aware that, if his Government lasted long enough, he would soon have to submit a name to the Queen for appointment as Viceroy of India, to succeed Lawrence, who was due to come home in January 1869. And there were difficulties. Stafford Northcote, the Secretary of State for India, was not sufficiently impressed by Lawrence's performance to suggest that the experiment of preferring a senior Indian Civil Servant should be repeated. Moreover, Lawrence's immediate predecessor, Elgin, had died in India, and before him both Dalhousie and Canning had returned to England broken in health – a circumstance that reduced the attraction of the office, despite its Viceregal prestige.

Mayo, with his impressive physique, had the stamina for the job; he had Ministerial experience, although in a limited field; he had the presence to be the Queen's representative in Hindustan; and in private conversation, if not in the House, he had flair and sparkle, enhanced by traces of an Irish brogue. It was enough to appeal to Disraeli's romantic impulse. As he opted for Mayo, Disraeli thought it fair to warn him that if the Government fell before the appointment became due (as happened), it would not be for him, as Prime Minister, to advise the Queen, and as an alternative the Governor-Generalship of Canada was more immediately vacant. This posed a dilemma for Mayo. He could take his wife and his growing family to Canada with less worry about climatic hazards, but India was a far greater challenge. Mayo made his momentous choice, and Disraeli went ahead. As the Tory Government tottered to its downfall, it was announced that the sixth Earl of Mayo would become the fourth Viceroy and Governor-General of India.

4
En Voyage

The news that Mayo was to be the next Viceroy was greeted by the press with hostility and derision. An unknown, or very little known, minor peer whose Parliamentary career had been spent addressing the sparsely-filled benches of the House of Commons during Irish debates seemed a singularly unlikely choice. Part of the reaction was simply due to his being Irish, at a time when English public opinion – still with traces of a guilt complex over reports of the horrors of the famine and more recently outraged by the Fenians' activities – was not well disposed to those across the Irish Channel. But many years later Sir George Campbell, who had served with admiration under Mayo in Bengal, wrote in his Memoirs that the appointment 'was denounced as a job'.[1]

Mayo, despite his political experience, was distressed at the outcry, as is evident from an early letter he wrote to Sir Stafford Northcote, the Secretary of State for India. 'I own I am sorely hurt at the mode in which the Liberal Press is abusing my appointment. I care little for myself for I am used to the scurrility of the Irish newspapers, but I am not without apprehension that these attacks may damage the Government and hurt my influence if I ever arrive in India. I never sought the office. I never asked for anything myself in my life – I accepted it because I felt I could do it.'[2] It was no doubt because he was still smarting at his treatment by the press that he wrote in the will which he made on 12 October 1868, 'I desire that nothing may be published at my death which is calculated to wound or to annoy any living being – even those who have endeavoured by slander and malignity to injure and insult me.'[3] Signs that his critics had drawn blood can also be seen in the speech he made when taking leave of his constituents at Cockermouth. Referring to his appointment, 'In the performance of this great task I ask no favour; let me be judged according to my acts.'[4]

Lawrence was not due to relinquish the Viceroyalty till January 1869, and it was unusual to name a successor so many months in advance. Apart from party manoeuvring, the announcement had been made earlier than was customary because Mayo made it known that he wanted to familiarise himself with the duties and issues involved, both at the India Office in London, and in Hindustan, before he took up office in Calcutta. This he now proceeded to do (having officially ceased to be Irish Secretary on 1 October), his normal energy redoubled by his determination to confound his enemies. His diary discloses a long series of meetings in October and November 1868 with Northcote and the old Indian hands who made up the India Council, and who were, of course, very keen to tell him how the country should be governed.

Many of the topics raised were to engage much of Mayo's time in India, and the opinions of those he met were carefully noted for future digestion. Sir Bartle Frere, who had been Chief Commissioner in Sind and Governor of Bombay, talked about keeping the peace with the frontier tribes. He also warned Mayo about the dangers of meddling with land tenures or anything affecting religion – 'a danger to which you will find your experience in Ireland makes you more alive than 9/10ths of the men you will meet in India'. William Massey, the historian and former Finance Member of the Viceroy's Executive Council, recommended some form of financial devolution to the Indian provincial governments (an idea that Mayo took up and made his own), and, ironically as it turned out, said it was impossible to reimpose income tax in India. Discussions with Mr Andrews, the Chairman of the Sind Railway, and Sir Arthur Cotton, the great irrigation engineer, foretold future preoccupations, and Sir Henry Rawlinson counselled a more active policy towards Afghanistan. After going down to Shoeburyness to see the new Moncrieff gun-carriage, Mayo paid a farewell visit to the Duke of Cambridge, now in his twelfth year as General Commanding-in-Chief of the Army, at the Horse Guards. Mayo, even at this early stage, was ready to take a long, cool look at the Indian Army establishment. So much is clear from his note of the meeting. 'I pressed upon him the desirability of devising, if possible, some means of retirement for the large number of inefficient officers who are connected with the army in India, in order to make room for young and active men.'[5]

Florence Nightingale, her Crimean reputation still undimmed, was flattered when Mayo turned up at her house in South Street to ask her views. But she had met Lawrence in the past, and when she learned that Mayo knew nothing about Hindustan and – to her mind even more unfortunately – very little about field hygiene, she thought that his appointment was 'another instance of our incurable frivolity with regard to India'. Mayo was simply 'a big Irish Child'. But she wrote to her friend Dr Sutherland that he asked 'most sagacious questions', and was 'not insensible but essentially Irish'.[6] She liked his frank and open demeanour, and was amused when he told her he was certainly the only Viceroy who had ever sold his own cattle in the open market. Later however, enthusiast as she was, she did not think that Mayo had done as much as he should to improve sanitation in the soldiers' quarters.

Two of those who held senior office in India – Sir Henry Durand the Military Member of the Executive Council, and Clive Bailey the Secretary of the Home Department – were coincidentally in London and Mayo gave them a preliminary cross-examination on their work. After an audience with the Queen on 7 November, at which Her Majesty told him he was to be a Knight of the Most Illustrious Order of St Patrick, he had a long discussion with the downiest of the Indian satraps, the elderly Sir George Clerk. Then, with final goodbyes to Northcote and the India Office staff he sailed from Dover.

The Viceroy-designate had to recruit a Private Secretary, and he had asked Northcote if he could suggest someone 'who liked hard work and would do as he was told.'[7] The choice fell on Major Owen Tudor Burne, and it proved to be a good one. If Burne was not so dynamic as his successor Evelyn Baring (later Lord Cromer, the ruler of Egypt) who went out with Northbrook as Viceroy's Private Secretary, he was, as Mayo required, very hard-working and was popular with his colleagues. As the Private Secretary is a person of considerable influence, being the single channel through which all must approach his master, Burne's career can be briefly recounted.

Born in 1837, he was the son of an eccentric clergyman who, even by Victorian standards, had an enormous brood of children.

Burne was number eleven out of nineteen, one elder brother eventually becoming Secretary of the Military Department in India. Gazetted as a subaltern in the XXth Regiment (Lancashire Fusiliers), he reached the Crimea shortly before peace was declared on 3 April 1856. He had only a few months at home before going out to India as a Mutiny reinforcement, and after the final relief of Lucknow he took part in the cleaning-up operations in Oudh. For a time he served under Sir James Hope Grant, and they made a fine musical pair. Grant was 'almost always accompanied by an enormous violincello, carried on a camel', while Burne took his hand piano with him.[8] In 1861 he was appointed Military Secretary to Sir Hugh Rose (Lord Strathnairn), the Commander-in-Chief, and was present with him at Canning's great Allahabad durbar when, as Burne noted, the effect of the Viceroy's high-flown sentiments was ruined by a comically inadequate translation. Next year, however, he was involved in some of Rose's disciplinary measures, and in the Horse Guards the view was taken that he was too young for the job. So he was eased out, though Rose softened his dismay by offering a lesser post on his staff.

He left India in 1865 with Rose and accompanied him to Ireland when he was appointed to command the Forces there. Rose had to explain to Burne that lack of seniority meant that he could only offer him the junior, and badly paid, post of ADC. In Ireland Burne joined in the skirmishes with the Fenians and found time to marry the beautiful Evelyne, the daughter of Lord Kilmaine, before he learned from Rose that a letter had arrived from Lord Aberdare at Dublin Castle, saying that Mayo wanted him to be his Private Secretary. After an interview with the Viceroy-designate, Burne was glad to accept and was present at many of Mayo's briefing sessions in London. One point in particular he noted – Mayo's surprise at discovering that in India alone the Queen governed 'nearly four times as many Mussulmen as were contained within the Turkish boundaries'.[9] Mayo never forgot his obligations to the Muhammadan communities.

Burne and his wife did not join the Mayos till they reached Alexandria on 26 November. Meanwhile the Viceroy-to-be and his family (he took his brother Eddy as Military Secretary) stopped for a few days in Paris, where Mayo took time to inspect the French Archives in the old Hotel Soubise. The storing and cataloguing of public records was something of a fetish with him. In his last appointment he had brought forward the bill on which the organisation of the Irish Record Department was based; he had been warned by the India Office that Indian Records were no better than chaotic; and with this at the back of his mind he paid a visit to the Paris Department. But he was not greatly impressed with what he saw, as there did not seem to be any 'calendaring' being done, apart from producing facsimiles of curiosities. 'The use to the public appears to me doubtful,' he wrote in his diary.[10] On the way south he inspected work on the Mont Cenis tunnel before crossing the Pass to find, on arrival at Ancona, that even Viceroys are not immune from having their luggage misdirected – in his case to Florence. At Brindisi he embarked on HMS *Psyche* and landed at Alexandria, to be received in state by Ismail Bey and taken by special train to Cairo.

At Cairo there were ceremonial visits to the Khedive and the obligatory trip to the Pyramids, where Mayo noted with innocent glee that Lord Napier of Magdala (Commander-in-Chief of the Bombay Army), who had now joined the party, fell off his horse twice. Mayo next went to see progress on the Suez Canal, still about a year from completion. Like everyone else, he was fascinated by the whole project and examined the works in detail. His own conclusion was that there might be problems with navigation, difficulties with drifting sand, and doubts about the canal's commercial prospects, but 'whatever be its results, it will ever stand forth as the greatest work which the French nation has attempted'.[11]

Ferdinand de Lesseps not only showed Mayo round the construction sites; he also intrigued him with his views on Biblical topics. They had an interesting, somewhat unreal, and at this distance slightly comic, discussion about the precise spot where Moses was left in the bulrushes – according to Lesseps at Saine, the only place where the water was calm enough to avoid his being swept away in the stream. Lesseps also had strong views on the route taken by the Israelites when, as the Bible says, 'the Lord caused the sea to go back by a strong east wind all that night, and made the sea dry land, and the waters were divided'. Lesseps concluded that the Israelites passed over somewhere near Toussoum.

Mayo noted these imaginative flights in his diary without indicating whether he was convinced by them. (Burne, who went through Mayo's diaries, said they were hurriedly dictated on his travels, not embellished by private comment, and merely 'a rough record of certain journeys and acts for future reference'.)[12] Mayo did, however, retain a warm admiration for Lesseps and his work. Later, when the Canal had been opened, he enquired about the possibility of acquiring some of the dredging equipment for use in India. He also asked Lesseps to be his guest at the ceremonies to mark another great advance in communications – the completion of the Bombay-Calcutta Railway. It is a pity that the Frenchman did not accept, because there is no knowing what might have transpired if he had addressed his inventive mind to the problems of Hindustan.

Arriving at Aden on 8 December, Mayo was for the first time within the bounds of his future bailiwick, as Aden at that time came within the Viceroy's purview. He was far from satisfied with the arrangements for the defence of this British outpost which, he realised, would become more important strategically with the opening of the Suez Canal, bringing 'large numbers of armed European steamers to these waters'. The fort, he thought, was badly designed and was not really a fortress at all. Mayo forwarded proposals for the improvement of the defences and the water supply, then hopelessly inadequate. With his usual practical sense he suggested that a large supply of pipes dumped at the time of the recent Abyssinian campaign should be used. Meanwhile he wrote to Bartle Frere, '"The Gibraltar of the East" as far as artificial defences are concerned, is a mockery.'[13]

Burne in his Memoirs says that it was at Aden that Mayo learned that Disraeli had resigned as Prime Minister after the general election, to be succeeded by Gladstone. In his diary Mayo notes that on 19 December, while lying off Bombay, he heard for the first time about the change 'which was a matter of great astonishment, as it never occurred to me that Disraeli would have found it impossible to meet Parliament'. This is a little ingenuous, since in the preceding months Disraeli's fall had been widely predicted.

Mayo's own appointment now seemed in question. There was a precedent for preventing a Governor-General of India designate from taking up office because of a change in the Home

Government. In 1835 the unfortunate Lord Heytesbury was actually being measured for his kit before embarking when the Tory Government went out of office and his appointment was cancelled. (This was the same Heytesbury who appointed the young Mayo as 'gentleman at large' on his staff at Dublin Castle when he eventually succeeded to a Viceroyalty, albeit an Irish one, in 1844.)

In the previous autumn *The Times* had reported that Anglo-Indian society was trying to persuade itself that one of the Queen's sons should be sent out as Viceroy. (A pertinent comment was added. Suppose the royal Viceroy went astray? Would it be convenient to snub him in a letter from the Indian Secretary?) In September *The Times* quoted an Indian paper which argued that the Duke of Edinburgh – whom Mayo was later to welcome as a visitor to India – should be appointed, and that if the Queen's first son was Prince of Wales, her second should likewise be Viceroy of India.[14] Gladstone, from later correspondence, apparently took the view that a dying Government should not have made such an important appointment towards the very end of its lifetime, and Lord Derby told Disraeli that he feared Mayo would be brought back and replaced by the Duke of Argyll. Speculation was still rife when *The Times* of 17 December 1868 quoted a passage from the *Western Morning News* as ignorant as it was confident. 'On the highest authority', it said that a decision had been taken to recall Mayo and prolong Lawrence's tenure for another year, after which he would be succeeded by the Marquess of Salisbury. *The Times* did have the caution to head the report 'Alleged Recall of the Earl of Mayo'.

In the event, Argyll was content to be Secretary of State for India and at once wrote to Mayo, 'You will have heard before this reaches you that I have received the seals of the India Office in the new administration. Indian politics are fortunately for the most part unconnected with the party struggle at home, and I hope there will be nothing to prevent me from having open and confidential communication with you on every question affecting the government of India.'[15] Mayo replied a month later 'I am happy to be able to confirm your opinion that party politics have no place here, and I shall ever labour to keep them at that distance where they fortunately are.'[16]

It may be suspected that both men were speaking tongue in cheek. Not all Mayo's predecessors had found it impossible to keep Home and Indian politics disentangled, and some of his successors, Northbrook for example, found it quite impossible. But as Argyll made clear in his obituary speech in Parliament after Mayo's assassination, both of them stuck to their original undertaking, and though belonging to different parties, their relations were as harmonious as affairs of state allowed. Mayo was, as it happened, fortunate in the Minister with whom he had to deal. George Douglas Campbell, eighth Duke of Argyll, was not as famous, or as notorious, as some of his forbears as head of Clan Campbell. Dry in manner, sometimes pompous in his utterings, he was an experienced politician who had been a prominent member of the Whig party since he first held office as Privy Seal in 1853. He had a fair amount of influence in the Cabinet and, at his leisure, was something of a scholar, publishing works on religion and science as well as on politics.

Mayo landed at Bombay on 19 December, to get his first taste of the red carpets, avenues of troops and gun salutes that were to recur wherever he made a formal appearance. He had polite talks with the Governor of the Presidency, Sir Seymour Fitzgerald, and other leading officials, all eager to make their number with the new Viceroy. But his ten days at Bombay were marked by the same enthusiasm, relentless energy, and practical attention to detail that were to feature prominently throughout his rule. On the morning after his arrival, for instance, when a leisurely tour of introduction might have been in order, Mayo was out at six o'clock to inspect the city's sewage system and see the discharge of one of the main sewers into the sea, 'the stench from which was sickening'. After breakfast he was off to see that the horses he had brought from England were in good shape. (To Arbuthnot he had earlier written 'I have taken your advice and have only ordered 3 carriages to take out – we must have something smart to begin with.')[17] In the following days there were visits to the gaols, a formal reception for a native chief, a strenuous journey to Poonah and back, and visits to the new Deccan College and to the Sassoon Hospital. He received in audience the High Priest of the Parsees, a venerable figure who had been decorated by Her Temporal

Majesty for his loyal behaviour during the Mutiny. He saw the works of the Elphinstone Land Company on the harbour foreshore, and it may well be that Fitzgerald broached the question of the government acquiring the Elphinstone interest – on which Mayo later took a firm line, so far as public funds were involved. The cotton-presses naturally engaged his attention and the Chamber of Commerce argued their special case with the vehement eloquence that was apparent in most Indian, or Anglo-Indian deputations. Lord Napier ensured that the new Governor-General saw a full-scale review of the garrison and visited various barracks. But Mayo was soon wise to what was behind Napier's attentive presence, noting acidly that 'the expense of erecting the Kolaba barracks is almost inconceivable'. Still Mayo's furious activity continued. 'Although we were not in bed till 2.30 we started this morning at six to visit the Vehar water-works.'[18] Then, on 30 December, he left on the *Coromandel* for the journey to Beypore, where he was met by the Madras Governor, Lord Napier and Ettrick (not to be confused with the military Lord Napier of Magdala), who took him on the 400-mile train journey to the headquarters of the Presidency.

For 4 January there was an entry much to Mayo's liking. 'Went out hunting in the morning. Had a short run of about five minutes with a fox, and afterwards a run of about twenty-five minutes with a jackal. A large number of people were present; and considering that the thermometer was at 80° the hounds, which had just come from England, ran remarkably well.'[19] During his time at Madras Mayo had time to reflect on the size of his new domain. Of the two Presidencies he had visited so far, Bombay was the size of Germany, while the area of Madras equalled that of the United Kingdom. He also perceived the difference between the intense commercialism of Bombay and what his private secretary described as the 'ancient patriarchical simplicity' of the Madrasees. The climate, the vegetation, even the religion of the inhabitants differed markedly from what he had seen in Bombay, and he had still to visit Central and Northern India.

On 6 January he went on board the *Feroze*, observing that as the pier was dilapidated it was necessary to cross a large chasm in a basket attached to wire ropes. His diary for the next day contains what was for him an unusual admission. 'Paid the penalty for my imprudence and over-exertion at Madras, being attacked sharply by fever this morning.'[20] But he had recovered when he reached the Hooghly two days later.

5
Brave Men before Agamemnon

The Viceroy and Governor-General of India, to whose office Mayo was to succeed, was one of the 'great suns of glory', a ruler possessing power equalled only by the President of the United States and the Czar of All the Russias.

To most Indians the Viceroy was the visible personification of the British Sovereign. When he conducted full ceremonial occasions he was seated on a throne surrounded by officials and servants bearing the symbols which Indians – princes and lower orders alike – recognised as signifying royal power, the peacock fans and the *chowri* of yak's tail. He had palaces at Calcutta and Barrackpore, and, for the hot weather, a separate headquarters at Simla. He travelled in regal state with a vast retinue and he had his own, élite, bodyguard of lancers glistening in their scarlet uniforms.

He held the chief executive office in British India, presiding over a small Executive Council. He was meant to accept their decisions, but he could overrule them – though this was seldom necessary. He could not, however, dismiss members of the Council, who were appointed by the Government at Westminster. He had a Legislature, which gradually became more representative but could be overruled by the Viceroy.

He was his own Foreign Secretary and represented the Raj in relations with the rulers of the princely states, who governed an area amounting to forty per cent of the country. The degree of Viceregal interference in these states varied according to the nature of the Chiefs' administration. The disposition to be adopted towards the princes, depending on the minute observance of protocol, mutual confidence, and in the last resort an assessment of how far each could push his luck, was a source of perpetual friction.

The title of Viceroy dated from 1858, in the aftermath of the Mutiny. Previously the country had been governed by the East

India Company, though it purported to be acting under the nominal authority of the Moghul, latterly an impotent pensioner in his court at Delhi. Gradually the affairs of the Company were brought more and more under the control of the Westminster Government, with responsibility shared, often uneasily, by the Company's Chairman and the President of the Board of Control in London.

In brief detail, the 'Company of Merchants of London', given its charter by Queen Elizabeth in 1600 to trade 'into the East Indies', despatched four ships from England carrying goods for trading and gifts for local rulers. Their immediate objective was no more than to bring back a cargo of pepper, then a scarce commodity in the home market. They went to Sumatra in 1608 but finding conditions unfavourable there moved on to Surat on the Indian coast. There were clashes with the Portuguese who were already established in the port, but by 1614, with the embassy of Sir Thomas Roe, the English had taken root, dealing principally in fabrics and indigo.

From this modest start the Company prospered, and by 1700 its stock was selling at a high premium in London. But expanding trade needs security and security in time requires the provision of troops, the levying of taxes, and the imposition of a system of law and order. The Company's agents, by now extending to Madras, Bombay and Calcutta, were zealous in all these fields, and the time was propitious. The great Moghul dynasty was in decline and the native rulers in disarray. The Persian Nadir Shah, and then for the first time tribesmen from Afghanistan, swept down to raid Delhi. In 1761 the Afghans thrashed the Mahrattas, the strongest force in Central India, before returning, heavy with loot, to Kabul.

Apart from the fragmenting and feuding of the Indian princes, the Company had another reason to adopt a more military posture. This was the presence of the French, anxious to expand their own trading facilities. A new phase started with the arrival in India of the indomitable Stringer Lawrence, a professional soldier who had served in Flanders, after Fontenoy, and had fought at Culloden. Lawrence emulated the French in recruiting native infantry and more than held his own in the Madras area. Clive's subsequent triumphs at Arcot and Plassey are part of military history, but once the Company had gained control of

Bengal it was drawn inexorably towards further acquisitions, however much this policy might be depored in London at the Leadenhall headquarters. In India the Company would assert that it was fighting defensive battles (which ironically extended its boundaries) but this period was marked by widespread exploitation. The Government in London now intervened more directly with the Regulating Act of 1773 and with the India Act of 1784 which in effect brought the Company under the Crown. The Board of Control was appointed with the right to issue instructions to the Company's agents in India. In time the Secret Committee of the Directors of the East India Company, despite its sinister title, became little more than a channel for transmitting the fiats of the President of the Board of Control. For all practical purposes the President was now Secretary of State for India, and from 1812 onwards he was a member of the Cabinet.

In 1774 Warren Hastings, the Governor of the Calcutta Presidency which was now more important than the other two Presidencies of Madras and Bombay, was made the first Governor-General. Hastings consolidated Clive's gains by vigorous campaigns against the warrior Mahrattas and the French, but his real claim to fame rests on his far-seeing administrative innovations, including the establishment of the Supreme Court at Calcutta. These very innovations, however, coupled with Hastings's overt interest in the welfare of the Indian peasant, were not popular with some of his colleagues, particularly Philip Francis, with whom he had to fight a duel. Thanks to Francis's intrigues, with the support of Edmund Burke, Hastings was impeached in 1788, two years after he returned to England, and was only acquitted after protracted proceedings that extended over seven years.

For a short time he was succeeded by a Scot, Sir James Macpherson. A charming scoundrel, Macpherson, who had been a member of the Supreme Council in Calcutta since 1782, held office as Governor-General for only a single year (1785–6), and earned no marks for probity. Macpherson was replaced by Lord Cornwallis, the soldier who surrendered Yorktown (but preserved his own reputation) in the American War of Independence. In India he stuck to his profession and personally led the successful campaign against Tipu Sultan of Mysore. Cornwallis was universally esteemed during his seven years of office (1786–93), and eliminated many corrupt practices. Unusually for his time, he gave up his prize money in the Tipu Sultan war for the benefit of his troops.

In complete contrast, the next Governor-General, 'Honest John' Shore, a Company officer and a scholar of the classics and oriental languages, lacked the personality to rule successfully. On demitting office in 1798, he was created Lord Teignmouth and found more congenial employment at home in evangelical circles. His successor Richard Wellesley, Earl of Mornington and soon made Marquess Wellesley, was intent on playing the part to the full. The building of the magnificent new Government House at Calcutta was typical of his determination to do everything on the grand scale, whatever the cost. Although he had been enjoined to follow a peaceful policy, the military campaigns during his time as Governor-General (1798–1805) were spectacularly successful, thanks mainly to his brilliant brother Arthur, the future Duke of Wellington. Together they finally put paid to Tipu Sultan at Seringapatam, and tamed the troublesome Mahrattas at the closely fought Battle of Assaye. But Wellesley's seemingly endless expenditure on his building projects was too much for the Court of Directors. He was summoned home, and Cornwallis was coaxed out of retirement to institute a policy of retrenchment. He had scarcely embarked on his economies when he died after a couple of months in his second term.

Sir George Barlow, a Member of Council who today would be described as a good Treasury man, took over as acting Governor-General and carried on the austere policy which Cornwallis had started. But he had not enough clout to earn the approval of the Westminster Government. His appointment was not confirmed, and in 1807 the job went to Sir Gilbert Elliot, first Earl of Minto. A barrister with diplomatic experience, Minto had several links with India, since one brother had been private secretary to Warren Hastings and another was later Governor of Madras. More to the point, he was President of the Board of Control for the year before he went out to succeed Cornwallis. In India he attempted to put the Government's finances into better order and insisted on religious toleration. Prohibited by instructions from London from waging war by land, he mounted two expeditions, against the French in Mauritius and the Dutch in Java, and himself took part in the Java campaign.

The Earl of Moira was said to owe his preferment in 1814 to the good offices of his friend the Prince Regent. An impoverished Irish peer keen to obtain the emoluments of office, Moira was in the Wellesley stamp. He fought an unnecessary war against the Ghurkas when Nepal was deemed to be intransigent over a frontier dispute. For a time the British forces were held at bay by the much smaller Ghurka army, but the tenacity of the skilful General Ochterlony prevailed and Moira was rewarded by being made Marquess of Hastings. He also took on the Pindari tribesmen and finally crushed the Mahrattas, acquiring the territory that included Poona. In more peaceful pursuits Hastings aped Wellesley's extravagant example, and together with his wife – the first consort to grace Government House with her presence – encouraged Calcutta society to assume habits of grandeur.

His successor Lord Amherst is best remembered for the remark 'The Emperor of China and I govern half the human race and yet we find time to breakfast'. Otherwise there is little to recount regarding his term (1823–28) apart from the first Burmese War, which produced some exceptionally vain-glorious despatches from his successful commander Sir Archibald Campbell.

Under the peaceful rule of Lord William Bentinck (1828–35) many humane reforms were carried out. Bentinck was more concerned than any of his predecessors with the welfare of the native Indians. He abolished *suttee*, admitted Indians to official posts, and initiated an ambitious educational programme. With the help of Thomas Babington Macaulay, a Member of Council, he ordained that Indians should be taught in English. But there were many who thought that Bentinck was too informal in his approach. He lacked style; he went about on horseback without an escort, or on foot carrying an umbrella. Invitations to Government House now went much lower down the social scale than previously, though Eurasians were not admitted.

Some confusion followed Bentinck's resignation on health grounds in 1835. The Court of Directors wanted to confirm the acting Governor-General, Sir Charles Metcalfe, an experienced and respected civil servant, but were displeased when he abolished restrictions on the Indian press. Then the Tory Lord Heytesbury was chosen, but before he could pack his kit the Government had fallen, and the appointment went to the Whig, George Eden, Lord Auckland. Amiable but indecisive and something of a party hack, Auckland went out full of good intentions and keen on liberal reforms. But events were too much for him. He had an obsession, in which he was strongly supported by Palmerston at home, with the threat of a Russian invasion of India through Afghanistan, and in 1838 he launched the 'Army of the Indus' to replace the Afghan amir Dost Mahomed by the aged puppet Shah Soojah. Kabul was occupied and there was a deceptive calm. Auckland's sister Emily, who accompanied her bachelor brother to India, wrote home to her friend Lady Campbell: 'Our George has done very well in India. You know we always thought highly of him even in his comical dog days.'[1] But the Afghans rebelled and when they massacred the retreating British force only a single European out of 16,000 soldiers and campfollowers reached the precarious safety of Jalalabad. Auckland arranged for an avenging army to be despatched under General Pollock, but his time had run out, and he returned to England discredited.

The Tories, back in power, sent out Lord Ellenborough, the second President of the Board of Control to be appointed Governor-General. Pollock reoccupied Kabul, burned a couple of mosques, and withdrew from Afghanistan – though permanent damage had been done since the sepoys had seen that the Raj was not invincible. Ellenborough, at indecent pains to dissociate himself from Auckland's policy, made an ass of himself with a ludicrous ceremony to welcome the returning troops and a pompous proclamation to the Indian people. Ellenborough was a soldier manqué – he had asked unsuccessfully for the old military title of Captain-General – and treated his civilian staff with contempt. The young George Campbell, at the start of a distinguished career, noted the resentment at Ellenborough's sneering references to civilians who wore moustaches as 'Cutcherry Hussars'.[2] Ellenborough soon engaged in two other wars, against the Amirs of Sind and the state of Gwalior. It would not be unkind to say that he was distracted by the concurrent amours of his wife, Jane Elisabeth Digby, whom he later divorced. Known as 'Aurora, the Light of Day', her lovers were to range from the King of Bavaria to her final spouse, a Bedouin Sheikh.

The Court of Directors had by now had enough of Ellenborough's frenetic activities, and after a reign of two years he was replaced in 1844 by the fifty-nine-year-old Peninsular veteran Sir Henry (later Lord) Hardinge. Trouble with the Sikhs had been looming ever since Runjeet Singh, the ally of the British and the one man who could control his fractious chiefs, died five years earlier. In 1845 a Sikh army of 60,000 men and 150 guns poured across the Sutlej to invade British territory. Hardinge took part in the campaign, insisting that he should serve under Sir Herbert Gough, his C-in-C, and was present at Ferozeshah, the most desperate battle since Assaye. He then installed the youthful son of Runjeet Singh as ruler at Lahore, with a British Resident to supervise him. Lest this should seem to be nothing but a list of military engagements, the rest of Hardinge's rule was relatively tranquil, and progress was made with such useful work as the Ganges canal and the stimulation of tea planting. In 1848 he asked to be relieved of the burden of office.

Annexation was the hallmark of the years (1848–56) of the Earl, eventually Marquess, of Dalhousie. Only thirty-five years old when appointed, Dalhousie was the son of a Scottish earl, and had already attracted attention while President of the Board of Trade. In that capacity he applied himself energetically to the problems of railway development, an interest he took with him to India. He was soon embroiled in another war with the Sikhs, but after Gough's Pyrrhic victory at Chillianwalla the enemy were finally defeated at Gujerat, and the Punjab was placed under a Board headed by the Lawrence brothers. This was but the first of the Raj's acquisitions under Dalhousie. Two years later he took up arms against the King of Burma, who was reckoned to have been oppressive to British merchants. Rangoon and Pegu were captured by assault and Dalhousie went to Rangoon to annex the new British province of Lower Burma.

It soon became apparent that Dalhousie was a born centraliser, as he relentlessly absorbed states in Central India. In some of them – Nagpur, Satara and Jhansi – a pretext was made of disputes regarding the succession; in Oudh the existence of a corrupt government was prayed in aid to justify intervention. Dalhousie's belief in the superiority of British rule was consistent enough, but he was accused, both at home and in India, of arrogance and insensitivity, and among the causes of the Mutiny that followed a year after he resigned in 1856 the annexations rank high.

Dalhousie, a slim figure who suffered from excessive self-confidence, inspired dread among his civilian colleagues, and his relations with his Commanders-in-Chief, Gough and then Napier, were abrasive. But his domestic policy was as ambitious as his attitude to the native states. The first Indian railways were built in his time and his legacy included a telegraph network that covered most of the country, the spread of irrigation schemes, and in administration the setting up of the first department exclusively charged with Public Works. George Campbell said the new department replaced the 'mongrel machinery' which had operated, or not operated, before.[3] Dalhousie's concern for the native population was seen in his extension of education and civil rights. He left India, already broken in health, to suffer vehement attacks following the events of the Mutiny, for which he was held to have a large share of responsibility. He died, a disappointed man, in 1860.

It was the fate of many Governors-General to earn obloquy and praise in almost equal measure, but Charles, afterwards Viscount and Earl, Canning remains exceptionally enigmatic. The son of Prime Minister Canning he seemed set for a golden future, but, though his career in India was illustrious, he did not entirely fulfil his earlier promise. An MP at twenty-four, he was offered the Foreign Office by Derby, but party considerations prevented his acceptance, and all that he had achieved before he went out to India in 1856 was the unglamorous portfolio of the Postmaster General.

He had also married the beautiful, and greatly admired, Charlotte, the daughter of Lord Stuart de Rothesay. As the most influential Lady Sahib since Emily Eden, she deserves a special mention. 'I am certainly getting to like India,' she wrote home in her first November. This compares with Emily Eden, who found it 'an abominable place' and wrote from Barrackpore, 'I cannot abide India, and that is the truth, and it is almost come to not abiding *in* India.'[4] Both of them found the insistent presence of bearers, bheesties and punkah-wallahs oppressive, but Charlotte made the most of it, introducing extensive improvements to the decor of the Viceregal establishments. Unlike Emily, who wrote bored, uncomprehending letters about the disasters of the First Afghan War, Charlotte earned a good name for her relief work during the Mutiny. Again in contrast to Miss Eden whose celebrated account of her journey *Up the Country* is punctuated with deprecatory comments on 'these brown, arid plains, and browner, arider people', Charlotte, though she did not really care for camp life, went with Canning on all his travels, and in 1860 explored the foothills of the Himalayas on her own. But Charlotte's real significance lay in the way in which she humanised much of Government House protocol and, as a lady-in-waiting to the Queen, brought a touch of regal style and elegance.

The first shock to Canning's peaceful intentions – Dalhousie had thought he would do well if times were quiet – came soon after his arrival. He had to declare war on Persia which was attacking Herat, always a sensitive area for the British who saw it as the invader's route to Hindustan, but the short-lived campaign ended in 1857. There had already been an outbreak of disaffection at Barrackpore when, in May, the Sepoy Mutiny started.

The causes of the rebellion have been extensively canvassed, but since later Governors-General always had them in mind, they can be briefly rehearsed. First, there was the resentment at Dalhousie's annexations, especially of Oudh which provided most of the sepoys for the Bengal army. Natives had also begun to realise that with the great vertebrae of telegraphs and railways the British were in a stronger position to impose their will, which was thought to be inimical to Indian customs and religion. Conversely, there was an undercurrent of belief that the century of British rule, dating from Plassey in 1757, was about to end. The Crimean War had reinforced the view that the Raj was not invincible in the field – a view that had been nourished by the Afghan debacle in 1842. The prospect of native troops being sent across the 'dark water' to serve overseas implied a defilement of caste, and many feared that compulsory conversion to Christianity would be introduced, an alarm given some credence by the issue to native regiments of cartridges greased with the fat of cows or pigs, sacred or unclean animals to Hindus and Muslims. (As soon as he heard of the rising at Meerut Canning issued a proclamation denying that the Government had an intention of interfering with Indian religion, but it was too late.)

While none of these circumstances, in themselves, might have provoked the Mutiny, it is clear, with hindsight, that together they provided the tinder which a single spark would ignite. The spark came on a Sunday afternoon at Meerut, and the next day the mutineers swarmed into Delhi. Within a month the rebels had gained possession of parts of the North West Provinces, most of Oudh and the Central Provinces, and the line of communication from Calcutta to Peshawar was cut. In the crisis Canning was at his most decisive. He did not panic though his European troops were desperately outnumbered. In Bengal, for example, the single British regiment compared with ten times as many sepoys; and conditions were no better in the other centres affected – Benares, Allahabad, Cawnpore and Lucknow. Reinforcements from home would take months in passage, but a timely signal to Lord Elgin, on his way to China with a punitive expedition, reached him at Singapore and the troops were diverted to India. By the end of the year the fortitude of Nicholson, Outram, Havelock and Colin Campbell prevailed. Delhi was retaken, Lucknow finally relieved, and the danger passed, though isolated pockets of resistance remained for another year and a half. The last Great Mogul, the aged Bahadur Shah, who had sided with the rebels, was put on trial and exiled to Rangoon.

Canning's perceptive strategy had persuaded John Lawrence not to abandon Peshawar, and he insisted on Colin Campbell recapturing Oudh, instead of making Rohilkhand his priority, as his Commander-in-Chief had proposed. In other ways Canning kept up morale in Calcutta; for long he refused to allow his Indian bodyguard to be replaced, and he even proceeded with the ball on the Queen's Birthday.

In the ensuing months Canning must have thought that all occasions informed against him. Apart from the £40m cost of the Mutiny and the increase of £10m in annual military expenditure, he was criticised by some for being too merciful to the rebels – thereby earning the honourable sobriquet of

'Clemency' – and by others for being too severe. His Resolution of July 1857 was designed to confine retribution to deserters and those convicted of atrocities, but his attempt to curb the understandable appetite for revenge was not well received, either by the Calcutta press or at home. As though to prove how difficult was the lot of the Governor-General, Canning's Oudh Proclamation, which offered merciful terms to the rebel chiefs, but confiscated most of the land in the province, was denounced for its alleged severity. Ellenborough, once again at the Board of Control, sent Canning a severe rebuke; it found its way into *The Times*; and significantly, it was Ellenborough who was forced to resign. Metternich's comment on Canning's policy was that 'he had exactly seized the proper medium'.[5]

For the rest of his time Canning continued to conciliate the Indian princes, allowing them to nominate heirs if they had none of their own – a right Dalhousie had removed, increasing the authority of local landowners, and, later, including Indians in his Legislative Council. He was paving the way to the future.

In England the political reaction to the Mutiny was to transfer the government of India from the East India Company to the Crown. The Court of Directors and the Board of Control were replaced by a Secretary of State advised by an India Council of those with experience there. The fiction that 'John Company' was acting in the name of the Mogul had, even before the Mutiny, been difficult to sustain, and the new regime was announced in the Queen's proclamation, read out by Canning at Allahabad on 1 November 1858, and subsequently at durbars in other principal centres. Canning, who retained the title of Governor-General, also became the first Viceroy. (The title of Viceroy is not derived from statute, though it appears in warrants of precedence and the regulations of the knightly orders. According to Curzon, when the Governor-General was regarded as representing the Sovereign, he was spoken of as the Viceroy, and when he was referred to as the Head of the Government of India, he retained his original title. But except in official papers the distinction was soon blurred.)

It did seem, however, that Canning's physical and mental powers had been impaired by the climax of the Mutiny, although he made imperial progresses throughout the country to emphasise the power of the Raj, and with the help of James

Wilson, a former Financial Secretary to the Treasury sent out from England, he set to work reducing the budget deficit. His conciliation plans now appeared to decline into indecision, but he loyally volunteered to serve another year to complete some of his reforms, before he returned to die a few weeks after he reached England. Canning, always a loner and sometimes a recluse – *The Times* unkindly referred to him as 'essentially cold, almost to repulsiveness' – had stuck to his beliefs, impervious to criticism.

In his place came James Bruce, eighth Earl of Elgin. Though descended from a Scottish family which claimed descent from King Robert the Bruce, he was of modest means, as his father had lost most of his fortune in bringing the Parthenon Marbles to England. It would not be unfair to describe him as a Scottish Peer on the make, a daunting thought, and one critic said he 'talked platitudes on principle'.[7] His earlier apointments as Governor of Jamaica and Governor-General of Canada had been reckoned successful, as had his conduct as Plenipotentiary with the expedition to China – interrupted by Canning's plea for help. There are, however, grounds for suspecting that he took pains to claim the credit, rather than Canning, for the diversion of troops to India – a clue to his careerist tendencies.

Elgin's reign was short, as he died of a stroke in the hills of Dharmsala in his second year of office. Before then he had tried to carry forward Canning's conciliatory programme, being fully conscious of the need to treat the mass of Indians less as an inferior race. He was more wary in his relationships with the princes. Although of noble stock himself, a rugged Scottish independence was apparent in his refusal to take rajas and maharajas at their face value.

John Lawrence was the first Indian Civilian to be preferred to the highest office since John Shore fifty years earlier. A colonel's son, his career in India had been exceptionally meritorious, and he was recognised in England, to which he had returned in 1859, as the 'Saviour of the Punjab', for his defence of the Province during the Mutiny. It was very largely his past reputation that prompted the Government to invite him to be Viceroy, after he had fretted for three years over his desk-bound work as a member of the India Council. A gaunt figure, Lawrence was a demon for work, and unlike his predecessors, he had a good knowledge of Indian languages. Strongly religious, he loathed the ceremonial of Government House and shocked Calcutta society with his informal behaviour. His Excellency in shirt sleeves at his desk, or strolling unaccompanied in the bazaars? It would not do. Under his regime, and that of his devoted but unstylish wife, the glamour of the Viceroy's court was dulled, croquet being one of the principal amusements. Owen Burne recalled: 'We of the younger generation at Simla never quite took to him. We thought him narrow-minded and obstinate, a man quite capable of ruling a province but less fitted in our opinion for governing an Empire.'[8]

Burne may have been prejudiced, but Lawrence had another disability. He lacked political weight at home – a fact soon noted by his colleagues – and depended too slavishly on the Secretary of State for instructions. He was often at odds with his Commander-in-Chief and with his Executive Council, especially the opinionated Sir Henry Durand, and he did not adequately control his Provincial Governors, as became apparent during the Orissa famine of 1866. (Canning had prophesied that Lawrence would upset all he had tried to do in Oudh and the Punjab, by not trusting the native 'gentry'.) This may seem hard on Lawrence, whose unremitting application only served to prove that at the topmost pyramid hard work by itself is not enough, but despite his lack of inspired direction, during his term there were notable advances in public works, railways and irrigation, and, in particular, measures to improve public health. The question of tenant's right was one of his personal concerns, but he got his proposals to improve the peasant's lot through his Executive Council only with the overt backing of the Secretary of State.

Soon after his succession a short campaign resulted in the annexation of the small frontier state of Bhutan, and otherwise in foreign policy he is best remembered for his declared policy of 'masterly inactivity' towards Afghanistan – a legacy which will be examined in later chapters. Lawrence demitted office in 1869, and was ennobled. Unlike his last three predecessors, he lived for another ten years before he was buried in Westminster Abbey. The man who followed him was of a different stamp.

6
His Excellency

> A hundred thousand speeches, and much red cloth
> And Smiths thrice happy if I call them Jones . . .
>
> KIPLING, 'Our Viceroy Resigns'

On the morning of 12 January 1869 the *Feroze* moved up the Hooghly from Diamond Harbour and about four o'clock in the afternoon cast anchor at Chandpal Ghat. The Governor-General and Viceroy designate landed from the official barge to be received by the Sheriff and the Commissioner of Police to the sound of a twenty-gun salute from the battery at the Ghat. The route from the quayside was lined with troops as befitted the arrival of Her Majesty's new representative.

Calcutta bore unmistakable marks of the conqueror's presence. First to be seen were the grim embrasures of Clive's citadel at Fort William, with its barracks and the spire of the Garrison Church as a reminder that the Queen had obligations as Defender of the Faith. The sward of the Maidan, which had once provided a clear field of fire, now served as a milieu for more sociable pursuits, with the peaceful emphasis repeated in the brilliant foliage of the Botanic Gardens. Finally the vista was closed by the dome and far-stretching wings of Government House.

It was an imperial city, and harking back to earlier empires a Graeco-Roman style of architecture was very apparent. Other writers have noted how, with occasional imperfections in detail, the classical rules had been followed, Doric columns decorating official buildings and Corinthian those for pleasure.[1] Among the most notable edifices, the Town Hall stood in the full magnificence of Tuscan Doric, while the Greek Doric Mint had a portico copied from the Temple of Minerva at Athens. The Church of St John's, where on Sundays the Viceroy and his consort sat on plush velvet, roped off to satisfy the curiosity of the worshippers, had a façade very similar to St Martin-in-the Fields in London. The imperial theme was given its apotheosis in the mighty pile of Government House. Nothing could be more palatial, truly palace-like, than the sweep of the porte-cochère, the huge colonnade, the white tropical birds that topped the urns on the balustrade. In front, the robot-like figures of the Governor-General's bodyguard, resplendent in their scarlet and white, stood sentry.

It was also a theatrical city. The elegant white villas that filled in the townscape down to the graceful curve of Garden Reach might, at first glance, glisten in the sun, but on closer inspection the stucco was flaking. Inside these pretentious dwellings there was no drainage or fresh water, and the rooms were often no more than half-furnished. Their owners did not seem to mind, because many of them were conscious of being in passage to make their fortunes, or to earn their pensions, or because they were resigned to the expense of keeping a second place in the hills for the hot season, or perhaps because they sometimes called to mind the sparse furnishings in the Scottish manses or crumbling Irish estates from which many of them came. At any rate the charade continued, given a sombre background by the slums of unbelievable squalor where the great majority of Bengalees lived.

Meanwhile, on the steps of Government House, stood Lawrence, wearing his official uniform for the last time and flanked, as Mayo noted in his diary, by, among others, Sir William Mansfield, the Commander-in-Chief, Sir Donald McLeod from the Punjab, Sir William Muir from the North West Provinces, and the Members of the Executive Council. The blue-and-gold, punctuated by occasional scarlet, of the uniforms worn by the reception path at the top of the stairs contrasted with the 'easiest of summer costumes, with a funny little coloured neck-tie' sported by the figure now dismounting from his carriage.[2]

The contrast became more poignant when Lawrence 'looking like a hoary weather-beaten rock, round which the elements had oft-times roared and dashed' shuffled forward the customary three paces to greet the athletic Mayo who bounded up the steps 'beaming with the brightness of health, buoyant in spirits'. Forty years of Indian service had taken their toll of

Lawrence, his face blanched and his tall figure shrunken. Mayo, in the words of Sir Richard Temple who was an eyewitness, was 'elastic with hope'.[3]

To Temple's mind the scene gained some added pathos because it was precedented. Six years earlier, Canning had looked 'pale, toil-worn and grief-stricken' when he handed over to Elgin, who 'came up gaily, ruddy in face, massive and square in forehead, buoyant in manner and stalwart in frame'.[4] The uncomfortable conclusion was that the office either killed those who held it (though only Cornwallis and Elgin died in India) or it broke their health. Temple mused on the differences between Mayo, known to be a sportsman, a hard rider and an excellent shot, and some of his predecessors – Hardinge quiet and genial, Dalhousie retiring and afflicted with pain, Canning naturally grave, Elgin bright and genial without any great physical stamina, and Lawrence drained by his labours. It was already apparent that a new man, in every sense, had arrived.

In the Council Chamber the formalities were soon completed. There, with Lawrence and the Members of Council in their accustomed seats, before the assembly of chief secretaries and senior officers and beneath the portraits of those who had gone before, Mayo took the oaths. Another salute was fired, this time from the ramparts at Fort William, to signify that the fourth Viceroy and ruler of the 196 million of British India had assumed power. In the evening he was entertained to a state banquet by Lawrence. This was strictly in accordance with protocol, but on at least one previous occasion things had not gone so smoothly. Auckland, on arrival in 1835, had the humiliation of being marooned in the Hooghly when his barge ran aground and reached land so late that the official dinner had to be cancelled. At the time onlookers saw this as an omen, and events proved they were right.

Lawrence lingered for a week to perform introductions and hand over to the new Viceroy. Mayo remained on friendly terms with Lawrence and later kept up a correspondence with him on current topics. 'Nothing', he wrote to Argyll, 'could equal the frankness and confidence with which he has treated me.'[5] He went on to praise Lawrence's generous disposition and his unrivalled knowledge of India and her people. This was written just before Lawrence left, but legend has it that Mayo was somewhat surprised when, at the end of their last drive together, Lawrence was annoyed that the *syce* had been too slow in opening the carriage door and leapt out to give the man's ear a hearty tug.[6] Recalling this incident, and knowing that he would not treat an Irish groom in this way, Mayo frequently inveighed against the 'abominable practice' of striking Indians. 'It is a cowardly and detestable practice, and ought, in my opinion, to be visited with the most severe censure and punishment.'[7]

Government House dated from the days of Wellesley. The 'Magnificent Marquess' was quick to decide that his existing headquarters did not match his ambitions. He had to emphasise that his status was superior to the Calcutta merchants who had mansions as grand as his seat of authority, and to this end he had a spacious site cleared adjoining the Maidan. He was fortunate in having to hand as his architect Lieutenant Wyatt. Although only a junior officer in the Bengal Engineers, he demonstrated the same vision and style that was exemplified at home in the work of the other members of his family.

The conception of the new palace – no other word would be appropriate – was derived from Kedleston Hall in Derbyshire. To signal the majesty of the Raj it was fronted with impressive Ionic façades, but, in contrast, its main rooms were marked by a clear simplicity of design, and it was surprisingly well ventilated by what breezes there were. The State Apartments were lodged in the centre, from which stretched four wings connected by curved corridors, and to the south the great dome faced across the Maidan towards Fort William. The ceremonial steps on the north front led to a room more than a hundred feet long, which was balanced by a similar room in the south front. The pattern was repeated on the upper floor with an elegant ballroom above the Marble Room. The Governor-General and his family lived in spendour in the two southern wings, while the northern ones housed Council meetings and rooms for distinguished guests who were favoured with His Excellency's invitation.

Most ladies of Governors-General were irritated by the size of Government House and the formality practised there. Lady Canning found that her sitting room on the upper floor made her feel giddy, as though she was recovering from a long illness, and insisted on moving to the floor below, where she reproduced a very English apartment, complete with chintz and prints of the Royal children. Lady Mayo, when her turn came, did not make great changes, but she imported furniture from Paris for the Duke of Edinburgh's visit. Soon after her arrival in India she enquired whether she could be present when the Viceroy, throned, received the Nepalese Ambassador. Burne's tart reply was that 'It has not recently been done, but there is no official objection. Lady Canning at times did it, and it lends interest to the ceremony.'[8]

Mayo also inherited a country place at Barrackpore, fifteen miles up the Hooghly, and this too originated with Wellesley. He had scarcely finished Government House – at a cost of £63,000 – when he started work at Barrackpore. But the Court of Directors had by this time had enough of his megalomania; they recalled him in 1805 and put a stop to building at the new country house. Barrackpore remained unfinished until, with the arrival of the Earl of Moira, grandeur again became the accepted mode. He levelled the site, and rebuilt a temporary house that Wellesley – who did nothing by halves – had constructed to house him while his new palace was rising, taking the opportunity to add a portico and colonnades of his own.

Barrackpore's subsequent history was not as peaceful as its rural surroundings. In Amherst's time there was trouble with the troops in the cantonment, and a much more sinister uprising by the troops at Barrackpore, occasioned by the introduction of the new type of cartridge, took place in April 1857. Canning was criticised for taking the outbreak too lightly, but before another month had passed the Mutiny proper started at Meerut.

Mayo did not make extensive use of Barrackpore. As he travelled enormous distances throughout the length and breadth of his domain he had little time for relaxation in his country retreat. But he did make the annual pilgrimage to Simla, now established as the summer capital. Simla, sardonically described by Kaye as that pleasant hill sanitarium which had been the cradle of more political insanity than any place within the limits of Hindustan, is worth a closer scrutiny, not so much for its history as for the light it sheds on the disposition of those who ruled India.

The settlement that became the summer headquarters was founded by a Lieutenant Ross in 1819 on land acquired during the Nepalese War, and was first visited officially by Amherst in 1827. For a time Governors-General spent occasional hot seasons there, leaving their Executive Council to swelter in Calcutta, but this caused much dissatisfaction. It was said, for example, that Auckland might have thought better of it if he had taken the advice of his Council in Calcutta before proclaiming his Manifesto from Simla to start the first Afghan War. In 1864, however, Lawrence insisted on a full-scale annual migration with his entire staff for six months every year.

Neither the site, nor the timetable, were free from controversy. Temple said that Simla had been chosen because it was by far the largest of the settlements in the mountains. It was the only hill station that could take so large an influx and could be reached by rail and road, even at the height of the rainy season. Politically, it occupied the most commanding situation in the Himalayan region, overlooking the North West Provinces, close to the Punjab proper, and comparatively near to the Indus frontier – but not too close to points that might be threatened. Others were less enthusiastic. Durand, pungent as always, minuted, 'It would be difficult to choose a point on the map of India that shall more successfully solve the problem of being as remote as possible from Calcutta, Madras, Bombay, and Kurrachee, and, of course, England.' The annual journey from Calcutta involved the loss of two months out of twelve for the transaction of business. Durand dismissed the climatic arguments, and contended that the Government should move for a year, or even two, throughout India, choosing locations for 'great administrative reasons', not merely for cool weather.[9] Mayo also came to have doubts. He told Temple that the proper place for the hill residence was the most central, and the most accessible, spot that could be found. 'Raneekhet fulfils these conditions – Simla does not.' But he did not press for a change when there were infinitely more important problems.[10]

The hill station as an artefact was entirely the work of the English, and in its surroundings exotic in the strict sense of the word. Morris noted that visually it was a 'neatly hatched compression of planes', with the buildings in their tiers on the hillside providing the horizontals. The verticals were the deodar and pine trees, while the diagonals were the slopes of the hills themselves which framed the settlement and intersected behind it.

No doubt the change of climate at Simla was very welcome to those who had come up from the torrid plains, but there were disadvantages. The highly rarefied air at a height of 8,000 feet affected the breathing and circulation of most newcomers. Often the clouds came down upon the mountains, while mists rolled up from the valleys, so that visibility was nil. 'In such a scene as this, you may perceive, if a lucid interval permits it, the Member of Council riding home from a meeting at the Viceroy's residence looking like a bathing-machine man, and caparisoned from head to foot in drenched waterproof garments.'[11] (Only the Viceroy was allowed a carriage.)

Burne, who had first visited Simla in 1862 as Sir Hugh Rose's Secretary, ignored these defects and rhapsodised about his 'Elysium' where picnics, dances, glee-clubs, and cricket (on a level patch of ground some 1,000 feet below, called Annandale) passed the time agreeably. Something of a performer himself, Burne took an active part in the constant amateur dramatics, that anti-social activity to which the Victorians were obstinately addicted, playing the lead in such masterpieces as *Alonzo the Brave* and *The Crimson Scarf*.[12] Burne accompanied Mayo to Simla for three summers, and for him it never lost its enchantment.

Simla was where the English could be themselves, and the only Indians there occupied an ancillary role as servants or dependents – unless they were visiting feudatory chiefs. The Viceroy and his family occupied a ridge-top house called Peterhof, which, with wooden verandahs and gables at each end, looked like a golf clubhouse in the Home Counties. It was not a lavish building, and monkeys jumped on the corrugated tin roof, which often leaked. (A later Viceroy, Dufferin, built the new Viceregal Lodge on the summit of Observatory Hill.) For the rest, W.H. Russell, the *Times* correspondent, who visited Simla in 1858, noted 'rows of detached bungalows standing amid flower-gardens and neatly laid-out compounds with English names on the gateways'. It was, in short, a suburban existence. The senior mandarins and generals did not come from quite such an elevated social background as they began to imagine as soon as they landed in Hindustan, and when they were relieved of the searching scrutiny of the Indian population there was something of a reversion to type. Not that the satraps would accept this analysis, pointing instead to the responsibilities they carried up from the plains and the meticulous pecking order that governed their polite society. (Lawrence thought he and his Council could get through in a day work that would have needed a week at Calcutta.) But while the English at Simla were, for the season, defiantly English, an odd parallel suggests itself. It is that of Arnold Lunn's disciples who colonised Swiss 'hill stations' towards the end of last century and imposed their own Anglo-Saxon customs on the Alpine resorts.

Mayo spent the hot weather at Simla each year while he was Viceroy, and it would have been out of character if he had not presided over the entertainments with his usual geniality – he enjoyed seeing Burne impersonate him in an amateur revue. But he was restless there; official business was conducted with despatch; and from Simla he carried out a series of vigorous expeditions.

The administration was carried out by a Cabinet, called the Executive Council, with the Governor-General as its President, subject to the authority of the Secretary of State in England and controlling in turn the twelve Provincial authorities. Technically, government orders proceeded in the name of the 'Governor-General in Council'. Canning had started the Cabinet system, and since then each Member of Council had been responsible for his own Department, much as at Westminster. (Previously, individual submissions had to be seen by each Member in turn, being transmitted in mahogany boxes from one Member's house to another.) Either Members or the Viceroy could bring important questions to the Council for decision, but John Strachey once advised that a paper should not be circulated without a note of Mayo's views, adding 'When the Viceroy has expressed a decided opinion on a question there is much less inclination to oppose than there is when each Member is left to form his own independent opinion.'[13] The Council seldom came to a formal vote, and the Viceroy could always impose his will by veto, but in the event Mayo was never outvoted.

Traditionally the Viceroy took charge of the Foreign Department, so that he was his own Foreign Minister. Additionally, and exceptionally, Mayo soon reported that he had 'been obliged to take the whole of the Public Works Department' to his own hand.[14] In 1871 he set up a new Department of Revenue, Agriculture, and Commerce, and rearranged the duties of the Home and Financial Departments. (As will become apparent, this was more than the whim of a new man trying to make his mark.) To complete the organisation, there were separate Military and Legislative Departments. Army affairs were, naturally, spoken for by a Military member in the Executive Council but the Commander-in-Chief also sat on the Council as an 'Extraordinary' Member.

Each Department also had a Secretary, who dealt with most day-to-day business and processed papers for his Member. Unlike Permanent Secretaries in Whitehall, however, they had direct access to the Viceroy, could consult him direct in an emergency, and had a weekly audience with him. Secretaries could, and often did, succeed to be Members, and they could also expect promotion to a Provincial post.

The Viceroy held a weekly meeting of the Legislative Council, comprising the Members of the Executive Council, the Lieutenant-Governor of the Province where the Viceroy might be residing, and non-official Members who were meant to represent the European and Native communities. The Legislative Council met in public, and its proceedings were reported in the press and published in the Gazette. But its powers were limited, as it did not initiate. Many of the bills it considered came up from the Provincial Governments for ratification, and they had all been previously approved by the Executive Council. The official Members, if they voted together, had a permanent majority on the Legislative Council, but legislation there had to be, and this was the forum where it was discussed and enacted.

Taken together, the time spend in studying official correspondence and despatches, the ceaseless round of interviews, the sessions in Council, not to mention the inexorable round of entertainments and formal appearances, made demands almost beyond the capacity of one man. But Mayo from the start attacked it all with gusto and found time to visit more parts of India than any previous Governor-General had done. His own recipe, as he confided to Sir George Campbell on his return to India to be Lieutenant-Governor of Bengal, was 'never to give the Sun a chance – to wear heavy Solar Topees, thick wadded back piece, and a heavy woollen girdle round my loins, and so I have often ridden 40 miles in fairly hot sun without any inconvenience but a good sweat.'[15]

That was written after Mayo had been in office for almost three years. A spurt of energy could be expected from a new man, but Mayo never lost his enthusiasm, although he did modify his original schedule, which occupied twelve hours of toil a day. Burne found his temper so equable throughout these long stints that he remembered working with Mayo as being 'really a recreation'. In his Memoirs Burne also quotes Mayo's old chief Lord Derby as saying that he did and said generous things 'not because it was polite, but because it was in his nature and he could not help it'.

Mayo clearly had a warm relationship with his Private Secretary, but he also had to work closely with his chief dragomen on the Council and in the Departments. Most of them appear in later chapters, but an introduction now will aid understanding of the intricate network.

John Strachey was the Member in charge of the Home Department until he moved to the new Department of Revenue, Agriculture and Commerce. Strachey, cool, intellectual, ambitious and certainly not over-modest – characteristics he shared with his able brother Richard, then Chief Engineer in the Public Works Department – was the antithesis of Mayo, but he enjoyed the Viceroy's complete confidence. It is evident from their letters that the Stracheys were more open, not to say caustic, than their colleagues in putting forward their views and this was something that Mayo relished. Strachey was succeeded in the Home Department by the scholarly Barrow Ellis from the Bombay Government.

The Financial Department was under the charge of Sir Richard Temple, known as 'Burra Dick' or the 'Great Tribulation'. With previous service in the Punjab and the Central Provinces, and as Resident in Hyderabad, Temple was able, fluent, possibly too fluent, and certainly too optimistic. One critic said 'He has nothing to learn, but if you are modest with him, he will teach you everything.' Mayo, as will become evident in chapter 14, simply did not get on with him.

While these mentioned so far were career civil servants, the Legal Member was normally a barrister of some repute sent out from England. Soon after Mayo arrived the learned Henry Maine, who had been Legal Member since 1862, returned to England and a chair at Oxford. In his place came James Fitzjames Stephen, the friend of Froude and Carlyle, who had already made a name for himself at the English Bar. In India Stephen displayed both his forensic skill and some determination to push on with codifying and consolidating statute law – that highly desirable work which everyone encourages but no one wants to do. Mayo relied heavily on Stephen for advice, particularly at the time of the Wahabi trials, but the barrister, who soon decided that he would be better off financially at home, was always threatening to resign and soon after Mayo's death he went back to England, eventually to reach the High Court bench. (Stephen and the Stracheys were uncles of Virginia Woolf and Lytton Strachey respectively.)

Now to Mayo's military chiefs – initially Sir Henry Durand, the Military Member, Henry Norman the Secretary, and Sir William Mansfield the Commander-in-Chief. The prickly Durand was difficult to handle. Very bitter, as he reveals in his letters, that he did not get the KCB for his services in the Mutiny, he had not been mollified by the belated award (in 1867) of the Star of India. Tall, broad-shouldered, with an impressive presence, his difficulties were compounded when he became deaf in his right ear, and he was always ready to take offence. But he was an upright man, loyal to Mayo, whom he strongly supported on non-military matters. Mayo always knew where he stood with Durand and wanted to appoint him to the new post which he had in mind as Agent-in-Chief of Rajputana and the Central States. Argyll was doubtful about Durand's qualifications, reminding Mayo that the India Council thought him 'imperious and harsh – especially towards Natives – apt to treat them with contempt and incapable of concealing what he thinks of them'.[16] But Mayo, relying on his own judgement, offered the post to Durand, who promptly turned it down, on the ground, among others, that it would amount to 'shelving' him. The Viceroy, not concealing his annoyance, made Durand the

Lieutenant-Governor of the Punjab, an appointment which he knew the old warhorse coveted.

Mayo had no problems with Norman, who succeeded as Military Member. Norman was not greatly given to arguing his corner, and his later career – in time he reached the highest rank in the army – was marked by his adroitness in not giving offence.

Sir William Mansfield was by nature more of an administrator than a fighting soldier, and though only an extraordinary Member took a lively part in Council business. (Charles Wood, while Secretary of State, had encouraged him to do this in Lawrence's time, as he thought Lawrence lacked experience in higher, imperial, business.) Mayo found Mansfield flexible and cooperative, and at one time thought of him for Durand's place as Military member, but nothing came of it and Mansfield went home, to be succeeded as Commander-in-Chief by Lord Napier of Magdala.

Napier's personal relationship with Mayo is not easy to disentangle. Napier had accompanied the Mayos on their journey out to India – he was on his way to resume his command in Bombay after the Abyssinian campaign – and Burne later thought their official relations were 'very cordial'.[17] But Napier's papers reveal that he did not really like the Viceroy, being infected with the professional soldier's contempt for politicians as a class, and suspecting, unfairly, that Mayo was intent on military reductions at any cost. 'Lord Mayo's proceedings are disclosed as systematic hostility to every military charge.'[18] Napier was also very deeply suspicious of the senior civil service. When Northbrook took over as Viceroy, Napier wrote acidly: 'Strachey is now applying the poultice to him as he did to Lord Mayo. I hope he may not be successful.'[19]

Inevitably, a new Viceroy was surrounded by advisers who had spent long years in Hindustan and who knew far more about the business of ruling the country. The surprising thing is that, from the moment he disembarked from the *Feroze*, Mayo took unmistakable charge, dominated these confident, authoritative satraps, and seldom had any difficulty in getting his own way. He persuaded them to work with him to carry out what he thought was his imperial mission. In a word, Disraeli had chosen a leader. To Disraeli Mayo wrote after a few months in office, 'The work here is tremendous. Everything comes to the Viceroy, and the bigness of the questions would surprise you. I do not think I have made a mistake yet. At least if I have, it has not been found out.'[20] The sapient Hunter confided in his wife that India was getting a new type of man, 'and Lord Mayo and Mr Strachey are the first of them.'[21]

To complete the *dramatis personae*, a word is needed about the rulers of the main Provincial Governments – the Governors of the Presidencies of Bombay and Madras, the Lieutenant-Governors of Bengal, the Punjab, and the North West Provinces. (The holders of these offices had often served their time on the Executive Council.) The distinction between Governors and Lieutenant-Governors was by now little more than historic, but a Governor had two councils – one for executive business, and a legislative council. He could proceed on his own in an emergency, but normally acted as Governor in Council. A Lieutenant-Governor had no executive council. He had less varied responsibility than a Governor, but was 'individually more potential'.

The Bombay Presidency, though still shaken by the collapse of the Bank of Bombay a few years earlier, still believed itself to be rather superior, and there was a long history of friction between it and the imperial administration at Calcutta. A later Secretary of State, Salisbury, complained bitterly about the arrogant bearing of the higher ranks of the Bombay service.[22] Mayo tried to keep a firm grip on Sir Seymour Fitzgerald, the Bombay Governor, but he found him distant, both geographically and in his approach to the Viceroy's policies. With Lord Napier and Ettrick at Madras Mayo had a better understanding, and Napier was very sympathetic to Mayo's reforms, even when they impinged strongly on the Madras army establishment.

In the latter part of 1870 Sir William Grey, the Lieutenant-Governor of Bengal, went home (to be rewarded in time with the Governorship of Jamaica). Grey had been very much a laissez-faire man, averse to over-exertion, mental or physical, and Mayo was often impatient with his reluctance to press forward with innovations. His successor, Sir George Campbell, was a complete contrast. A shrewd Scotsman, his dry manner and nasal accent irritated many of his colleagues, but his energy was not in question. He had conducted the important enquiry into the Orissa famine in 1866, had sat in the High Court of Bengal, and had been Chief Commissioner of the Central Provinces. Campbell was back in England, wondering about his future employment, when Argyll and Mayo decided he was the man to rule the 67 million inhabitants of the province. He proved to be a zealous reformer, starting the first Bengal census, founding a medical school for native assistants, and introducing examinations for native candidates for the civil service. The *Friend of India* commented gleefully that Campbell, who took up office in March 1871, 'had shaken the Bengal office till its official teeth chattered'.[23] Northbrook later thought he was guilty of 'over-administration', but Campbell found the tempo and temper of Mayo's government greatly to his taste.

Sir William Muir was an efficient and acceptable ruler of the North West Provinces, always alert to watch lest conditions of partial scarcity should deteriorate into a full-scale famine, to protect the peasantry from exploitation, and to maintain the rule of law in his troubled province. Mayo's correspondence with him shows their mutual respect – even extending to their shared concern that pheasant were being exterminated in the mass over the Mussoorie hills and their plumes sold to the London market.[24]

Lastly, the Punjab. Sir Donald MacLeod had wanted to retire soon after the new Viceroy's arrival, but Mayo retained the venerable Lieutenant-Governor for his advice and help in the discussions with the Afghan Amir. Then, as we have seen, Durand took his place. Unhappily, Durand had only a few months in office. On the last day of 1870 he met a grotesque death during a visit of inspection to Tonk, when the elephant on which he was seated with the local ruler passed under too low an arch and he was crushed to death. (Coincidentally, poor MacLeod was killed in November 1872 when his foot was caught while he was getting into a Metropolitan Railway carriage at Gloucester Road station.) Durand was succeeded by Sir Robert Davies, who had been Commissioner in Oudh, where he made his name in the long struggle with the Talukdars that led to the passing of the Oudh Tenancy Act in 1868.

There is an element of musical chairs in this, as in any hierarchy, and the effect was twofold. First, those concerned divided their energies between their existing duties and manoeuvring, if intriguing is too strong a word, for their future. There was also much jealousy and backbiting. For example, John Strachey thought William Muir was 'mendacious' and brother Richard was convinced that Grey hated him. Second, the correspondence between Mayo and Argyll indicates how much time it took to keep the pavane proceeding at a dignified pace. It was no autumn reshuffle. Mayo had no illusions. Writing to Argyll on the vexed question of retirement pay, he observed, 'This like every other service in the world is composed of respectable mediocrities and some Hard Bargains. Therefore they like a system which gives no advantage to genius, or brilliant success, which is rare but not uncommon. They are quite right, but the Public Service does not benefit as much as it might.'[25]

The question is how Mayo fared in moulding the senior officers, civil and military, to his will as he applied his mind to the various functions of government.

7
The Public Good

'I have only one object in view. I know we have not done all our duty to the people of this land. I know that millions have been spent on the conquering race which might have been and could be spent in enriching and elevating the children of the soil. We have done much but we can do a great deal more. It is, however, impossible unless we spend less on the "interests" and more on the people.'[1]

Mayo so wrote to Argyll, not in a moment of initial euphoria – most Governors-General started with the most admirable intentions – but on 1 September 1871, after he had been in office for two years and eight months. He had learned something of the hazards in steering his proposals through the Executive Council and in obtaining, where necessary, the approval of the Secretary of State, but he showed no signs of slackening in his determination to promote the prosperity of the people as the best way to contribute to the imperial vision. His strong resolve had been apparent since the first crisis with which he was faced.

On his arrival in January 1869 he was warned that, following the failure of the July monsoon, conditions of near scarcity, rapidly approaching famine, had been reported from the North West Provinces. Mayo at once wrote to Argyll saying that he might have to import corn from abroad, and he was sure His Grace would agree that anything was justified to save human lives.[2] No doubt, as already mentioned in chapter 3, Mayo recalled Peel's import of American maize in 1846 at the time of the Irish famine. He was also aware that starvation, particularly in populous centres, was the breeding-ground for serious insurrection. But in addition to this political consideration it was the welfare of the masses he had in mind. He also referred to his Irish experience when it was suggested that, on the Poor Law analogy, funds for famine relief should be raised by local taxation. A Poor Law system, he replied in scathing terms, might be well adapted for dealing with chronic pauperism, but to his certain knowledge it inevitably broke down when faced with a national calamity. He remembered very clearly how ineffective Lord John Russell's invocation of Poor Law measures had been during the potato famine in Ireland.

In much of the business that came before the Governor-General in Council, especially if it concerned the Financial, Foreign and Military Departments, the initiative was, for all practical purposes, Mayo's own. As regards the Public Works Department, which dealt with more bread and butter matters, the Viceroy might have been expected to content himself with a more general, supervisory role. But this was not Mayo's approach. He was too restless in his mind – and he was too active physically. He had to see everything for himself.

Mayo travelled throughout his domain far more extensively than any previous Governor-General had done. According to Burne, he covered nearly 6,000 miles in his first year, 9,000 in his second, and 4,000 in 1871. He used the railway wherever possible, but much of this extraordinary mileage was accomplished by dint of hard riding, sixty miles a day or more, and his staff were hard put to keep up with him. Often he was the first Governor-General to visit a particular locality, and his hectic anabasis reached remote posts where His Excellency was not expected. In April 1870, for example, after visiting Peshawar and the Khyber Pass he rode eighty miles to Kohat, where he held a durbar for frontier chiefs. The mountain men came armed to the teeth; some were said to be the greatest rascals in the country – 'all of whom spent their lives in plunder, and most of them had been engaged in many murders'. Mayo thought it curious to see the tribesmen ploughing with their matchlocks slung over their shoulders.[3] After a further 500 miles, most of it over rough hill roads, he was at Sialkot to meet the devious Maharaja of Kashmir before travelling a further 280 miles to reach Simla on the last day of the month. In three months he had covered nearly 3,000 miles.

Next year he left Simla on 1 November 1871 for his return to Calcutta. On the way he held an unusual 'rural durbar' at Palumpore, when the natives were encouraged to speak their minds. (The *Friend of India* commented with surprise on the 'openness' of the discussion.[4]) Mayo repeated one of his basic tenets to the assembled chiefs. His 'whole desire' was to make the Government 'suitable for the wants, and productive of advantage, of its many millions of inhabitants'.[5] On 12 November he went to Dharmsala to visit Elgin's tomb, and then there was an exciting journey down the River Ravee – Lady Mayo was in the party – on 'mussucks' of inflated cow hide. Next to Amritsar, Lahore and Sonepore for a diplomatic meeting with the highly respected Jung Bahadur, and on 27 November he was back in Calcutta, having done 2,500 miles.

All this provides an impressive tribute to the Viceroy's stamina. But there was more to it. Mayo was a good listener, as can be deduced from the objective tone of his diaries. There was no 'side' about him despite his exalted rank, and the District Officers he met were invariably impressed by the attention he afforded them. Just as his career as an Irish MP was based on his intimate acquaintance with those who worked on the land, so he built up a fund of knowledge from those who carried the burden of government in the Indian provinces. Burne was always impressed by the speed with which the Viceroy gathered real information.[6]

Mayo was keen to experiment, to try new ideas, but he was far from seeking to extend the tentacles of government. He had doubts whether the conquering race had been wise in imposing an alien, sophisticated system of administration instead of attacking the basic problems, particularly, as we will see, agriculture. But first he turned his attention to the Public Works Department.

On 9 May 1869 he wrote to Arbuthnot, saying that he had himself taken over responsibility for the Department.[7] There were several reasons for his decision. As a matter of principle, he was convinced that the first thing was to ensure that the funds required for the developments that the country needed were available, and he meant to achieve this by drastic economies in administration. Next, the money must be steered in the right direction – by applying it to building roads and railways, and by improvements in physical conditions by developing agriculture and irrigation.

Mayo had also come to the view that the Department, as it was run, was extravagant and inefficient. Estimates were a laughing-stock, and supervision of projects under way was unbelievably casual. 'There is scarcely a fault', he minuted, 'which could have been committed in the construction of a great work which has not been committed here.' As regards the building of the Calcutta High Court, he said sharply that the Department should stop waffling that an offending officer was 'not free from responsibility', and admit that he was not up to the job. Part of the trouble was caused by the shortage of qualified civil engineers, and this was not made good till graduates from the new college at Cooper's Hill, opened by Argyll on 5 August 1871, began to go out to India. Much of the inefficiency, however, was the direct result of poor accounting and budgeting. Mayo was absolutely opposed to financing non-remunerative schemes by borrowing, and it was cardinal to his policy that the money must be found before the work was begun.

What he achieved can be seen in the note he had prepared in answer to a mischievous letter that appeared in the Calcutta press on 13 April 1870, alleging that 'in an evil moment he [Lord Mayo] took personal charge of the Public Works Department, which means that he allowed the able and ambitious Col. Strachey to spend money as hard as he was able'.[8] The reply pointed out that, after discovering reckless excesses over the estimates and issuing stringent instructions which were 'most unpopular' both to the Department and to the local governments, he cut the Public Works ordinary grant by £500,000 and again by £800,000, and with other economies saved over £1.3m. in his first year (1869–70). In the next year he insisted on a further reduction of £400,000 and as a measure of the relative size of his economies, it is relevant that before his pruning exercise the annual grant exceeded £8m.

Reductions in expenditure and the elimination of waste, however desirable, are negative achievements, and Mayo was keen to make progress with the domestic fabric, the 'infrastructure' in today's jargon. Under his rule, roads were constructed on as large a scale as before. But all Governors-General had seen the need for more and better highways, and the work was largely carried out by the Provincial authorities. With railways it was different.

About 4,000 miles of rail had been laid by the time Lawrence left the country, but there were compelling reasons – military to connect strategic outposts, and commercial to facilitate trade – for pushing ahead with the development of the network.

Up till now the railways had been built by the 'Guaranteed Companies'. In theory there was a system of joint control with the Government Director and consulting engineers supervising every detail of the Companies' activities, but in practice the Companies got their own way. Two sets of establishments were doing the work of one, and complacency was rife. Mayo did not like what he saw of the railway organisation, and studying the papers he found 'grave instances of obstinacy, corruption, and neglect of local opinion'. (He was also incensed at the treatment of native passengers. 'They are packed much more closely in third-class carriages than in their ordinary modes of conveyance; and because a man is broiled in a *dak ghari*, there is no reason why he should be roasted in a railway carriage.')[9] Most unsatisfactory of all were the financial arrangements, since the Companies, as their name implied, were guaranteed 5% on their investment, and in consequence had no incentive to economise. The cost of construction was now running at £17,000 a mile, double Dalhousie's estimate.

In one of his last minutes Lawrence had questioned the equity of giving the Companies this free charter for extravagance.[10] He had earlier raised his doubts with Northcote, who was not sympathetic. Argyll, however, took a different line. In his Memoirs he stated what he thought of the Government taking over construction before he knew that this was Lawrence's view. He came to this conclusion on general grounds, then learned from papers already in the office that 'it was only in despair of this course being sanctioned that the Government of India was pressing for at least *some* improvement in the extravagant conditions allowed to the guaranteed companies'.[11] On 12 February 1869 Argyll wrote to Mayo suggesting that they should dispense with the Companies, since it was quite wrong that they should be given 5% when the Government could raise the money at 4%, with the possibility of greater native involvement and investment. But, he added cautiously, this was only his personal opinion, and 'many interests will be alarmed at the proposal'.[12]

Mayo readily accepted that this was the right course, and Argyll, with less trouble than he expected, obtained Cabinet sanction. Mayo sensibly allowed the Companies to continue with their immediate plans, and reserved for the state large tracts of country where no line had been begun – an unusual, but for once justifiable, example of nationalisation. The annual report on railways for 1871–2 recorded that there were 5,204 miles open for traffic. A further 2,400 miles were under construction, of which 940 were being built by the Companies and 1,503 by the Government.[13]

Rivett-Carnac, the Cotton Commissioner, gives a good example of Mayo's personal intervention.[14] Carnac, who had long been arguing for a branch line from Khamgaon to join the Great Indian Peninsula Railway at Jhellum and carry cotton, had made no progress till he was summoned to join the Viceregal camp assembled at Amballa to greet Sher Ali. The day after his arrival he had an interview with Mayo. The Viceroy, it appeared, had read the papers and told Carnac to discuss them with Richard Strachey. To Carnac's surprise, Strachey approved, and they went back to Mayo who promptly added his ukase to the scheme. He told Carnac that, as the man on the spot, he would be responsible for building the line, and that, for good measure, it should be finished by the following spring so that he (Mayo) could open it at the end of the Viceregal tour of Central India. This, the first of the State Railways, was completed on schedule, and at precisely 4 o'clock on 4 March 1870 Mayo hammered in the last rivet and declared the line open.[15] As an indication of the different attitudes in India and at Westminster, Mayo was warned by Bartle Frere that the India Council had solemnly proposed sending the Viceroy a severe reprimand for starting the Khamgaon line without the Secretary of State's consent; but Argyll was not prepared to be huffy and sent his approval.

Mayo was still determined to bring down the cost of construction. 'The truth about India is simply this, cheap railways or none; and I would rather do without railways altogether than incur the future risk of that abnormal increase in expenditure.'[16] He was attracted by the idea of reducing the gauge, which would bring the cost down to £5,000 a mile, and suggested to Argyll that they should seek the advice of an American engineer who knew about light railways. Argyll agreed to consult the British Legation in Washington, and with the engineer's arrival imminent Mayo had this cautionary advice for him: 'If a man is healthy when he comes out, and *sober* and careful when here, he can do very well. If he intends to drink he may bring his coffin with him.'[17] At home John Fowler, the doyen of the British engineers, pointed out that the cost of construction in America was no less than in India.[18] Professional jealousy had been aroused.

Thereafter the great gauge battle proved more controversial, and was much keener fought, than the Guaranteed Companies issue. In India the mercantile community was opposed to having two different gauges, which meant a break in transit; engineers denied that the smaller gauge would be cheaper; and there was a strong body of opinion that the existing, standard gauge of 5 ft 6 ins (nearly a foot broader than British lines) was best suited for military purposes.

Argyll took refuge in appointing a committee to examine the arguments. Richard Strachey from the Public Works Department was in London to put forward Mayo's case. As he reported to the Viceroy on 30 June 1870, he had seen Argyll, though it was 'difficult to get him to listen'; Argyll was 'quite staunch as to narrow gauge', but there was strong opposition.[19] In fact the Committee could not agree, and Fowler kept writing to Mayo that its proceedings were dominated by Strachey, although (unlike Fowler) he had no railway experience. Eventually Argyll, losing patience, left it to Mayo's discretion.

Mayo waited for a personal report from Strachey on his return to India before telling Argyll that he had decided in favour of a narrow gauge. After studying the views of the chief of the Norwegian railway department, and even examining the results of the little Festiniog line in Wales, he circulated a lengthy minute to the Executive Council, canvassing the merits of the various widths ad nauseam.[21] On 3 January he told Fowler that he had opted for the metric gauge of 3 ft 3 ins, and that he hoped the question could now be regarded as settled. He explained, somewhat ingenuously, 'It was not an easy matter for non-professional men to decide. However, I consulted no one as I could not do so without causing jealousy.'[22]

The significance of this dispute, as it wound its way to a conclusion, lies not so much in the merits as in the way in which Mayo obtained the agreement of the self-appointed experts on the Executive Council, and secured acceptance in

London. He now went ahead to authorise a cheap line from Agra to Ajmere and another from Lahore towards Peshawar, and by the end of 1871 900 miles, mostly on the smaller gauge, had been put in hand in Rajputana, the Punjab, and Berar. Sadly, Mayo's plan was not the success he hoped for, though he did not live to witness the growing volume of criticism that the metric gauge was only marginally less costly to build, was more expensive to maintain, and was less stable for carriages. After his death, Salisbury as Secretary of State was more inclined to listen to the critics, and in 1875 under a compromise the broader gauge was reinstated for the most important lines still to be built. Mayo, for a time, might have won a famous victory, but as little Peterkin could have asked 'What good came of it at last?'

Elsewhere on the railway front Mayo had some success, and his personal influence persuaded native princes to subscribe £2m for lines in their territories. In Hyderabad, thanks to the cooperation of the Nizam's enlightened minister Sir Salar Jung, a line was laid connecting the Nizam's capital with the Great Indian Peninsula Railway at a cost to the princely state of £1m. The line and profits were to belong to Hyderabad, but the construction and operation were British. In Indore, the Maharaja Holkar provided another £1m to link his state with the G.I.P. in return for 4½% interest and half the profits.

Other projects already begun were completed during Mayo's rule. The vital line connecting Calcutta and Bombay was joined at Jubbulpore, at a ceremony marked by the presence of the Duke of Edinburgh in March 1870. On 15 October in the same year, in Mayo's absence, the Maharaja of Patiala opened the Sutlej Bridge to put Lahore in direct communication with Calcutta and Bombay.

It seems, however, that Mayo, impatient for progress as he was, remained disappointed with what he had achieved. Writing to the loyal Richard Strachey on railway matters (dictated on board HMS *Glasgow* at Port Blair on the forenoon of 8 February 1872, it was his last letter, and after his assassination it was not despatched) he complained: 'I have subdued many demons, but obstruction and delay are many-headed monsters which bear on the present occasion.'[23]

Mayo believed that, wherever possible, the country should be self-sufficient. He carried out prospecting for iron and sought the services of an oil expert from the United States to examine petroleum possibilities. Rivett-Carnac recalled the beneficial effect of the Viceroy's interest in the Chandah coal mine.[24] Mayo sent for Carnac and asked his opinion about the file regarding an alleged deposit of coal at Chandah. Carnac outlined the doleful sequence of events. Lucie-Smith, the local Deputy Commissioner, thinking he had found a coal seam, forwarded a sackload to the Geological Department in Calcutta. He got a good bureaucratic reply. How could it possibly be coal when the Department had never reported coal to be there? After further importunities from Lucie-Smith the Department admitted that it was a species of coal, but it would not burn. Lucie-Smith, not discouraged, dug deeper and took several cartloads to the Chief Commissioner at Nagpur, where he started a monstrous conflagration. The Department, unbowed, countered by saying that it was too inflammable, and might have been used in fire-ships in former wars; that was all. Mayo, realising that Lucie-Smith was an original who should be encouraged, ordered the Head of the Geological Department to proceed at once to Chandah; the presence of a coalfield was acknowledged; and Mayo said he would attend the formal opening of the pit in the following spring, which he did on 1 March 1870.

The visit to Chandah further exemplified Mayo's very personal style. Lucie-Smith, delighted at the imminent arrival of His Excellency, was anxious to demonstrate the many local improvements he had made, but Calcutta thought he was getting above himself and sightseeing was cut out of the programme. The hand of the sapient Burne is apparent in what follows. The Viceregal party was encamped about fifteen miles from Chandah and the coal mine to be opened the next day. Mayo observed innocently that he had heard that Chandah had some fine ancient buildings, which he would have liked to see. He was told that a visit would have been included, had H.E. not been so pressed for time, and that horses could not be procured at such short notice. Mayo, not to be deterred, said he had in mind to try a bullock-coach after dinner. In the words of an eyewitness, 'The staff are amused; the Europeans not of the party are astonished; the natives are amazed; Lucie-Smith is jubilant . . . the red-and-gold chaprassies glide about like huge goldfish.'[25] The inspection was carried out; Lucie-Smith publicly congratulated; and Mayo returned to camp in time for breakfast.

The 'local fund tiger' provides a tragi-comic epilogue. Mayo had been promised some shooting on his way from Chandah to Jubbulpore. A tiger had been marked down, but in the intervening days it waxed fat on the relays of bullocks provided to keep it in the vicinity, and the civil surgeon on the station had to treat the sacrificial carcases with opium to keep it in condition. On the appointed day a flanker inadvertently killed the tiger before Mayo could get a shot, and an official file grew bulky dealing with the insistent claim that the opium and rations given to the beast were a proper charge on local funds.

8
Two Blades of Grass

As the only Governor-General who had farmed on his own account, and made a living from the land sufficient to allow him to spend half the year on his duties at Westminster, Mayo had no doubts regarding the need to improve, modernise and develop Indian agriculture, on which over 90% of the people relied for their subsistence.

As early as April 1869 he wrote to Lord Napier and Ettrick, 'I really think that the time has come when we ought to start something of an Agricultural Department . . . Agriculture, on which everyone here depends, is almost entirely neglected by the Government. I have seen enough already in my wanderings to know that there is an enormous field, not exactly for reform, but for the investigation of husbandry in India.'[1] Until now agriculture, like other matters not directly assigned elsewhere, had come under the Home Department, which had become an unwieldy conglomerate. Mayo, if he reflected on his Westminster experience, must have seen a parallel in the gradual transfer of functions from the 'omnium gatherum' of the Home Office. (In Scotland, history was repeating itself as recently as the 1960s. The old Scottish Home Department had acted, with some success, as a universal repository until the other, limited, Scottish Departments resented its primacy and there was a wholescale redistribution.) It is surprising that no Governor-General before Mayo saw the necessity of devoting far more official attention to the country's basic industry; it is perhaps not so surprising that in London the India Office should not have been anxious to disturb the status quo,as Mayo proposed.

What Mayo wanted was a Department of Agriculture and Commerce, because, in his logic, agricultural products were the most important of Indian exports, and it followed that the development of Indian commerce depended upon improving the quantity and quality of agriculture. His mind was moving towards creating an organisation which would combine the functions of an agricultural agency and a board of trade. But it was to be primarily an agriculture department. Its main job was to be to ascertain precisely what reforms were essential and then work out systematically how they could be implemented. It was to be headed by a Director-General of Agriculture, not a Secretary, and would be staffed by experts. The Director-General, who would be supported by Provincial Directors, would promote and coordinate the best practices, whether they were derived from Indian, European or American sources.

This was very much a counsel of perfection, and it owed a great deal to the advice of Allan Octavian Hume, an eccentric enthusiast who while a District Officer had farmed a small estate of his own. (Known as the 'Pope of Ornithology' for his vast collection of oriental birds, Hume later resigned from the service and was instrumental in founding the Indian National Congress.) Consultation with Hume showed that the cost of the scheme – £250,000 annually and an initial outlay of the same amount – while not extravagant, was not likely to be approved by the Government at home, and Mayo was prepared to settle for a modified plan.[2] But even this met with only a cool reception. Mayo proposed a 'Department of Agriculture, Revenue, and Commerce', but Argyll quibbled and ordered the name to be changed to 'Revenue, Agriculture, and Commerce' to indicate a different scale of priorities.[3] Moreover, though Mayo appointed Hume – surely the right choice – to be Secretary, Argyll made it clear that his successor must be a revenue man.

Mayo's eagerness was not diminished. On 9 June 1871 he had reported that the new department opened that week with John Strachey as the responsible Member of Council and Hume as Secretary.[4] Immediately he told Hume to get on with 'sound instructions in the Veterinary Act'.[5] In September he reminded Argyll that his main agricultural object was 'not to fill the coffers of the State but to stimulate the efforts of the people towards improvement in that industry'.[6] He even talked of taking over the new Department himself if a separate Member of Council could be appointed to relieve him of Public Works. But nothing came of it, and it was to be many years before his idea of a purely Agricultural Department was realised.

The Governor-General's far-seeing plan had not been entirely frustrated because there had been a sensible rearrangement of business. The new organisation took over forestry from Public Works, studs and horse-breeding from the Military Department, inland customs and salt questions from Finance, land revenue and settlements from the Foreign Department, and – from Home – agriculture and horticulture, and a miscellaneous bag including surveys, geology, meteorology and statistics. On paper it read well; on the ground it was less effective.

For example, Mayo as an experienced farmer recognised that the prime necessity was to enhance the fertility of the soil. When the use of ammoniac manure was recommended he commented scornfully that he might as well ask Indian husbandmen to manure their ground with champagne. He saw that the scarcity of manure was caused by the paucity of cattle, which in turn was due to the losses of stock from starvation and cattle disease. With Hume's keen cooperation, he wanted to set up an institution to carry out research into cattle epidemics, but he did not have time to put his proposal into commission.

He did, however, leave the Department with some salutary advice which could with advantage be followed by other Ministers of Agriculture. The Department must, he said be careful of two things: '1. We must not ostentatiously tell native husbandmen to do things that they have been doing for centuries. 2. We must not tell them to do things that they can't do and have no means of doing. In either case they will laugh at us, and disregard really useful advice when it is given.'[7]

If his new department foundered to some extent after his death, he had some success meanwhile in stimulating irrigation schemes, which he knew were indispensable to counter recurring crop failures. But here too he had a peculiar reverse. He thought that irrigation projects should be paid for by the districts which they benefited, and not charged to general revenue. On principle, he said, Madras should not pay for the enrichment of the Punjab, nor Bengal for the irrigation of Sind. But having got his proposals through a reluctant Executive Council, he was discomfited to find Argyll disallowing them. He did, nevertheless, secure the passage of a land improvement act which gave advances to landlords and tenants for minor works – wells, tanks, and subsidiary channels of irrigation. 'It is', he wrote at the time, 'a system under which money may be lent with perfect security for the great end of making two blades of grass grow where only one, or, more likely in India, none ever grew before.'[8]

It is a matter of peculiar irony that Mayo, with his farming background, his unusual capacity for seeing the picture steadily and seeing it whole, combined with his keen eye for the most earthy details, should have accomplished less in the agricultural sphere than he did in the more rarefied atmosphere of foreign policy, where he had no previous experience.

Still on domestic affairs, the task of providing even a basic education for the mass of the people was Sisyphean, though much had been done before Mayo took up office. Universities, which were examining bodies, had been established in Calcutta, Bombay and Madras. Each provincial government had an education department, and overall there were about 35,000 schools, but there were wide differences in the various areas. In Bombay, for example, schools providing popular education extended throughout the province, and in the North West Provinces the indigenous schools had been developed. In Lower Bengal it was a very different matter. Here Calcutta University dominated the scene, and policy had concentrated on higher education while the primary sector was neglected. In round figures, the Bengal government spent £150,000 annually on higher, but only £50,000 on elementary education.

Mayo was highly critical of this imbalance. To his mind it was not enough that annual educational expenditure in India had trebled in the ten years to 1870 and was now running at nearly £1m a year.[9] More than his predecessors, he saw education as playing a vital part in his conception of much closer links between the Raj and the people, and despite the long-term nature of the problem he could claim two innovations.

First, he set the tone, rejecting the 'filtration' theory, under which it was supposed that the benefits of education provided for the upper and middle classes would eventually 'filtrate' downwards. He pointed sarcastically to the failure of this proposition in England, where, though there were ample facilities for the schooling of the nobs and the bourgeois, 'the masses in the big towns and a great portion of the agricultural poor are as ignorant as, and more vicious than, they were in the days of Henry VIII'. He continued in the same vein, 'If you wait till the bad English that the four hundred Baboos learn in Calcutta filters down into the forty millions of Bengal, you will ultimately be a Silurian rock instead of a retired judge. I am by no means in favour of stopping any education. Let the Baboos learn English by all means, but let us try to do something towards teaching the three R's to rural Bengal.'[10] Mayo found an ally in Sir George Campbell, and between 1870–71 and 1874 when Campbell left Bengal the number of children being educated at Government expense there had risen from 160,000 to 400,000.

Mayo's second innovation was to insist that more money should be spent on teaching in the vernacular, at the expense of that previously spent on the higher reaches. This was not universally popular. Mayo's motives were misunderstood, and the Bengalees, fearing that fewer opportunities for learning English would impair their prospects of government employment, organised public protests at Calcutta Town Hall. A memorial was sent to the Secretary of State, but Argyll did not intervene. Mayo was adamant that, while English might be the medium for higher education, the masses could only be reached in their native tongue, and it was for this reason that he encouraged teaching in the vernacular.

This was particularly necessary for the Muslims. Mayo realised that while Hindus readily accepted all education facilities, Muslims, because of their religious beliefs and national traditions, did not. In short, they would not go to a Hindu school to be taught by a Hindu teacher. Intent on redressing this unsatisfactory situation, Mayo proposed that Arabic, Persian and Urdu should be given a more prominent place in the curriculum. In 'avowed English' schools in Muslim districts, qualified Muslim English teachers should be appointed, and the Muslims should be given grants to create schools of their own. Mayo's projected reforms were supported by Campbell, Napier and Ettrick, and Muir, and his initiatives were developed by his successor Northbrook.

In circulating his proposals to Council, Mayo could not refrain from citing an Irish precedent. In 1832 Lord Derby introduced a scheme of national education on a strictly non-denominational basis. The Roman Catholic clergy and people participated fully and the Catholics actually managed three-quarters of the schools. To Mayo's mind the Muhammadans were now behaving in the same way as a section of the Protestant party in Ireland who had held aloof.[11]

Mayo was, of course, very conscious of the political dangers of deepseated disaffection among the Muslims, who in Bengal accounted for a third of the population. He was aware that within the frontiers of British India it was in Bengal that subversive Muslims could enlist most support, and, as discussed in chapter 15 which treats of the Wahabi conspiracy in more detail, he seemed to be preparing the way for further changes to improve the general status of the Muslim community. In the education field some of these reforms would have come without his intervention, but it is to his credit that he pushed ahead with them. In establishing the college at Ajmere for instance, he was alive to the advantages of giving the future rulers of the princely states facilities for better instruction.

In his earlier manifestation as Chief Secretary for Ireland Mayo had earned a reputation for his expertise in getting his bills through Parliament. He soon learned from his Legal Member – Henry Maine till December 1869, and thereafter Fitzjames Stephen – and from the Secretary of the Legal Department, Whitley Stokes, that legislation in India was a very different matter.

It is sometimes forgotten that in India, even after the Mutiny, there was a strong body of opinion that the government of the country should be based on equity, and not on written law at all. On this basis, for example, the courts should be able to decide not only whether a contract had been broken, but also whether it should have been made. In practical terms, the District Officer should be allowed to settle day-to-day cases at his own discretion. There was also an ingenious theory that since the Raj had now assumed the absolute power of the old native states, any law passed amounted to a restriction on, or a diminution of, that power. Another source of friction arose from the long-standing hostility between the Government and the Supreme Courts at Calcutta, Bombay and Madras, which had originally been set up to act as an independent check on the powers of the executive. Against this background, Indian civil servants and the mercantile community tended to regard the acts passed by the Legislative Council in Calcutta as an irritation at best, and lawyers as potential obstructionists, the latter view being fortified by the fact that law was by far the most popular profession for educated natives.

Nevertheless, the Government of India was committed to proceed by rule of law – the (comparatively few) enactments affecting India passed by the Westminster Parliament, the acts of the Governor-General in Council, applying to the whole country, and those passed by the Legislative Councils for Bengal, Madras and Bombay. But there were difficulties. The legal draughtsman in India had a problem not faced by his brethren at Westminster – the belief shared by Hindus and Muslims alike that law and religion were, if not the same thing, at least two sides of the same coin.

The procedure was lengthy and cumbersome. After formal introduction in the Legislative Council, bills were first circulated for comment to the local governments, who then passed copies to the District Officers. As the game of snakes and ladders continued, the District Officers might be directed to canvass local opinion among native leaders and others who might be affected. The text of the bill was also published in the *Gazette*. Next, a Select Committee collated the views received, deliberated on them, and made amendments as necessary. A revised edition was often published before the bill was again brought before the Legislative Council. Then followed a debate on the principle and a discussion of any further amendments before the motion was put 'that the bill do now pass'. The bill obtained the force of law with the Governor-General's signature, though it could be disallowed by the Secretary of State at home.

Fitzjames Stephen, in his learned contribution to Hunter's 'Life', summarised the four main categories of legislation: (a) acts fundamental to British government, where it was necessary to interfere directly with native practices, e.g. the abolition of *suttee*, and two acts passed in Mayo's time – the Act VIII of 1870 to prevent the murder of female infants, and the Act XXVII of 1871 to prevent eunuchs from possessing themselves of boys; (b) codifying acts which reduced unwritten law to a formal shape, e.g. the Evidence (1872) and Contract (1872) Acts; (c) acts relating to judicial procedure, including the Code of Criminal Procedure (1872); and (d) acts governing land revenue. The last was the most important, arising from the relationship between the Government as owners and collectors of the Revenue and those who cultivated the land.

Since the process of consultation and passing of legislation was measured in years, not months, it is not easy to be precise regarding Mayo's own contribution. Some of the bills which reached the Statute Book in his time had been put in hand by Lawrence, while some of the measures which owed much to his initiative were only passed after his death while Lord Napier and Ettrick was Acting Governor-General *ad interim* pending Northbrook's arrival.

Twenty-six acts received the Viceroy's assent in Mayo's first year. Most of them are not now of interest, but there were three which did not fit into Stephen's categories, dealing as they did with a section of the community not so far mentioned – the Europeans in India. Act II of 1869 made various provisions regarding the appointment of justices of the peace, the only magistrates who could try European subjects, and put the earlier fragmented enactments on a more satisfactory basis. Act IV applied the English Divorce Act of 1858 to the marriage of Christians in India, and under the European Vagrancy Act (XXI) any vagrant for whom employment could not be found in India could be shipped back to the country whence he had come.

For the rest, it will be sufficient to say that codification and consolidation, those wearying, but essential, part of the legislative corpus, made steady progress with Mayo's encouragement. His last public action in Calcutta was to declare, in the Legislative Council, his firm support for the bill (eventually Act III of 1872) to make possible a non-denominational form of marriage for those who did not have their own religious prescription. A vestige of the problems caused by doctrinal differences in Ireland clearly remained in his mind.

Politicians do not always get on with their legal advisers – at home there is evident record of vocal disputes between the Law Officers of the Crown and their colleagues – but Mayo had an amicable relationship with his Legal Members. Fitzjames

Stephen fully shared Mayo's objective of trying to make the statute book at once as short and as complete as possible, to have only one act on each subject, and to pass no acts that were not really required. Admittedly most Governors-General would have subscribed to these principles, but Mayo went further than most in putting them into effect. The cool, detached Fitzjames Stephen, who never doubted his own ability, admired the way in which Mayo kept a watchful eye on the Legislative Department without any irritating interference.[12]

Two aspects of Mayo's attitude to legislation deserve comment. First, he was a Conservative, and Conservatives, either at home or in charge of overseas administrations, are not notorious for their enthusiasm to legislate for the sake of legislating. In matching the legislative programme to what he saw were current needs he was content to provide a framework within which the good might prosper and the wicked find it more difficult to pursue their evil ends. Second, he had the unusual Ministerial gift of asking awkward questions as a layman, and, if he was satisfied with the answers, letting his draughtsman proceed. He was then brisk and precise, both in securing the passage of bills in the Legislative Council and in defending them if the Secretary of State showed signs of disapproval.

Preserved among Mayo's Indian papers is a voluminous correspondence with friends, acquaintances and others who invented a transparent excuse to write to the Viceroy seeking preferment for their sons or relations. All of these received a firm, polite response indicating the correct procedure for appointment or promotion. Mayo no doubt disappointed some of his admirers when it became clear that he would not consider 'personal interest or feeling when the good of the public service is involved', and that he did not regard India as a refuge for unemployable Irishmen. Judging by their sheer numbers it is probable that many of these replies were drafted by his Private Secretary.

In the fashion of the time, however, Mayo did not feel inhibited from asking the Duke of Edinburgh for a commission in the Rifle Brigade for his son, still a schoolboy.[13] He was not confident of the outcome. Writing soon afterwards to thank the Duke for his good offices in trying to find a vacancy in the regiment for young Dermot, he continued ruefully: 'He will not go up for his exam for some little time. It is not creditable, I think, to the system of education pursued at Eton that after having passed three years there a boy should have to go to a Private Tutor's for some months to enable him to pass the ordinary Examination for a Direct Commission.'[14] On further thought, Mayo overcame his paternal pride to realise, as other fathers have done, that for a son of limited educational attainments the cavalry was a better bet. So he wrote again to the Duke of Cambridge suggesting that Dermot might be commissioned in the Tenth Hussars, who were due to come out to India soon.[15] Still not sure that his request would be granted, he tried once more, this time writing to the Prince of Wales, whom he had met in Ireland, with the hope of a cornetcy in the Tenth for his son.[16] These high-powered approaches were eventually successful, and Dermot got his commission in the cavalry.

Entirely in character is the touching, sympathetic letter of condolence to Lord Derby's widow on the death of her husband. Derby, his first political patron, had three times given him Ministerial office. Yet, as Mayo wrote elsewhere, regretfully but realistically: 'His departure can have no political effect whatever, though a year and a half ago he was "the greatest of the Subjects of The Queen".'[17]

In lighter vein, Mayo wrote to Lord Bloomfield, the British Ambassador in Vienna, asking him to send out a qualified Austrian bandmaster to take charge of the Viceroy's band. 'Our evenings are made hideous by its discord,' he complained.[18] Bloomfield, who had been at the Embassy in St Petersburg during Mayo's visit there in 1845, though they do not seem to have met, replied that he had just missed obtaining the bandmaster of the Württemberg Regiment.[19] Bloomfield thought the salary offered (£250) was not attractive, but he managed to enlist someone suitable. Mayo acknowledged his arrival in November 1869;[20] and harmony was restored to Government House.

Mayo's equine interests extended far beyond his official concern for the Stud Department – where he was often critical of both the policy followed and its execution. For a time he ran his own racehorses, and he was always keen to encourage turf clubs and horse shows. He wrote to Admiral Rous, the scourge of corruption on the racing scene, asking him to recommend a jockey, 'a boy who can ride 7 st 2 lbs, who can finish, keep sober, and do as he is bid. I will give him £10 or £15 a month with his lodging and tips for wins.' He went on to add, 'It is a capital country as long as you can eat, drink, and sleep. I can do all these, and tho' the work is tremendous I never was better in my life.'[21] Rous had to send a discouraging reply to another query from Mayo about the purchase of horses. 'Owing to the cupidity of race horse owners and the facilities for railroad travelling, our nags are generally used up, legs and feet the worse for wear before they are 5 or even 4 years old.'[22]

Mayo was a keen and, from the start, a good hog-hunter. As the *Oriental Sporting Magazine* recorded affectionately, 'He was always magnificently mounted on first-rate weight-carrying hunters, and when riding his favourite pigsticker "Mr Cox", clad all in white from his *pugree* to his boots, he looked a perfect model of a thorough sportsman.'[23]

Mayo's sense of humour is apparent in the last of these miscellaneous extracts. In reply to Lord Calthorpe, who had asked for a white elephant, apparently for the zoo, Mayo solemnly explained why it was impossible to despatch one home. White elephants were really a chocolate colour, with a dull whiteness in the eye and quite white in the orifice of the ear, and were greatly venerated. The only one which had been caught recently was now in the possession of the King of Burma, and was attended by twelve young ladies of noble family, tending and suckling him.[24]

9
'Heaven's Light Our Guide'

No Viceroy's social calendar ever lacked oriental pomp and circumstance, but the biggest spectacle of Mayo's time was provided by the visit of the Duke of Edinburgh, the first member of the British Royal Family to set foot on Indian soil.

His Royal Highness Alfred Ernest Albert, the second son of Queen Victoria, was something of an oddity. Educated for the Navy, he was also a keen musician and a good violinist – not accomplishments common in the wardroom. His naval career was meritorious; he served in many parts of the world and was Commander-in-Chief in the Mediterranean and at Devonport before being promoted Admiral of the Fleet in 1893. In 1862 the Greeks, having got rid of the despot King Otho, elected Prince Alfred to succeed him. This was a surprisingly near-unanimous decision, as 230,000 of the 241,000 who voted were in his favour. Queen Victoria liked the prospect of her son becoming an Aegean monarch, but Palmerston knew it would be contrary to the agreement with Russia and France for a prince of any of these countries to ascend the Greek throne, and the invitation was politely declined.

In 1874 Prince Alfred married the Grand Duchess Marie Alexandrovna, the only daughter of Alexander II, the Czar of Russia (the Czar to whom Mayo later sent his own envoy). In 1893 he succeeded his father's brother as Duke of Saxe-Coburg and Gotha, at the same time relinquishing his seat in the House of Lords, though after a solemn debate he was allowed to keep his naval rank. His death and his burial at Coburg in 1900 attracted little comment. *Punch* could do no better than note his obsequies in a quatrain of staggering banality.

Summoned to lordship in a stranger land,
He left his English birthright of the Main;
Now, swiftly touched by Death's restoring hand,
He is the QUEEN's again![1]

When Prince Alfred, Duke of Edinburgh since 1866, paid his visit to India at the end of 1869 he was twenty-five years old and already had some experience of showing the flag overseas. In January 1867 he commissioned HMS *Galatea* and in her made a lengthy voyage to Rio Janeiro, the Cape and the Australian colonies. (He also wrote, and had published, a 'Galatea' waltz named after his ship.) He was generally well received, though a disaffected Fenian called O'Farrell tried to assassinate him at a very formal picnic just outside Sydney. This was thought to be an unsporting aberration. The Duke escaped with a fleshwound and O'Farrell was hanged. His Royal Highness returned to England in the summer of 1869 and plans were already in hand to send him off again, this time with India on the itinerary, when Mayo started his own homework in preparation for going out as Viceroy.

Snags, which consumed a great deal of official time and temper, soon appeared. At what time of the year should the Duke's visit take place? What orders should govern the ritual exchange of gifts with native princes? Should there be a durbar, and if so where?

The original intention was that the Duke should reach India in early March and remain in Bengal till mid-June. From Simla, Lawrence had been the first to observe that this was nonsense. A protracted visit in the hot season would not appeal to Europeans, anxious to take to the hills, or to Indian princes who would probably refuse to come to Calcutta. Mayo, though as yet only Viceroy-designate, took the same point very forcibly with Northcote, still Secretary of State. The message seems to have got home, because in writing to Fitzgerald on 19 October he was delighted to say that the visit had now been postponed till the autumn, and that he had discussed the programme at an amicable meeting with His Royal Highness.[2]

The question of the ceremonial presents proved more intractable. The practice invariably followed in India was for gifts received by the Viceroy or senior officers from native potentates to be handed over to be lodged in the Toshakhana, the central treasury. Thereafter they were either sold, or recycled when gifts had later to be made to other princes. (Argyll and Mayo agreed that public sale in India was objectionable, and that the products of the princes' munificence should be catalogued and sent home for discreet disposal.) There was, however, no precedent to suggest what should be done with the gifts which a royal personage like the Duke would certainly receive, or what was to be done about defraying the cost of the reciprocal presents. Mayo wrote home seeking guidance, and Argyll replied that he had consulted the Queen. Her Majesty's view was that the gifts should be considered 'Private and Personal and therefore to be accepted', i.e. to be retained by her son.[3]

Mayo, not happy with this predatory arrangement, wrote again on 12 August asking for more precise orders, adding that it would be much better if the presents were treated in the normal way 'which is well understood in this country'. According to his calculations the Duke would be offered about £8,000 worth of gifts and have to give about £10,000, which was surely excessive.[4] Mayo was still hammering this point when he wrote again on 30 November, and on the same day his Foreign Department addressed a formal despatch to the Secretary of State objecting to even a reduced figure of £5,000 each way for the exchange of gifts, since 'in the existing state of our finances, the expenditure of £5,000 from Indian revenue for such an object would certainly occasion much dissatisfaction, and would inevitably lead to remarks of an unpleasant character being made not only in this country, but probably in Parliament, and on the part of the public at home'.[5] Argyll, now understandably weary of this tiresome correspondence, replied on 28 December leaving it to Mayo's discretion, adding that he was not so worried about 'the abuse which would be heaped upon him for allowing the Duke of Edinburgh to gratify some of the Native Princes by keeping some of their presents'.[6]

The outcome of this matter of great pith and moment was a happy one and, though there is no written evidence, may have been due to the diplomatic talents of Owen Burne and Neville Chamberlain, the Duke's principal aide. On 2 January 1870 His Royal Highness, by now in Calcutta, sent a note to Mayo saying that £5,000 was a 'very large sum for such a purpose', and proposing a more modest exchange of arms, curiosities or 'specialities' manufactured locally.[7] Mayo quickly assented and provided £1,500 for return gifts.

The original programme had included the investiture of the Duke with the Star of India at a durbar at Agra, but on 12 August

Mayo added the first note of caution when he wrote to Argyll. 'Unless the season promises very well, I shall not hold a durbar at all. Nothing will induce me to order large bodies to march through Famine Stricken Districts, and so materially aggravate the sufferings of the people.'[8] At the beginning of September he told Argyll he had published notice that the durbar must be regarded as uncertain, but that he would not decide for another month. Finally, with the threat of famine not yet passed, Mayo reported to the Queen on 2 October, regretting that the Agra durbar had been cancelled because of the 'scarcity and dearness of provisions which still exists in Rajputana, Central India and parts of the North West Provinces'.[9]

On 26 December – the original programme had slipped somewhat – the loyal citizens gathered to greet their royal visitor. According to the *Times* correspondent, 'In the conversation of patient Orientals, who stood or squatted for hours in the sun, nothing was heard but the Prince.'[10] But their vigil was poorly rewarded, because the *Galatea* could not get up the river, abreast of the landing stage at Prinsep's Ghat, by the scheduled time of four o'clock. The sun set about five, when the landing was at last effected, so that it was dark before the procession had got half way to Government House. If the crowds could not see the Prince, shrouded in crepuscular gloom, he could not see the full majesty of the seventy richly-caparisoned elephants mustered in a semi-circle to receive him. But HRH had recovered sufficiently from the hazards of navigating the Hooghly to attend a gala performance of *Lucrezia Borgia* in the evening.

The festivities lasted for the next fortnight. Burne gave up his quarters in Government House to the Duke and his suite; special furniture for the State Drawing Room had been brought from Paris; and as it was Christmas time Lady Mayo had mistletoe fetched down from Simla. In the course of the celebrations, enhanced, as Burne observed, by the presence of Scindia, Maharaja of Gwalior, the Maharaja of Jaipur and other leading Indian rulers, there were levees, drawing rooms, fireworks and race meetings. On the Sunday the Bishop of Calcutta preached on board the *Galatea* with the Viceroy and his wife among the congregation.

The balls to which invitations were most eagerly sought were those given by the Viceroy and by HRH in return. At the fancy dress occasion at Government House, Burne and his wife – with a poor sense of history and no sense of the ridiculous – appeared as Darnley and Mary, Queen of Scots. Burne thought he looked 'tolerable and she lovely'. But the social climax was undoubtedly the entertainment on board the *Galatea*. *The Times* rhapsodised over the huge canvas awning that had been erected on deck. 'Never was there so unique a ballroom, and loud were the exclamations of chiefs who rule millions and count their revenue by half millions that truly this was Paradise.'[11] The young prince shared in the collective euphoria and took partners for every dance, to the delight of Calcutta matrons.

In the midst of these frivolous activities the most solemn, and most public, ceremony was the investiture of His Royal Highness with the insignia of the Star of India. The Chapter of the Most Exalted Order held on the Race Course Encampment on 30 December was intended to take the place of the cancelled durbar, and to the minds of some of the princes it was an indifferent substitute. But it is doubtful whether Mayo, or any of his predecessors, really understood the significance of the traditional durbar.

Originally, the Moghul's durbar represented an act of incorporation between the prince who made his obeisance with the offer of *nazar*, gold coins, and *peshkash*, valuables such as jewels or elephants, and the Moghul who reciprocated by presenting a *khelat*, a formal dress of honour, including shawls, turbans, jewels, and so on. When this had been done, everyone felt better and the suppliant prince was in theory incorporated as part of the person of the Moghul.

The British from the start took a more pragmatic view of the meaning of this ceremony, and to them it seemed that the proffering of *nazar* and *peshkash* was simply a payment for privileges and trading rights. Prior to 1858, while the East India Company operated under the nominal authority of the Moghul – as his *Diwan* (chief civil authority) from 1765 and later as his 'Protector' after Lake captured the Moghul capital of Delhi – Company officers frequently returned to England laden with booty at least partly derived from the receipt of *nazar*. The Government at home eventually became disturbed at this practice – put another way, public opinion was scandalised at the more flamboyant manifestations – and *nazar* was declared to be bribery. So the dilemma persisted. The Moghul, though in Kaye's words nothing more than 'a pensioner, a pageant, and a puppet', was still the fountain of honour for Indians, but not for the British, who could not take part, and be incorporated, in ritual submission to a foreign ruler. But they had to act the part, and the East India Company Officers continued to present their own *khelats* in return for *nazar* at ceremonies styled durbars. The gifts received, however, were no longer pocketed by British officials but consigned to the Toshakhana.

Meanwhile the Moghul was still receiving his *nazar* from Indian princes, handing out *khelats*, and issuing *sanads*, royal charters to vacant thrones. But all this came to an end with the passing of the Government of India Act of 1858 which vested the sovereignty of India directly in the British monarch, and removed the inconsistency of acting under the 'nominal authority' of the Moghul. The British now set about regularising Indian royal titles, a process which involved enquiries which were often not to the taste of the princes. Entitlement now depended on evidence of loyalty to the Crown and good administration of the territory within the princes' domain. Partly as a sweetener in this process, and partly to provide a replacement for the old Moghul's durbar, the Order of the Star of India was introduced in 1861.

According to Michael Maclagan in his authoritative study of 'Clemency' Canning, the idea of the new order came from the Queen. Canning was certainly consulted and wondered if the awards were to be accompanied by more substantial favours, such as grants of land or money. 'The honours of the House of Delhi were seldom barren gifts.'[13] Canning also pointed to the risk of causing jealousies between princes, and to their overdeveloped sense of amour propre. He cited the occasion when he was advised that protocol required him to kiss a visiting raja. Fortunately the raja did not make his appearance – very fortunately, since Canning later learned that he was a leper.

The new Order of the Star of India was gazetted in London on 23 February 1861. It bore a ribbon of light blue with white edges, and the splendidly Victorian motto 'Heaven's Light Our Guide' – a translation of the Latin phrase suggested by Prince Albert. The Viceroy of the day was designated Grand Master and the order was restricted to twenty-five knights. In India the Nizam of Hyderabad, the Maharajas of Gwalior, Kashmir, Indore and Patiala, the Gaekwar of Baroda, the Begum of Bhopal and the Nawab of Rampore among the princes, together with Sir George Russell Clerk and General Sir Hugh Rose, were the first to be invested. At home Her Majesty invested Viscount Gough, Lord Harris, Lord Clyde, Sir John Lawrence, Sir James Outram, Viscount Combermere and Sir George Pollock, all venerable old India hands. Although this was not a full complement, in 1866 the Order was enlarged into three grades – GCSI, KCSI, and CSI, and so remained until the end of British rule.

The Star of India was recognised as the principal honour conferred by the Raj, but the investiture was essentially a British ceremony, with the new knight kneeling before the Sovereign or her representative, the Viceroy. Moreover, unlike the *khelat*, the insignia had to be returned on the death of the recipient. It could be argued that this was very much a 'contractual' ceremony, and a poor thing compared with the full religious significance of the Moghul durbar, but that was how it was.

Whether Mayo gave much thought to these theological distinctions is at best uncertain, but he did address his mind to another complication. It was he who embodied the full authority of the Raj, not Prince Alfred, and there was to be no confusion on this point. 'His Royal Highness during his stay in India is the *guest* of the Government. He does not visit India as the representative of Her Majesty, nor does he in any way represent the Viceroy of the Government of India while on his tour.' He went on to say that 'There should be no general Durbar, and no presentation of *nuzzers* and *kuilluts*,' and only private visits from chiefs would be allowed.[14]

Mayo was a born impresario, as he had already shown at Amballa. He realised that while the princes must be encouraged to see that the ceremony was, symbolically, intended to bind the British Royal Family closer to India and her 'feudatory chiefs', the Bengalees must also be given their circus. Nothing was spared to make the whole business as imposing as possible. On 1 January 1870 Mayo penned his report to the Queen. 'A street of large tents 400 yards long and 70 yards broad was closed at the end by the Viceroy's durbar tent and four large Shemianas or Portico tents under whose shade were seated 2,000 Native and European Ladies and Gentlemen.' This was the setting.[15]

The Viceregal procession was more than half a mile in length as it drove along the straight line of troops a mile and a half from Government House to the Encampment. Most ceremonies of this kind are remembered best if something goes seriously wrong to add a comic touch – Ellenborough in his time was furious when the elephants refused to kneel to welcome the 'Illustrious Garrison' on its return from Afghanistan – but on this occasion the staff-work was impeccable, and honour was satisfied. Durand, however, struck a carping note. 'The trumpets were a miserably squeaky production, of a penny-trumpet plaything kind . . . There was something funereal in our march up to and back from the durbar tent. I expected every moment to hear the dead march in Saul.' He thought Europeans believed such ceremonies unsuited to the time and that while the natives admired the cavalcade they wondered about the significance of the robing of HRH.[16] (According to Trotter, the multitude cherished a wild belief that the Duke had come to remove the income tax, which Mayo had recently doubled.)[17]

One man who was not present in the Encampment was the mysterious Mr Bentine, and thereby hangs a strange tale. The editor of *The Englishman* received a report that one Bentine had been overheard to say that his wife had been seduced by Lieutenant Fitzgeorge of the *Galatea*, and that he intended to take his revenge. The police were informed, and it appeared that Bentine, who was staying at Spence's Hotel, where he 'consorted only with American rowdies', had obtained an engagement with a circus but seldom turned up, saying he had more important things to do.[18] Often drunk, he had bought a revolver, and it was thought that his threats might extend to His Royal Highness. With commendable despatch Bentine was deported to Australia in the *Isabella Browne*, in the nicest possible way, being offered an assisted passage, which he was strongly advised to take. This might be considered a gentlemanly but efficient example of internal security, and as the Duke was due to return to Australia, the authorities there were warned to keep Bentine under surveillance. Mayo later thought this was not enough and suggested that the hapless Fitzgeorge (who had been on the strength of the *Galatea* since June 1867, and against whom there was no evidence of illicit sexual behaviour) should be transferred to another ship.[19] Argyll replied that he had warned the Admiralty and the Home Office – no doubt bearing in mind the earlier attempt on the Duke's life – and Bentine sinks into obscurity.

The Duke now left Calcutta to complete his tour of other parts of India, allowing Mayo to get down to his arrears of work. HRH had of course to be exposed to the full range of sporting rigours, starting with a boar hunt at Dewan Sorai, where some twenty-seven elephants were brought out to beat the jungle. 'A fine boar was secured before luncheon, and after that three great tuskers fell before the spear.'[20] A week later Mayo joined the party at Benares. The Maharaja, a loyal and important prince, had early written to offer his invitation to the Duke to try his shooting at Chukea, which had 'often afforded good sport, tigers and bears being sometimes met with, whilst deer and wild pig are numerous'.[21]

The sport proved disappointing. On the first day HRH shot a tiger which escaped. Two days later the Duke dismounted and followed a wounded beast – then thought to be a dangerous practice – but Mayo ran after him and brought him back. The Viceroy and the Duke then parted company, Mayo going back to Calcutta and the Duke continuing on his way to the North West Provinces, but the royal shooting was seemingly dogged with ill-luck. On 6 February Mayo sent a rocket to Neville Chamberlain. 'I am sorry to see by the Papers that HRH has been following a wounded tiger on foot. I thought it was settled at Chukea that this was not to happen again, and certainly if it does take place it is entirely contrary to my wishes.'[22]

Mayo rejoined the Duke at Jubbulpore, where there was to be a ceremony to mark the completion of the Calcutta–Bombay railway line. At the banquet it was significant that the first toasts were, in order, to the Queen and then to the Viceroy. Mayo then tactfully recalled that the French Engineer-General Vauban at the end of a siege, when victory was near, used to ask for a member of the royal family to witness the success of his soldiers. Tonight, Mayo went on, they were in the same position – their celebration being graced by the presence of HRH, whose health he now proposed. A bit laboured, but sufficiently apposite.

After a formal reply by the Duke, Mayo proceeded to the principal toast, the Great Indian Peninsula Railway, and ended on a prophetic note: 'Dynasties and kingdoms are not immortal, and it is possible that, in the far futurity, some power still unborn may reign in India. Our insular greatness may not last for ever . . .' But, he concluded, the railways would remain as a lasting memorial of the good the British had done and of the benefits they had conferred on the people of India.[23]

Owen Burne was moved to note that Mayo had come to India with an undeserved reputation as a dull orator, but developed in time into a good and fluent speaker, and he attributed this to his having a first-rate shorthand writer in the worthy Mr Latimer to take his dictation. At a distance, Mayo's speeches are not inspiring to read, but an occasional flash of inspiration is apparent. It is also clear from the manuscripts preserved among his papers that he took great pains to polish his first draft, trying to find the memorable phrase – though he did not go as far as Canning, who used to make so many changes that his private secretary could not recognise the original.[24]

Mayo took his personal leave of the Duke at Jubbulpore, but His Royal Highness had several weeks still to spend in India before he finally sailed from Bombay with an exchange of telegrams as fulsome as convention required. Had the tour been a success? Had it served its primary purpose of strengthening the bonds between the Crown and Her Majesty's Indian subjects? The *Times* correspondent, writing for home consumption, thought so, and the Government were sufficiently satisfied with the visit to send out Alfred's elder brother, the Prince of Wales, on another foray five years later. The Indian press was less enthusiastic, and Mayo evidently thought the criticism had some validity, since he kept extracts among his private files.

The *Madras Times* regretted that the Duke had accepted all the deference and tributes as due to his mother in person, 'as if there were no British nation, no British parliament, no British statesmen, who have something to do with the beneficient rule of which we hear so much'. The editor would have liked to see HRH soaring above the *Almanack de Gotha*, but concluded 'It is perhaps as well as it is', since it would all be arranged for him and he need not take note of 'the trifling influences that help, perhaps more than the personal characters of sovereigns, to make history'.[25]

The *Pioneer* touched on the matter that had already exercised

Mayo. The Duke's visit was bad

precisely because it discredited the kingly office represented by the Viceroy and no one else, and interposed between him and the Chiefs of India a sham figure of royalty. It is because English writers see where the real power lies, and to whom it rightfully belongs, that they object to the parade of a lay royal figure who can only fill the natives of this country with delusive and mischievous ideas. The Chiefs of India have been taught to look beyond the Viceroy, and even beyond the Secretary of State, and the consequences cannot be other than pernicious.

The *Pioneer* observed that the Duke's visit certainly occupied a good deal of Mayo's time, and probably interrupted a lot of secretarial drudgery, and added maliciously: 'It staved off for a while the impending financial discussions. It cost the State a few lakhs, and it entailed private expenses on a few officials. Possibly the Duke's tour, as with all commotions, was the incidental cause of less or more private bickerings, envy, and uncharitableness.'[26]

On the cost of the visit, Mayo, though not a particularly rich man, ignored Argyll's suggestion that it would be a fair charge on public funds, and the more explicit proposal from his Executive Council that £10,000 or whatever was needed should be added to the Durbar fund. Instead, he met the expenses from his own purse, adding 'what is done now need not in any way bind my successors, who must take their own view of public duty'.[27] In one respect, however, he was not going to be imposed upon. Some time later he was approached by an artist called Nicholas Chevalier, who claimed that the Viceroy had commissioned him to paint a picture of the investiture ceremony for a fee of £1,000. Mayo not normally forgetful, could not recall doing this, and promptly wrote home to enquire about Chevalier's credentials, and to ask if his work would be worth the price he wanted.[28] Some inconclusive correspondence between Chevalier and Burne ensued, and the matter was still unresolved at the time of Mayo's death. Chevalier did not get his fee, and so far as can be traced did not depict the investiture, but he seems to have become something of a protégé of the Duke's, since he painted his wedding in 1874.

10
Sepoys and Sabres

Sifting through the papers at the India Office before he left for Coromandel, Mayo had been left in no doubt that he would be expected to reduce military expenditure. He had already told the Duke of Cambridge that he suspected that the army establishments contained a great deal of adipose tissue (chapter 4), and though the service chiefs at Calcutta argued their case with some vigour, he remained critical. 'The majority of the officers in command of the Divisions or Brigades of the Bengal Army', he later wrote to Napier of Magdala, 'are, from age, infirmity, and other causes, unfit either to command the force under their orders in the field, or to give to the Regiments which compose their force the military instruction which was always indispensable, and the absence of which has now become a national danger.'[1] A healthy scepticism is useful when undertaking a review that is going to cause upsets.

Any study of army requirements had to be coloured by recollections of the Mutiny. Looked at from a strictly military point of view, a basic cause of the sepoy rebellion was that the native army was much too large and the European force far too small. Lawrence certainly thought that the sepoys had become too numerous, and would not have risen unless they thought they had a chance of success. In his view, 'it was the sense of power that induced them to rebel', and while the issue of the cartridges was important, it only affected timing. In 1856 the native army of 250,000 men had outnumbered the European regiments of 46,000 by more than five to one. In the aftermath of the Mutiny the native army had been halved and the British troops substantially increased. Following some modest reductions under Lawrence as the country became more accustomed to peaceful conditions, the native army on 1 April 1869 stood at 133,000 of all ranks, and the European element at 62,000. (These figures are rounded up to make the reader's task easier; in the minutes, reports, and abstracts of statistics of the period they are given in confusingly different forms that would defy even the latest computer; but the sense, and the trend, is clear.)

To assist him in considering what should be done, Mayo had the benefit of three military advisers, very different characters whose personalities have been touched on while discussing the makeup of the Government of India (chapter 6). They now appear in high relief.

Sir Henry Durand, the Military Member of Council, had started his service in India as a subaltern in the Bengal Engineers in 1828, and first came to notice in the Afghan War when he was one of the intrepid band who crept up by night to blow open the gates of Ghuznee. Private Secretary to Ellenborough in 1843, he had fought in the Sikh War and the Mutiny before holding political appointments in Gwalior and Bhopal. He had a spell at home on the India Council, and then returned to Calcutta to become Secretary of the Foreign Department in 1861, eventually assuming his present post in the Executive Council. He felt, with some reason, that his knowledge of Indian affairs was unequalled, and he had no inhibitions in putting his views forward, either by forceful speeches in Council or in lengthy, lapidary minutes.

Mansfield, originally an infantryman in the 53rd Foot, is in some ways the most interesting of the three. He held diplomatic posts at Constantinople and Warsaw before becoming chief of staff to Colin Campbell during the Mutiny. In the fighting at Cawnpore after the relief of Delhi he was criticised for allowing large numbers of mutineers to escape because of his indecision in pursuing them. According to Fortescue's history, Mansfield possessed a very remarkable intellect, but not the instincts of a soldier.[2] The *Friend of India* thought fit to sum him up as 'a failure as a soldier, as the commander of soldiers, as a general commanding in the field – witness Cawnpore – Sir William Mansfield's administrative capacity is beyond all doubt'.[3]

However that may be, he was appointed Commander of the Bombay Army in 1860, and had been Commander-in-Chief, India since 1865. Now that his appointment was coming to an end, Mansfield, quite simply, wanted to succeed Durand. There was a respectable argument, to which we will return, about the odd arrangement whereby the C-in-C sat on the Executive

Council as an additional or extraordinary member. Mansfield thought this anomaly could best be resolved by making the C-in-C the Military Member, but his view did not prevail, and for the time being he and Durand continued to fire volleys from their entrenched positions. On his return to England he was given command of the forces in Ireland, and in 1871 was ennobled as Lord Sandhurst.

In 1870 Norman, who had been made Secretary of the Military Department under Lawrence, took over Durand's seat on the Council. Good at processing papers, he was regarded as a safe man.

To complete the picture, Mansfield was succeeded as C-in-C by Lord Napier of Magdala. Like Durand a Bengal Engineer by origin, he had been responsible for many innovations in engineering works. (The cantonment at Sirhind became known as 'Napier's system'.) He commanded a division in the China expedition of 1860, was Military Member from 1861 to 1865, and had already been invested as Commander of the Bombay army when he made his name in charge of the Abyssinian campaign in 1867. Then he went back to Bombay. Napier was very conscious of his prestige – in India, the C-in-C ranked second only to the Viceroy – and he did not often see why his views should be questioned. But it was with his three original advisers, Durand, Mansfield and Norman, that Mayo began his review of military expenditure.

Argyll's reminder that he wanted to see cuts was not long in arriving. In his despatch of 26 January 1869 the Secretary of State pointed out, in a pained way, that although there had been some reductions, expenditure had risen from £12.75m in 1856–7 to over £16m in 1868–9. A new and expensive police force had been organised, but consequent savings in army costs had not been effected. The despatch concluded with the pious hope that savings of £1.5m could be found.[4] This was, no doubt, a good Treasury opening bid. Mayo, however, set about his task with such vigour that when his proposals reached England, and what they meant in terms of troops on the ground became apparent, they were more than the Duke of Cambridge, ever zealous for the officer corps, was prepared to stomach, or Argyll to approve.

In his review Mayo stuck firmly to two principles. The first – which met with the entire agreement of Mutiny veterans – was that he could not condone the removal of a single British bayonet or sabre from India. On this point he was emphatic: 'We are strongly impressed with the belief that we have not one British soldier too many in this country. We would most strongly object to any reduction in their number.'[5] His second tenet may on the surface seem contradictory. Mayo never forgot that military charges accounted for just over half the net available revenue of the Government of India, and he was convinced that, even if the country were in a more prosperous state, 'we should not be justified in spending one shilling more upon our army than can be shown to be absolutely and imperatively necessary . . . Every shilling that is taken for unnecessary military expenditure is so much withdrawn from those vast sums which it is our duty to spend for the moral and material improvement of the people.'[6]

Initially Mayo found that, as he expected, retrenchment was distinctly unpopular. As he explained to Argyll, 'Sir William Mansfield is an economist. Sir H. Durand conscientiously believes that reduction in many cardinal points of military expenditure, especially as regards barracks, is undesirable.'[7] Durand had himself confided much earlier to his old chief Ellenborough: 'The latter [Mansfield] is an able man in many respects, but his tendencies are, I think, rather dangerous; for ignoring the fact that peace in India is not the same thing as peace in England, he is disposed, in pursuit of military economy, to reduce our European force almost beyond a safe minimum.'[8] Again, to Sir Robert Vivian, the veteran of the Burmese War forty years before, he wrote: 'Having seen the empire once nearly lost, and experienced what it cost to recover it, I shall not be swayed by either Lord Mayo or Sir W. Mansfield in recording my views on possible reductions.'[9]

Eventually Mayo, tactful but firm, secured Durand's consent in principle to most of his proposals. There was no real problem in taking the axe to the staff at the various headquarters. Mayo was convinced that examples were ready to hand of units where the officers had at best nominal commitments and were seldom distracted from their curry and claret. The Bombay Command, he told Argyll, teemed with Inspecting Officers who had little or nothing to inspect, and 'Doing Duty' officers who had no duty to do. Reductions in this category, saving £79,000 a year, were proposed, and accepted by Argyll.

Adjustments in the complement of European troops proved more complex. The underlying problem was that the strength of individual regiments had declined so that too many separate regiments had to be maintained in order to keep up the total number of fighting men. Put another way, there were too many officers to other ranks. Durand agreed, observing that in a European infantry regiment there was now one officer to 23½ muskets and in the cavalry one officer to thirteen sabres.[10] Mayo's proposal would have resulted in a reduction of seven infantry and four cavalry regiments, but through cross-postings would have ensured that there was no diminution in the rank and file. Argyll agreed to reductions of two regiments in each arm.

As regards artillery, Mayo readily accepted advice that for once was nearly unanimous. First the retention of the brigade system, where each brigade comprised a number of batteries, had produced far more field officers than could be found work. 'I am besieged', minuted Mansfield, 'by the applications of Artillery Lieutenant-Colonels for the command of depots or indeed for any situation which affords even the semblance of employment.'[11] Second, the batteries were seriously undermanned – with the consequence that on going to war, either half the guns would have to be left behind, or the number of gunners would have to be doubled in an awkward hurry. The solution proposed was the replacement of ninety-four batteries insufficiently manned by eighty brought up to full strength. There would be fewer guns, but this would be offset by the introduction of rifled, instead of smooth-bored equipment. These recommendations were broadly accepted.

When it came to possible reductions in the native troops, Durand and Mansfield were anxious not to be too hard on the Bombay and Bengal armies, but everyone agreed that the Madras establishment was overloaded. Even the Governor of Madras agreed that the cost of the army 'far transcends the wants of the country'.[12] The Madras force was much larger than was needed for local defence, and the C-in-C would not employ Madras troops elsewhere. It was also an extravagant army, operating the 'family system' whereby Madras sepoys took their wives and children with them, a factor which greatly impaired their mobility or their use in other areas of India. Mayo wrote cogently to Argyll representing the poor morale and indifferent promotion prospects of the officers. Argyll, however, was not impressed by Mayo's strictures, observing that the evidence did not come from Madras.[13] He evidently suspected there had been some collusion to do down the reputation of the Madras contingent.

In the upshot Mayo proposed that in Bombay the Sind Horse should be reorganised with two larger regiments instead of three small ones, and that four infantry regiments could be spared. In Bengal the proposal was to dispense with one cavalry and four infantry regiments. This gave rise to a continuing dispute with the Secretary of State. After various compromises had been canvassed, Argyll suggested cutting the native armies in each of the three Presidencies by 9,000 men. This was unacceptable to Mayo, and his colleagues, and the argument was still unresolved at the time of his death. So far as a figure can be extracted from the welter of returns, estimates, proposals and counter-proposals, Mayo submitted plans that would have saved £950,000 a year; the items agreed by Argyll produced economies of about £600,000.

In the course of Mayo's review it became increasingly apparent that the whole structure of separate Bengal, Bombay and Madras armies, each with its long administrative tail and costly headquarters, was out of date. This was certainly Mayo's opinion, and it was shared by both Mansfield and Durand, who minuted in typically trenchant terms that he could not see the need to maintain in 1869 the same number of commands-in-chief as was kept in 1857 for a very much larger number of troops 'when neither railways nor steam communication presented the facilities of locomotion they now offer'.[14] Mayo went as far as ordering Mansfield's plan for unifying the command structure to be printed for transmission to the Secretary of State, but on second thoughts he suppressed it. He was shrewd enough to see that such a drastic reduction in career prospects would not find favour in army circles at home, especially with the Duke of Cambridge at the Horse Guards. But he remained convinced that there were too many Cs-in-C, as is clear from a private letter to Argyll. 'I have long made up my mind that the Presidential Commands have become unnecessary and that they must go soon.'[15] He added that he was very much against centralisation, with two exceptions – military and foreign affairs. (It was not till 1879 that the Army Commission recommended that the Presidency army system should be abolished, and the necessary legislation took even longer, being passed in 1893.)

Mansfield had also referred to the peculiar arrangement which required the Viceroy to consider, and possibly arbitrate on, advice on military matters from two sources – the Military Member and the C-in-C who sat on the Executive Council as an additional member. Mansfield argued that he could not be effective as C-in-C if he had to hang about Calcutta to attend the Council, but in proposing to combine the two posts he was not disinterested. He cited the French precedent, where the Minister of War (Mansfield's suggestion) held the superior rank of Marshal, and since both he and Durand would before long demit their present appointments, was this not the time to create the new post? And who better to hold it than an upgraded Mansfield? Durand, whose ambitions lay elsewhere, agreed that it was anomalous for the C-in-C to sit on the Council, in effect reviewing his own performance, and that he should be free for travelling, inspecting and other duties.

Mayo was aware of what was going on. He had raised with Argyll the possibility of making Mansfield the Military Member to succeed Durand. This would pave the way for excluding the C-in-C from the Council's deliberations.[10] Argyll was not satisfied and played it long. Eventually, as we have seen, Mansfield went home, to be succeeded in India by Lord Napier of Magdala, and Norman got Durand's seat. The thorny question of dual military representation on the Council was to vex more than one future Viceroy, and in 1905 Curzon resigned when Kitchener's proposal to abolish the Military Member and set up an Army Department under the C-in-C was accepted in substance.

Mayo was involved in two disputes about the supply of arms, but in only one of them was he successful, and then only in part.

He had been in office for a bare three months when he wrote to Bartle Frere at home expressing his emphatic view that wherever possible military material for use in India should be manufactured there.[17] Everything but small arms, he said, could be made locally. This was consistent with his ambition to make India self-sufficient. He could scarcely expect to secure an immediate change in ordnance policy, but following his representations factories for rifle ammunition, and for guns and gun-carriages, were eventually established.

This was the time when the Enfield rifle, a muzzle-loader, was being converted into a breech-loader according to the design of Mr Snider. (By later standards, the Snider bullet, which was hollow and made an enormous hole on impact, was inhuman.) By 1869 the Snider was the standard weapon in the British Army at home, and at the same time the Martini-Henry, a new hammerless rifle, was being distributed for trial, and soon after for issue. Lawrence, remembering the Mutiny, had wanted to restrict the latest weapons to European regiments, but Mansfield disagreed. So did Mayo, as he told Argyll. Lord Napier and Ettrick was of the same view. To give native troops inferior rifles, he argued, implied a suspicion of their loyalty. 'An army cannot be a good army unless it is well-treated, and it is not well-treated if it is ill-armed.'[18] But neither Lord Napier of Magdala nor Argyll were persuaded, and Mayo had to be content, for the time being, with breech-loaders for European troops and muzzle-loaders for the native soldiers. By March 1871 thirty regiments in India had Snider rifles.

One of Mayo's earliest observations on the soldiery was concerned with a very human matter – the incidence of drunkenness and venereal disease among British troops. One remedy, he suggested, would be to make spirits more freely available in regimental canteens. 'It might seem that free trade in spirits is rather an Irish proposal for stopping drunkenness, but there is a great deal to be said in its favour.' Mayo hoped that it would keep the troops out of the bazaars, where they drank 'the abominable liquids made from rice and the juice of trees'.[19] To control venereal disease, he proposed to extend the provisions of the Contagious Diseases Act to every station in India, even if it meant building more hospital accommodation.

With the general health of the troops very much in mind, he also continued to correspond with Florence Nightingale. Never giving up her battle for better sanitation, she had been elected a member of the Bengal Social Sciences Association, to whom she sent a paper on the prevention of cholera. After an earlier exchange of letters[20] she wrote on 24 March 1870, ready as always to hand out her prescription for improving barrack conditions, '(a) plaster and whitewash the outside to protect the walls from sun radiation. (b) fill the verandah arches with Venetians to protect the room walls.' With a pleasant little barb she added: 'I am afraid India is rather short of that (not unknown) article, a pump', and went on to offer to present one, 'provided you will guarantee me from being thrown into my own well by the Bheesties or Coolies whose trade I shall have damaged'.[24] Mayo noted her views and gallantly sent her two white shawls.

Mayo was not satisfied with the way barracks were being designed, built, or financed. 'You can hardly conceive the extent to which military works are being carried out and the Palaces that are being built all over the country,' he wrote to Arbuthnot in January 1869. 'I am all for giving everything that can secure health and comfort to the soldier, but I am inclined to believe that we are overdoing it in some places.'[24] The application of 'specimen' plans throughout India was, he told the Executive Council, absurd. In Bengal twenty-nine stations had closely adhered to the specimen, and in only ten cases, mostly hill stations or fortified places, were there any deviations. 'I cannot believe that it was wise to provide costly accommodation at Rawal Pindee (almost the healthiest station of the British Army) that may possibly have been necessary at damp and sultry Barrackpore, or in the burning plains which surround Allahabad or Gwalior.'[23]

The building programme was too far advanced for Mayo to have the effect he wished, but he did introduce cottage-barracks in hill stations, a healthier and arguably a more economical course. He was also resolutely in favour of transferring as many troops as possible to the hills. The outbreak of the Mutiny had revealed that much of the army was in the wrong place, but with better road and rail links and a more settled outlook Mayo did not consider that his redeployment was dangerous, and in the autumn he proposed that ten more regiments should be moved into the hills forthwith.

Previous administrations had borrowed to meet the cost of barrack building, but Mayo strongly disagreed, insisting that the cost should be treated as ordinary expenditure and met from the current year's revenue. On this he had to overrule Durand, who contrasted the niggardly amount allocated to barracks with the sums found for railways and canals. Elsewhere Durand complained about 'a paroxysm of military retrenchment, accompanied by very petty civil parings'. He was unrepentant in his view that 'for every consideration of security, of necessity, of humanity, and of the soundest economy' the money needed for troops' accommodation should be spread by loan over a period of years.[24] But Mayo had his way.

Today these arid arguments about organisation and expenditure are primarily of interest to the military historian, but they show how readily Mayo grasped the main issues. Sometimes in discussion with the gnarled veterans of earlier campaigns he would joke about his commission as a junior officer in the Kildare Militia. Sometimes he was near to despair. 'We have useless Regiments, hosts of useless officers, we have in some cases three establishments where one would do the work *better*, we have Presidential jealousies and divided authority which penalises control . . . we have no right to be here at all unless we use *all* our power for the good of the blacks.'[25] But he did not overlook the needs of internal security, and he was fully aware that the maintenance of morale in both native and European regiments was a delicate business.

A military masquerade to end this chapter. One of Mayo's last engagements before he sailed for Burma and the Andamans was to attend a review at the Camp of Exercise at Delhi on 6 and 7 January 1872. Some 15,000 troops took part and the manoeuvre programme required a division under General McMurdo to defend Delhi against an attack by two other divisions under these mighty warriors, both holders of the Victoria Cross, General Sir Henry Tombs and General Travers. So successful was the attack that the battle ended a day earlier than had been expected. Mayo, in one of his periodical reports to Queen Victoria, added 'The natives could not understand it – they were convinced that some great military operation was intended, and they are said to have begun to hide their money and jewels.'[26]

11

Petty Wars and Princes

Mayo was not going to have his reputation as a peace-loving statesman marred by petty wars or punitive expeditions against troublesome tribesmen who harried the borders from time to time. He believed that every shot fired in anger over the frontier reverberated through the whole of British Asia, and gave to natives who were no friends of Christian or European rule 'the notion that among our own subjects there are men still in arms against us'.[1] He told the Lieutenant-Governor of Bengal that he was decidedly opposed to the defence of the frontier by military reprisals if they could be avoided.[2] When explaining to Argyll that he intended to maintain a system of constant vigilance and defence, instead of spasmodic raids, he was even more explicit: 'This will undoubtedly be unpopular, for when honours and thanks of Government and promotions and KCBs or CSIs are to be got marching up a high hill with an overwhelming force and burning a few wooden huts and the crops of corn, these things will always find favour with local Governments and their subordinates.'[3]

At the end of 1870 the Punjab Government wanted to carry out hostile operations following a tribal raid on the village of Jascote in the Agror valley on 24 August, when four men were killed and seventeen wounded. As a matter of routine, they sought the Viceroy's approval to reprisals in this, and future cases. Mayo was not amused.

No one can read the Lieutenant-Governor's letter without coming to the conclusion that there still exists in the minds of the authorities of the Punjab an ardent, though partly concealed, desire for that avenging policy which the Government of India is anxious to avoid.

I frankly own that it is not to the credit of our administration that, after 25 years of constant contact with these people, unlike our officers in Scinde, the Punjab authorities have devised no better means of dealing with them and of repressing their outrages than by copying their own savage mode of warfare.

Many of those who served in the Punjab or the North West Provinces sincerely believed that punitive expeditions were necessary and had to be severe, but not the Viceroy. After delivering his rebuke, for this was just what it was, to the Punjab Government, he gave their proposals 'a decided negative'.[4]

On only one occasion did he agree that it was necessary to measure swords with recalcitrant neighbours. In July 1871 he told Argyll, with evident regret, that a small expedition would have to be mounted against the Looshai.[5] This was an idea which seems to have originated in the minds of the Commander-in-Chief and Grey while still Lieutenant-Governor of Bengal. Certainly Campbell, on his return to Calcutta to succeed Grey in March 1871, was quite clear that he was 'in no degree responsible for the policy of the expedition', though it fell to him to attend to the facilities for its despatch.

What had happened was that the Looshai who inhabited the densely wooded hills that stretch along Eastern Bengal from Kachar southwards to Arakan had been causing havoc among the Kachar teaplanters. The raiders had even taken prisoners, including a little English girl, the daughter of a planter (Mr Winchester) who had been killed in the attack on his estate. The Calcutta press, who had long been nourished on a diet of Looshai misbehaviour, were demanding action, and now the offending tribesmen had to be disciplined.

The plan was that two columns, one under General Bourchier (with the future Lord Roberts on his staff) starting from Assam, and the other under General Brownlow from Chittagong in the south, should eventually effect a junction. Mayo kept a close eye on the number of troops and the expense involved, but Bourchier still got three regiments of native infantry, while Brownlow was given one native infantry and two Ghurka regiments. Both columns had guns from a mountain battery and a company of sappers and miners – in sum a sizeable deployment. Mayo, highly sceptical about the whole manoeuvre, told Napier, much to his irritation, that he doubted whether the two British commanders would easily succeed in making contact – events proved he was right – and he did not want the operation prolonged while separate British contingents vainly sought for each other in unfriendly terrain. In fact the two columns penetrated well into Looshai country, Bourchier, who had already reported the rescue of Mary Winchester, describing the events as 'from first to last sheer hard work'.[6] At Mayo's insistence, it was not a purely retaliatory exercise; it was to demonstrate the necessity, and the benefits of peaceful coexistence with the Raj. Campbell added his own snide comment. 'The whole thing was, I am sure, most efficiently conducted – the tribes were punished and frightened, and we were able to claim that they had submitted; we made terms and conditions which they observed for some years till their next outbreak.'[7] Campbell apparently shared Mayo's doubts whether the game was worth the candle.

The Viceroy was not only responsible for the 200 million population of British India, with its annual revenue of about £46m. In a different way he also controlled the 153 feudatory states, where the 50 million natives provided their chiefs with an annual income of £15m. (The term 'feudatory' has been challenged in favour of 'semi-sovereign'.) In area, British India, including British Burma, extended to about 900,000 square miles, while the territory under the feudatory chiefs was equivalent to two thirds of that figure.

It is unnecessary for our purpose to go into the long history of conquests and acquisitions by the East India Company, but when Mayo took up office relations with the feudatory states were still, inevitably, coloured by the Mutiny little more than a decade earlier. Paradoxically, one lesson of the Mutiny was that the sepoys, on whom the Company depended for the core of its army, had proved disaffected, while the ruling princes generally stood firm behind the Raj. The lapsed dynasties, however, were hostile. Of these, the Muhammadans were symbolically represented by the aged King of Delhi who took the rebels' side; the Hindus, descended from the Mahrattas, contributed leaders like Nana Sahib and his follower Tantia Topi; while the states whose rulers had been deposed when there was no direct heir contributed the Rani of Jhansi. But the great mass of the feudatory princes did not join the uprising.

Before the Mutiny the most powerful princes were bound by

tightly drawn treaties; the weaker ones were taken over when a pretext could be found; and annexation, always a cardinal feature of East India Company policy, was given a new impetus under Dalhousie. But in 1858 the Raj renounced interference with the right of an independent prince to choose a successor when he had no heir to his body, and the practice of adoption was recognised. Canning's *sanad* of 17 March 1862 to the Hindu feudatories conveyed an assurance that 'on failure of natural heirs, the British Government will recognise and confirm any adoption of a successor made by yourself or by any future Chief of your State, that may be in accordance with Hindu law and the customs of your race'.[8] A similar patent was granted to the Muhammadan chiefs, and both contained a further assurance that nothing would disturb these engagements as long as the chiefs remained loyal to the Crown and faithful to their obligations to the British Government. The corollary was that the princes had a new interest in the good government of their domains and in cooperating with the sovereign power.

Subsequent events, however, had cast a gloss on this interpretation. Put most simply, Canning was thought to have gone a long way to conciliate the feudatory chiefs, but Elgin, in his short tenure, had been less forthcoming. He persuaded himself that his predecessor had 'never intended to let the chiefs get the bit into their mouths', and that his deference to native princes had been only a means to an end – the reestablishment of British rule. Lawrence also had been more disposed to consider what he regarded as the rights of their subjects rather than the princes' sense of their own propriety.

John Strachey, in a formal minute he wrote after Mayo's assassination, summed up the late Viceroy's policy towards the native states.[9] There was to be no meddling or spasmodic interference in their affairs, and, in general, they were to be left to govern in their own way. When improvements were required in their administration, they should be encouraged to come spontaneously, but when he had to interfere his actions should be sharp and effective. There was to be no coveting of their territories, and the chiefs should be led to see that they had nothing to fear from the British, but their arbitrary power was not to be used merely for personal aggrandisement. It was essential that they saw that the identity of their interests with those of the Raj, set out in the treaties, was a reality. Finally, since ignorance, often inescapable in young princes brought up in the confines of the *zenana*, led to misgovernment, the better education of the next generation was a priority.

This was an ambitious programme, not capable of being achieved in the short term, and Mayo was well aware of the inconsistency inherent in the relationship with the feudatories. Reduced to practicalities, it was ill-defined.

> We act on the principle of non-interference, but we must constantly interpose. We allow them to keep armies for the defence of their states, but we cannot permit them to go to war. We encourage them to establish courts of justice, but we cannot hear of their trying Europeans. We recognise them as separate Sovereigns, but we daily issue to them orders which are implicitly obeyed . . . In fact, all our action with regard to these petty despotic states is governed by the circumstances of the time and the character of the ruler; and it must ever be so if we are to influence them for good.[10]

There was occasional friction with individuals. The Foreign Department at Calcutta had strict rules prescribing the official courtesies between the Governor-General and the princes, and Mayo was content to observe them. A month after he took office he reported to Argyll that he had refused to grant the tiresome Nawab Nazim of Bengal a public interview unless he complied with the ancient custom of presenting a *nuzzer*. Nazim had pursued a long, vexatious claim for increased privileges derived, he argued, from earlier treaties, and he was now on his way to London to make his case in person. He also intended to lease a sporting estate for the autumn, and Mayo added, rather patronisingly, 'If your Grace could put his people in the way of getting a place where there are plenty of grouse, you would do him a great kindness.'[11] Argyll replied in the same vein that he would do what he could 'to be civil to him'. Later, after consulting the Governor-General in Council, as required by precedent, Argyll rejected Nazim's claims very firmly.[12]

Then, when the Maharaja of Jodhpur absented himself from an official ceremony at Ajmere in circumstances regarded as a deliberate insult, Mayo recommended that he should be stripped of his Star of India.[13] The Secretary of State thought this would be rather petty, and Mayo wrote again that he quite understood that Argyll did not want to go further in this momentous matter.

More seriously, Mayo kept a careful watch on the affairs of Kathiawar, where the 188 small component native states were administered by a British Political Agent. Until the excellent Colonel Keatinge introduced his reforms in 1863 there had been no written law and nothing resembling a judicial system. Since then some progress had been made in suppressing the predatory activities of outlaw bands, but the Agent complained that he had only 89 police to cover 20,000 square miles. There was also a complicated, and unsatisfactory, arrangement with the Gaekwar of Baroda for the collection of revenue, but Mayo decided to hold his hand, conscious that if things in the honeycomb of states at Kathiawar were not right, they were at least a great deal better than they had been.

In Alwar, however, the misbehaviour of the prince made intervention inevitable – the only occasion when Mayo took such a course. There was always the possibility of conflict between the Hindu nobles and the disaffected Muhammadan population in this state in the north-east of Rajputana, and matters were brought to a head when the young prince officially came of age in 1863 and abolished the Native Council of Regency. He then embarked on a time of extravagant debauchery, and in seven years transformed the £170,000 he had received on his majority into a deficit of the same amount, also squandering the state revenue of £200,000 a year. Hunter records that large sums were assigned to men whose sole duty was to make salaams to the Prince, to singers and dancing girls and wrestlers, and that he was daily seen drunk 'with low Muhammadans'.[14] Faced with the prospect of the entire state of three quarters of a million souls being thrown into upheaval, some of the Viceroy's more cynical advisers thought it would be best to let the parties fight it out. Mayo thought otherwise. In his view the Raj could not permit civil war in any state in India,[15] and he accordingly favoured arbitration by a senior officer, assisted by the respected Maharaja of Jaipur. But events moved too quickly to allow this leisurely process to take place. 'The Chief', wrote Mayo, 'is incorrigible; he never keeps a single promise; he is able and crafty, but is constantly drunk.'[16]

But the Viceroy did not agree to deporting him, and instead

issued orders to set up a Native Council under the presidency of Major Cadell, the British Agent. The Maharaja of Alwar was given a seat on the council, with a liberal personal allowance, and his state subsided into an uneasy peace. Exhausted by his excesses, he died in 1874 at the age of twenty-nine.

Relations were sometimes touchy wih two of the most powerful chiefs –the Maharajas Holkar of Indore (according to Burne, 'one of the greatest impostors in India'), and Scindia of Gwalior, though Holkar was persuaded to cooperate in building a railway line to connect Indore with the Great Indian Peninsula Railway. The relationship with Scindia over the fortress of Gwalior merits further scrutiny.

Briefly, in 1853 Dalhousie had said that Scindia's fort should be restored to him, and in 1860 Canning gave the same undertaking, a promise later confirmed by Elgin; but nothing was done. The proposal under discussion towards the end of 1871 was that the British should withdraw from the Gwalior fort and the cantonment of Morar, but not before Scindia had built a railway at his own expense from Gwalior to Agra. There would be a slight increase in the British contingent at Agra, with agreement that Scindia would, for his part, consent not to strengthen the fort, and that his private army should be reduced to the strength fixed by the treaty of 1844.

Mayo thought this arrangement would get the British out of a station which was unhealthy and unsafe militarily; that it would provide free of charge about a hundred miles of railway; and that it would restore good faith, which in the case of the fort was 'not unassailable'. In his despatch to the Secretary of State, Mayo confidently disposed of minutes of dissent recorded by Napier of Magdala and Temple. Military authorities since Sir Hugh Rose's time had agreed that Morar was unsafe as a garrison site, and on the point that Scindia himself could not survive without the presence of a large subsidiary force, Mayo observed that, should the Maharaja's troops be mutinous, Morar could be reoccupied within forty-eight hours on the new railway.

It may be thought that Mayo had the better of the argument, though Napier was writing home that the treatment of Scindia had been 'paternal towards a wilful child, stimulated and instigated by artful men about him, who hate us for our supremacy'. Napier was also apprehensive about creating a precedent. 'If we withdraw from Gwalior because Scindia dislikes the curb on his power, we shall have no better reason for not withdrawing from Secunderabad because the infant Nizam may want to play at soldiers when he gets a little older, or from Mhow, because it threatens Indore.'[17]

Mayo, undismayed by his colleagues' criticism, proposed to open discussions with Scindia at the end of 1871, and there can be little doubt that he would have prevailed, if he had been spared to continue in office. In the event the garrison at Morar remained for many years, and the fort was given back to Scindia in 1886.

With some of the princes, notably the Maharajas of Jaipur and Patiala, Mayo maintained a close friendship. He also had an amicable understanding with the elderly Prince Gholam Mahomed. (As the wheel of fortune turned, the last surviving son of Tipu Sultan was now a KSCI and a loyal supporter of the Raj.) Like his advisers, Mayo greatly admired the little Begum of Bhopal. Her mother, the famous Sikander Begum, had stood behind the British at the time of the Mutiny, and was proud to be included in the first appointments to the Star of India before she died in 1868. Her daughter, the thirty-year-old widow who succeeded as Begum, was equally well-disposed and carried out many liberal domestic reforms. She was invited to Calcutta as an honoured guest and presented to the Duke of Edinburgh. Her Anglophilia extended to learning English and, exceptionally and entirely contrary to precedent, Mayo gave her permission to write direct to Queen Victoria.

Mayo's relationship with the feudatory chiefs is best exemplified by his visit to Jaipur and Ajmere in October 1870. After enjoying the genial hospitality of the Maharaja and some excellent sport in the field, the Viceroy and his entourage moved on to the great Sambhar Lake with its limitless supply of salt, that valuable commodity. (The rulers of Jaipur and Jodphur had been persuaded to grant the Government a permanent lease.) On 20 October Mayo entered Ajmere in solemn procession to be welcomed by the provincial chiefs mounted on their ceremonial elephants and ranged in rank along the route. Greetings were extended by the municipality, since this was the first time that a Governor-General had visited the ancient capital of Rajputana. Next day Mayo received eight of the principal feudatories in private durbar, before attending the foundation of the new college for the sons of nobles that was to bear his name.

This was a project very dear to Mayo's heart. He knew how defective was most of the chiefs' education, and he believed that the prospects of stable government would be greatly enhanced if they were taught on English lines before succeeding to the seat of power in their states. Another establishment, the Rajkumar Chiefs College, which was opened at Rajkot in Kathiawar in December 1870, met with plenty of teething troubles. Some of the reluctant entrants, disliking school discipline, soon returned to the blandishments of the *zenana*; others went about accompanied by bands of armed retainers, 'strange wild-looking creatures who might have come out of the Middle Ages'; but the first Principal, Chester Macnaughton, gradually asserted his authority.[18] Meanwhile, Mayo was full of hope as the foundation stone was laid. As an indication of how much Ajmere remained in his thoughts, a year later he was writing to General Chamberlain to draw his attention to the new seminary whose 'main object and end' was 'to make young chiefs into Gentlemen', and to invite him to become its first President. Knowing that the title would be important to Chamberlain, he suggested 'Governor of the Nobles College of Rajputana'.[19]

Mayo's philosophy is seen at its clearest in the remarkable speech he made to the assembled Chiefs at Ajmere on 21 October, defining, as it does, his attitude towards the imperial mission.

I, as the representative of the Queen, have come here to tell you, as you have often been told before, that the desire of Her Majesty's Government is to secure to you and your successors the full enjoyment of your ancient rights and the exercise of all lawful customs, and to assist you in upholding the dignity and maintaining the authority which you and your fathers have for centuries exercised in this land.

But in order to enable us fully to carry into effect this our fixed resolve, we must receive from you hearty and cordial assistance. If we respect your rights and privileges, you should also respect the rights and regard the privileges of those who are placed beneath your care. If we support you in your power, we expect in return good government. We demand that everywhere throughout the length and breadth of Rajputana, justice and order shall prevail; that every man's property shall be secure; that the traveller shall come and go in safety; that the cultivator shall enjoy the fruits of his labour, and the trader the produce of his commerce; that you shall make roads, and undertake the construction of those works of irrigation which will improve the condition of the people and swell the revenue of your states; that you shall encourage education, and provide for the relief of the sick.

Be assured that we ask you do all this for no other but your own benefit. If we wished you to remain weak, we should say; Be poor, and ignorant, and disorderly. It is because we wish you to be strong that we desire to see you rich, instructed, and well-governed. It is for such objects that the servants of the Queen rule India; and Providence will ever sustain the rulers who govern for the people's good.

I am here only for a time. The able and earnest officers who surround me will, at no distant period, return to their English homes; but the Power we represent will endure for ages. Hourly is this great Empire brought nearer and nearer to the throne of our Queen. The steam-vessel and the railroad enable England, year by year, to enfold India in a closer embrace. But the coils she seeks to entwine around her are no iron fetters, but the golden chains of affection and peace. The days of conquest are past; the age of improvement has begun.

Chiefs and Princes, advance in the right way, and secure to your children's children, and to future generations of your subjects, the favouring protection of a Power who only seeks your good.'[20]

The speech was worthy of the occasion, and happily when Charles Aitchison, the Foreign Secretary, followed with the translation in Hindustani, 'contrary to all former precedents, he did it most admirably'.

The only discordant note was struck by the unseemly conduct of the Maharaja of Jodhpur. He had never been willing to agree that he ranked after his rival the Rana of Udaipur. 'In a fit of hesitation and folly as to their precedence', noted the *Friend of India*, 'he was too late for the Durbar and he will be very sorry for it.' It appears that the drunken potentate was eventually persuaded by his nobles, and even his son, casting their turbans before him, that he should attend. But he had missed his chance, and the Viceroy took his misbehaviour as an affront. Jodhpur was ordered out of Ajmere without the usual salute or guard of honour, and forbidden to fly his flag. Mayo, as we have seen, also thought that expulsion from the Order of the Star of India would be justified, but this was a small blemish on the accord of the day, which went a long way to convincing the feudatory chiefs that they could place their trust in the Viceroy. It is not surprising that when Scindia heard of Mayo's death, his comment was 'I have made a friend and lost him'.

If the chiefs were being warned to put their house in order or depart, there was also an element of idealism. Both Mayo and Aitchison were good Victorian optimists who believed in 'improvement' and the power of moral suasion.

The continuing, often tortuous relationship between the Viceroy and the princes was one of the most fascinating aspects of the history of the Raj. Shorn of its rhetoric, and its very acceptable public presentation, Mayo's policy proceeded on two assumptions: the feudatory states afforded a useful reserve of military power for use in an emergency; and, secondly, rule by the princes, encouraged to adopt liberal practices, could be made a channel for modernisation and stability. His view was not inconsistent with that of a later Viceroy, Lytton, who assured Disraeli that the Indian peasantry was an inert mass which, if it ever moved, would 'move not in obedience to its British benefactors, but to its native chiefs and princes', however tyrannical they might be. Mayo would have shared Lytton's conclusion: 'If we have with us the Princes, we shall have with us the people.'[21]

The sad reflection is that Mayo's attitude was a refinement of that originating with the East India Company, which practised 'subordinate isolation' towards the princes – subordinate because the feudatory states were not allowed to carry out their own foreign policy, and had no international life, and isolated because, unless they misbehaved too outrageously, the chiefs were left to go their own way. Sad, since in time the princes' protected existence carried with it the seeds of their own destruction. They became more like puppets, increasingly impotent, and vulnerable to rebellion from within and pressure from outside their states. But that was long after Mayo.

During his rule there was no dispute about his personal standing with the princely states. Daly, the Agent for central India, wrote:

> His prestige with the Chiefs and Princes of India stood romantically high. He had made their position and personal interests his special study. Hardly any predecessor had seen so much of India and so

carefully marked the characteristics of its native rulers. There was that in his presence and manner which touched Asiatics, and charmed those who came into contact with him, while his character for earnestness commended itself to all.[22]

12
The Afghan Amir

Nothing in Mayo's time – the initial impressions he had garnered at Bombay and Madras, the reception by the senior mandarins and provincial governors on the red carpet at Government House, the obsequious addresses from the merchants and zemindars at Calcutta, or his involvement with the chiefs and princes – distracted him from what was to be his principal personal concern, foreign affairs.

The Foreign Department was very much the Viceroy's bailiwick. As his own Foreign Minister, he looked for advice not, as with other aspects of government, to a designated member of the Executive Council, but to the Secretary of the Foreign Department. Mayo was fortunate in having as his Foreign Secretary Charles Aitchison (later to hold high office in British Burma and the Punjab), but it was soon clear that the impetus would be the Viceroy's. John Strachey, who knew Mayo better than most, said that from the moment he set foot in India he threw himself into international questions with a vigour, sagacity and foresight which had a pronounced effect beyond the limits of his domain. Durand, who as Military Member kept a wary eye on defence matters, strongly supported Mayo's foreign policy, and, for once, had no captious comments to make.

British India's relations with the states which were her immediate neighbours had in recent years been fairly peaceful. Lawrence had followed a deliberate policy of *laissez-faire*, and there had been no accessions of territory since the short war against the Himalayan state of Bhutan at the beginning of his rule. But the frontier states, remembering how the British, from the days of John Company onwards, had spread their tentacles across the continent, could be forgiven for doubting whether the Raj. had really lost the appetite for further acquisition. The states in the west and the north west were also aware that the

Great Bear had swept down to the Oxus, which did not make their intermediate position any more comfortable.

From the imperial point of view, both at Calcutta and at Westminster, Russia still represented the main threat to British India. An immediate invasion did not seem probable, but the Russian advance throughout Central Asia was apparent for all to see. The Russians annexed Tashkent in 1866; in 1868 they moved into Samarkand; in the same year they subdued the Khan of Bokhara; and they were consolidating everywhere, with roads and telegraphic communications.

These developments were in Argyll's mind when he sent Mayo a comprehensive memorandum on foreign policy. Argyll's main conclusion was that none of the Great Powers, especially Asiatic Russia and Persia, whose interests might be inimical to British India, should march with its boundaries. In effect, there should be a *cordon sanitaire* of friendly states round the Indian frontier.[1] By the time he read the memorandum at the end of 1869, this was Mayo's own policy, which he pursued in a highly individual way. One of his gifts was an ability to sieve through the relevant material and pick out the cardinal points. He saw that the first objective must be to convince the frontier states of Britain's peaceful intentions, and of her wish to be of assistance but not to interfere in their domestic politics. He had already made a start with Afghanistan.

Apart from the necessity of creating a bulwark against possible Russian encroachment, Mayo had good reasons for wanting to reach an effective concordat with Afghanistan. A stable regime in that country, and one that was well disposed to the Raj, would help to keep the peace in India. It would cease to be a haven for subversive elements. There was also the commercial argument, and Mayo never lost sight of the need to expand trade in central Asian markets.

Relations with Afghanistan had improved since Auckland's aberration in launching the Army of the Indus in 1839 to replace the Afghan ruler Dost Mahomed by the puppet Shah Soojah. In 1843, after one of the worst débacles in British history, Dost Mahomed was allowed to return to the throne of Kabul, and his authority was formally ratified in one of the East India Company's last treaties. In 1855 Dalhousie engaged to respect the territories 'now in His Highness' possession, and never to interfere therein.'[2] The treaty remained valid throughout the Mutiny, when Dost Mahomed refused to give aid to the mutineers, but after his death in 1863 at the age of eighty the affairs of Afghanistan were once again thrown into turmoil.

The Dost had nominated his son Sher Ali as his rightful successor, but when the new Amir asked for a closer alliance with the British, Lawrence would have none of it. Without formal British recognition, Sher Ali's position was more vulnerable, and for the next five years he was involved in a bitter struggle with his various relations (Dost Mahomed had left at least sixteen sons and six grandsons). Sher Ali, though he had prevailed in some of the earlier battles, was driven out of Kabul in 1866 by his brother Afzul, who then sought recognition from Lawrence. The Viceroy replied that, while he would recognise Afzul as ruler of Kabul, if he could consolidate his power there, Sher Ali still ruled at Kandahar and Herat, and he must continue 'to treat him as ruler of that portion of Afghanistan over which he retains control'.[3] Another request a year later – by this time Sher Ali was penned in Herat – met with a similar reply. In 1867, when Afzul died, Lawrence acknowledged his brother Azim as ruler of Kabul, though his hold over the city was distinctly precarious. The Viceroy's declared policy remained not to interfere and to recognise the warring chiefs only as Amirs of the area which he considered was under their authority.

Durand summed up the confusion. 'Afghanistan cannot support so many chiefs, but the people do not seem to know how to get rid of their plague; and as soon as one overgrown family has managed to get extirpated, polygamy builds up another, so that the process of having to get rid of superfluous chiefs is endless.'[4]

This was not the most decisive episode in British diplomacy. Lawrence might argue that we should leave the Afghans to settle their own hash, but his critics held that it was both morally wrong and politically dangerous 'to stand by and see a neighbouring state torn to pieces by internecine factions, and liable at any moment to become the theatre of successful Russian intrigue'. Moreover, did we not claim to be the great ameliorating power in Asia? In that event we were disregarding our most solemn duty and falling into 'the blunder of exalting the influence of our European rival upon the ruins of our own'.[5]

The chiefs, for their part, realised that the British, whom they suspected of wanting to prolong the civil war, were simply waiting to see how the cat jumped. In Sher Ali's words, 'The English look to nothing but their own interests and bide their time; whosoever side they see strongest for the time they turn to him as their friend. I will not waste precious life in entertaining false hopes from the English and will enter into friendship with other Governments.'[6]

Lawrence was unmoved. Strangely, though he had a poor opinion of Sher Ali, he was more favourably disposed towards Afzul and Azim. He was still adhering to his policy of 'masterly inactivity' – a phrase coined by John Wyllie, a former under-secretary in the Foreign Department, writing in a famous article in the *Fortnightly Review*.[7] Lawrence's difficulty was that he could not see a middle course between doing nothing and active intervention on the ground. That is the real case against him. He believed it was 'a delusion, and a mistake to suppose that we could bring about amicable relations by the mere influence of negotiations'.[8] This almost amounted to not having a foreign policy at all.

In the autumn of 1867 and throughout 1868 Sher Ali, resilient if nothing else, managed to overcome his rivals and to convince Lawrence that he was now the ruler of Afghanistan. Lawrence suddenly changed his tune. He formally recognised Sher Ali by letter, and as a token of goodwill sent him a present of 3,000 muskets and six lakhs of rupees, with a promise of six more to come. He also consented to receive a visit from the Amir, and said he was willing to travel to Rawalpindi, or even Peshawar, to meet him. Why did he abandon the policy he had followed so obstinately? It may have been mounting criticism, both in India and at home. Northcote, as Secretary of State, told him not to be 'too ostentatiously indifferent' towards the rulers of Afghanistan. Sir Henry Rawlinson, the foremost opponent of 'masterly inactivity' and now a member of the India Council, minuted on 20 July 1868: 'The fortunes of Sher Ali are again in the ascendant. He should be secured to our interests without delay. Provided he is unentangled with Russia, the restoration of his father's subsidy, and the moral support of the British Indian Government, would probably be sufficient to place him above all opposition, and to secure his fidelity.'[9]

No doubt these expressions of view influenced Lawrence, weary after his years in India and seldom keen to engage the authorities at home. Anyhow, though he had never been impressed by the Russian menace, even contending that the further the Russians advanced into Central Asia the more problems she would have,[10] Lawrence had made his belated friendly overture to Sher Ali, and that was the situation when Mayo arrived in India.

Lawrence had to leave Simla and return to Calcutta before the rendezvous with Sher Ali could take place. Mayo's first reference to meeting the Amir came in a letter to Sir Donald Macleod, the Lieutenant-Governor of the Punjab, and was prompted by a report that Azim had sought refuge in British territory.[11] At the same time Mayo wrote to Argyll that 'this terminates the civil war in Afghanistan and renders Sher Ali's position apparently more secure'. He added that if Sher Ali had caught Azim and his nephew he would have blown them from a gun or put out their eyes, and that it was very important to capitalise on the Amir's friendly feelings towards the British.[12] (A fortnight later he learned that Azim had not, after all, crossed into British India. He had fled to Turkestan, and died there.)

By the middle of February 1869 plans for the meeting had begun to take shape in Mayo's mind, and he told Macleod that he would be sorry if anything happened to prevent it. He hoped to see the Amir in March, at Amballa, and the reasons he gave for his choice of date and location – Sher Ali would have preferred Peshawar – are interesting. In March the Government normally moved to Simla, so that it would not appear that the Viceroy had gone far out of his way. Since Amballa was on the railway, it would be much easier to assemble the ceremonial troops that would be needed, and the requirement that the Amir should travel to Amballa would emphasise that 'the meeting was sought for more by him than by us'. Did Mayo perhaps remember that Canning had held a great durbar at Amballa for the cis-Sutlej princes of the Punjab, when awards for loyalty were presented to the rulers of Patiala, Jind and Nabha?

Argyll's lack of enthusiasm – 'you should maintain that policy of reserve, and of abstention from interference which was pursued by your predecessor'[13] – and his insistence that

Lawrence's gifts to Sher Ali should not bind the Government to repeat them, did not discourage Mayo, who agreed that on principle he disliked regular subsidies. Mayo also told Macleod that he intended to follow the precedent of Auckland's meeting with Runjeet Singh in 1838, being the last occasion when anything of the kind took place. Either this was an Irish way of putting it, or Mayo had forgotten his Anglo-Afghan history. Auckland's great *tumasha* at Ferozepore had been designed to solemnise his treaty with Runjeet, which enabled the latter, for the price of providing a token force, to join in the invasion of Afghanistan and help to overthrow his enemy, Sher Ali's father. The Ferozepore circus was acclaimed at the time for its colourful ceremony, though the Misses Eden, accompanying their brother, the Governor-General, were disgusted by the extravagant drinking habits of the Sikh ruler, pockmarked after a lifetime of constant debauchery. Even then many feared, rightly, that the outcome of the junketings would be disastrous, and it was certainly not an auspicious precedent for Mayo.

This, the only time when Mayo came face to face with Sher Ali, was popularly described as the Amballa Durbar, but, for reasons discussed in chapter 9 on the significance of the ceremony, it was not really a durbar at all. For example, the official notification said explicitly that while presents would be given to the Amir, 'no *khilluts* will be conferred on, and no *nuzzurs* will be taken from, those Native Gentlement who are present'. An essential part of the durbar ceremony was accordingly prohibited. As though to reinforce this point, Mayo, who had some difficulty in persuading the Punjab chiefs that they should attend an assembly in honour of someone they had no reason to like, had emphasised that this was a unique occasion, and that it was their duty and privilege to join with him in welcoming the head of another country. 'I have endeavoured', he wrote to Argyll, 'to give the visit the character of a meeting between equals to show the world that we look upon the Amir as an independent, not as a feudatory prince.'[14]

The Amir, accompanied by his youngest son Abdulla Jan, started from Kabul in February, and on 2 March he was received at the mouth of the Khyber Pass by Major Pollock, the Commissioner at Peshawar, and Brigadier-General Stewart with his brigade and a guard of honour from the 19th Bengal

Lancers. Thereafter the business of conning him – for it was no less than that – proceeded apace. Sher Ali was impressed by everything he saw at Peshawar (which Runjeet Singh had seized from his father) except for the appearance of the local ladies, about whom, in Burne's account, he said 'Ah, you sly people, I see you keep your pretty girls at home.'[15] During his slow march through the Punjab he was treated with every mark of respect, so much so that when he reached Lahore, the very seat of Sikh power, he exclaimed joyfully that he now began to feel himself a king.

Mayo wrote enthusiastically to Argyll that the muster at Amballa included 8,000 troops of every form and hue, from the camel corps of the Maharaja of Patiala, armed with the matchlocks of 300 years ago, to the newly formed mountain battery of steel guns. The formalities on 27 March started at five o'clock and ended within the hour. 'After a conversation of about fifteen minutes duration, fifty-one trays of presents were brought into the Durbar tent for His Highness the Amir; twenty-one trays for His Highness's son; and five trays for each of His Highness's six principal Sirdars. Six horses were also led to the entrance of the tent for the acceptance of His Highness.'[16]

The chiaroscuro caused by the satraps of the Raj, squeezed into their dark blue uniforms, sashes and medals proclaiming their orders of chivalry, tense as though on parade, facing oriental chiefs apparently relaxed beneath their jewel-crusted turbans, had long been a commonplace. But Amballa was an occasion for the connoisseur. There was no doubt who was in charge as the Viceroy, tall, broad-shouldered, clean-shaven, with an eye like Jove to threaten and command, radiated confidence. Beside him, the Afghan Amir, short of stature, aquiline in profile, was for the moment subdued, but – as Temple noted – his hooded eyes searching round the tented pavilion scarcely suppressed flashes of fierceness.

Mayo presented a sword of honour, which he hoped the Amir would regard as a symbol of the Viceroy's desire that he should be victorious over his enemies in defence of his 'just and lawful rights'. Sher Ali gallantly replied that he would never unsheath it except in the service of his friends the British, and in return gave Mayo his own sword which had been handed down to him by Dost Mahomed. Despite later arguments, Sher Ali retained the warmest recollections of Amballa, so much so that two years later he sent Mayo the oozing gift of a hundred camel loads of fruit, ranging from 8,000 boxes of grapes to ten loads of pomegranates and three of apricots. The *Friend of India* expressed the confident hope that His Excellency would 'feel bound, in honour, to himself eat [the fruit] even to the last fragment'.[17]

Not all the chiefs who were present were equally pleased at the magnificence of Mayo's arrangements. Holkar was reported as exclaiming: 'I think you are making too much of this adventurer – but I suppose Russia is considered to be approaching very close, therefore you spend such thousands on Sher Ali and are so delighted at his coming to you.'[18] The Maharaja Scindia was even more acid. 'Distinctions as great as the light of the sun and of night are not pleasing to us who are better friends than the Amir is.'[19]

Mayo, if he was aware of this understandable jealousy, took no notice of it. He had to pay a return visit to the Amir's lines, and thereafter Sher Ali, who had declined an invitation to dinner because 'he was not used to the European mode of eating', attended an informal evening reception. There he was astonished to witness British officers in full uniform singing operatic airs at the piano. According to Burne, one of the performers, the delighted chief said 'Ah, I will make my Generals do that when I return.' Mayo was moved to wonder what Runjeet's shade would have made of it, if he had seen the Afghan Amir sitting in the Viceroy's tent in the middle of the Punjab, between a Sikh chief and an English General. Durand had his own reflections. 'Considering that I was with Lord Ellenborough at the durbar when Dost Mahomed was allowed to return to Afghanistan and that Sher Ali, his son, was one of those present, it is not without some special as well as general interest. Sher Ali and I must have met some six or seven-and-twenty years ago . . .'[21]

The social frivolities were but the trappings and the suits. In the intervals between the celebrations Mayo and his advisers had serious private discussions with the Amir. The only Englishmen present with Mayo were Sir Donald Macleod, Seton-Kerr from the Foreign Department, and Captain Grey as interpreter;

Sher Ali was supported by Nur Muhammad Shah, his chief Minister. Strangely, Sher Ali hardly referred to the Russians and did not seem, at the time, concerned about any threat from that quarter. Sher Ali had come wanting a treaty, a fixed annual subsidy, arms and troops when he, not the British, thought he needed them, a promise that the British would not acknowledge 'any friend in the whole of Afghanistan save the Amir and his descendants', and the acceptance of the young Abdulla Jan as his heir.[22] He got none of these.

Mayo wrote to Argyll that the Amir had been told that what he would receive would be 'all the moral support in our power and that in addition we are willing to assist him with money, arms, ammunition, native artificers and in other ways, whenever we deem it desirable so to do'. Mayo was clear that there should be no embarrassing entanglements, but, he added, the Afghans had been our friends once and would be again 'when we may find the advantage of possessing on our frontier an almost imprenetrable country, manned by some of the best hill troops in the world'.[23]

The extent of Mayo's commitment was set out in the formal, but friendly, letter he sent to the Amir to record their agreement. The crucial paragraph read:

> Although, as already intimated to you, the British Government does not desire to interfere in the internal affairs of Afghanistan, yet, considering that the bonds of friendship between that Government and your Highness have lately been more closely drawn than heretofore, it will view with severe displeasure any attempts on the part of your rivals to disturb your position as ruler of Cabul, and rekindle civil war; and it will further endeavour from time to time, by such means as circumstances may require, to strengthen the Government of your Highness, to enable you to transmit to your descendants all the dignities and honours of which you are the lawful possessor.[24]

Sher Ali declared that the letter from the Viceroy was worth a crore of rupees to him.[25] (He also got six lakhs of rupees – the balance of the twelve promised by Lawrence – 10,000 arms, six siege guns and a mountain battery.) Argyll, however, thought Mayo had gone too far. The letter quoted above might, for example, commit the British to support Sher Ali against a rebellion he had brought on himself. The reference to 'rightful rule' could also be taken as implying that they recognised his house could claim sovereignty *de iure*. Mayo replied, somewhat stiffly, that it would have been ungenerous and imprudent 'to have addressed His Highness in uncertain sounds', and Argyll did not pursue his objections. But Mayo was nettled at the London reaction to Amballa, as is clear from a letter he wrote to Lawrence on 3 June 1869, in which he complained that he had been misrepresented.[26]

On Sher Ali's return to Kabul the principal Sirdars, including chiefs who had been hostile, offered their submissions, although Ishaq Khan fled across the Oxus and Abdur Rahman took himself off towards Bokhara. For all practical purposes the civil war was at an end, and Mayo was entitled to claim that, without interfering, he had helped to restore peace.

Sher Ali had been so impressed by what he had seen on his journeys, and at Amballa, that he changed many Afghan customs to follow the English model, as he conceived it to be. He told his shoemaker to devise footwear on the English pattern; he affected the English costume of coat and pantaloons and made his officials do the same. He ordered his troops not to carry arms in Kabul between dusk and dawn. He appointed a judicial officer to hear petitions and organised a Council of State. His most radical proposal was to change the practice of paying officials in kind by introducing cash payments, but this was too radical for the Sirdars, and the scheme was dropped. In time Mayo became slightly alarmed at these Anglophile tendencies, and advised Pollock at Peshawar to give Sher Ali a tactful reminder not to push his reforms too far or too fast.

After the great gathering at Amballa broke up, Mayo with characteristic energy completed a rapid march through the lower Himalayas to Mussoorie and Roorkee, and reached his summer headquarters at Simla on 15 April. For the rest of his time in India he remained proud of what he had accomplished at Amballa. In fact, he went on about it.

Was he justified? Certainly Amballa had been well stage-managed, and Lawrence would not have done it with the same panache. On the surface, the policy followed by Mayo in the secret sessions carried forward that which Lawrence had – finally and reluctantly – adopted. But Mayo added one element of his own, which was of prime importance in an Asiatic context

– his friendly presence and enthusiasm. He made it clear that, while the British were no longer an aggressive power, there would be no more of the indifference to conditions in border states that had appeared throughout most of Lawrence's rule. To convince Sher Ali and his Sirdars of a positive friendly intent was a significant step forward. Mayo had not finished with Afghanistan, as will become apparent in the next chapter; but the most important thing about Amballa was the way in which it marked the beginning of a foreign policy which he now proceeded to develop along the frontier.

13
Masterly Activity

'Gallop' is not a verb normally associated with the conduct of diplomacy, but it comes readily to mind when examining Mayo's attitude, after Amballa, to external states. Not for nothing had he been a Master of Foxhounds; as he looked over the frontier, he went straight for his fences. 'With Asiatics', he told Durand, 'a bold front is the first element of success, and a bold front can, I firmly believe, be well maintained without aggression, oppression or injustice; without foreign conquest or domestic tyranny.'[1]

The way his mind worked can be seen in three private letters. In May 1869 he wrote to Disraeli: 'If I am allowed to carry out my policy I shall be able to form round our frontier from the Mekram coast to the confines of Northern Turkestan and China a cordon of friendly and independent states whose interest it will be to keep in with the great English Raj.' (He ended with some caustic comments on a recent Irish debate, and as Disraeli was in Opposition, added 'You had better burn this.')[2]

Next January he wrote in high glee to Lord Derby, 'Some people may admit that the Poor Paddy that the Times told everyone was not fit to be trusted with the care of a West Indian Island has, without firing a shot or moving a soldier, made British influence paramount in Regions which have been for years the hard nut of Anglo-Indian politics.'[3]

A few months later, in May 1870, writing again to Disraeli, he summarised the success of his departure from 'masterly in-activity' – a year's peace in Afghanistan and 'absolute obedience' by Sher Ali to British wishes; Russia's agreement not to meddle in the affairs of Kabul, and her enquiry as to what the British thought should be the northern boundary of Afghanistan; the despatch of an envoy to Eastern Turkestan; Persia's acceptance of arbitration on her border dispute with Afghanistan; and the establishment of direct trade between

British Burma and Western China. 'Pretty well for one year,' he concluded with unconcealed pride. The MFH reasserted himself as he added that he had travelled nearly 3,000 miles in the last month, 400 on horseback, 'and was all the better for it'.[4]

We will see how far his claims are valid. Relations with Persia, always an unreliable neighbour, can be disposed of first. The Shah had lately been troublesome by making claims to territory that traditionally belonged to the Khan of Khelat at Mekram, and by encroaching on Seistan, the swampy desert through which runs the Helmand river, and – more important in Afghan eyes – the route from Persia to Kandahar. Mayo succeeded in persuading the Persians to accept arbitration in both disputes – with the Khan over Mekram, and with Sher Ali regarding Seistan. But it was a tortuous business.

In August 1870 Colonel (later Sir) Frederick Goldsmid, an able Engineer officer, was nominated to arbitrate on Seistan and proceeded first to Teheran, where he was discomfited to learn that Sher Ali had not yet formally agreed to arbitration. To save time, Goldsmid, with Mayo's ready agreement by telegram, proposed to deal first with the Mekram boundary. Goldsmid reached his objective in Baluchistan in January 1871, and though hindered by suspicion from both sides he was back in Teheran in July with his report. Fortified by Alison, the British Minister, he had an audience with the Shah on 6 August, and on 4 September the boundary – as defined by Goldsmid and approved by Mayo – was accepted *pur et simple*. So far so good.

Seistan proved more difficult. The Persians were at first reluctant to accept Goldsmid's intervention, and Mayo had to persuade Sher Ali not to start open warfare. Goldsmid returned to Calcutta on 7 December 1871 for further instruction from Mayo. The Viceroy had meanwhile written to Argyll on 24 October saying how glad he was that the Persians were cooperating, and at the same time he sent a generous message to Alison for his help in bringing this about.[5] Goldsmid's mission, including Pollock the Commissioner at Peshawar, encamped in Seistan in February 1872, and by June had returned to Teheran with his proposals. Both sides appealed against his recommendation – a Solomon's judgement giving each half of what they wanted – but Argyll confirmed the award, and the Shah's visit to England in 1873 was made the occasion of his imperial assent.

By the time this oriental pavane had come to an end, Mayo was dead, but he had played his part. While the Persians agreed to arbitration under Article VI of the Treaty of 1857, Sher Ali said he had refrained from taking up arms over Seistan 'out of deference to the wishes of the Viceroy of India'.[6] That was the extent of Mayo's influence.

Incidentally, Mayo strongly believed that relations with the Persian Gulf should be transferred to the Government of India, and that the British Mission in Teheran should come under the Secretary of State for India and not the Foreign Secretary. According to Burne this was still very much in his mind when he was assassinated.[7]

Next to Khelat. Under the 1854 Treaty, the Khan was required to rely on British advice in foreign affairs; to protect merchants and stop raids into British India; and to allow the stationing of British troops in Khelat, should that be deemed necessary. In return he received a small annual subsidy. But the luckless Khan could not exert real authority over the warlike Beluchees, the problem being whether, as his Sirdars claimed, he was merely the head of a confederacy of chiefs, or whether, as the Khan asserted, he was entitled to regard himself as the supreme ruler in his own right. In 1871 the powerful Brahui tribe rose against him and the Beluchees speedily revived their old sport of attacking caravans in the Bolan Pass.

The latest rebellion was but one incident in a dispute which had long worried the British. In Lawrence's time Bartle Frere wanted to occupy Quetta to safeguard traffic through the Bolan, and this course was now strongly advocated once more. But Mayo would have nothing to do with it. 'I am not going to play the Shah Soojah game over again,' he wrote to Argyll.[8] Instead, he authorised Sir William Merewether, the Commissioner of Sind, to arbitrate between the Khan and his discontented chiefs. As time dragged on, it could be said that, for once, Mayo's merry diplomatic gallop had come to a halt, but – in Hunter's words – 'the internal consolidation of a State is a work of time, not less than the pacification of its frontier .[9] It was not till 1876 that Northbrook could point to a fragile settlement of the Khelat wrangles, and that after several frustrated missions. Mayo could at least claim that he had not acceded to committing British troops to what might have been a lengthy guerrilla campaign in most unpromising territory.

In the autumn of 1870 it suddenly appeared that the tranquil Afghanistan which was so important to Mayo was again about to be riven by civil war. Yakub Khan, the eldest and ablest of Sher Ali's sons, rose against his father and fled, first to Kandahar and then to Herat. Yakub's rebellion had been caused by the insistence of Sher Ali's young, favourite, wife that her son Abdulla Jan – who had been brought to the famous meeting at Amballa – should be formally recognised as the heir to the throne. Mayo's reaction was cool. To Argyll he recalled that he had promised not to interfere in the domestic affairs of Kabul, and commented ruefully that 'whenever an Afghan meditates some act of treachery he is always most affectionate for some time previously'.[10]

The internecine struggle continued for six months or so, but Mayo held back. In June 1871 it seemed that Yakub was installed as master of Herat, probably with Persian support, but a week later there was better news. Yakub had apparently asked his father for forgiveness and Mayo at once wrote to Sher Ali urging him to be magnanimous. He did this despite his undertaking not to favour one side or the other, but admitted it was a last throw.[11] On 7 July he was happy to record that Yakub was on his peaceful way to Kabul, and reiterated why he had not intervened on the ground. If he had supported the Amir he would have antagonised Yakub, who was bound to be an influential figure in future. Conversely, if he had taken Yakub's side, Sher Ali would have set the sons of the Prophet against the Kaffirs and Britain would be drawn into another Afghan war. He put this point very forcefully. 'Afghans do not fight when they can murder or bribe. I believe they have done a good deal of both lately.'[12] As British officers did not engage in the latter business, he went on, they would have been assassinated – and then they would have had to be avenged. Mayo did not see himself mobilising another Army of Retribution, as Auckland had done. In short, Mayo's intervention by letter was prudent and timely.

Its effect was only temporary, as he suspected. Sher Ali replied that he would honour the Viceroy's commands and pardon Yakub. On 26 September Mayo told Argyll that Yakub had been made governor of Herat, but 'they are one and all such an infernal set of scoundrels that it is impossible to prophesy what will happen'.[13] After Mayo's death, Sher Ali proclaimed Abdulla Jan as his heir, and when Yakub protested, shut him up in prison. For the time being, however, a semblance of Afghan harmony prevailed.

While Mayo's disposition towards Persia and Afghanistan was firm but friendly, it was in his attitude to Russia that he appeared at his most imaginative. True, he started with the advantage that, as a young man, he had seen the Russians at first hand when he visited St Petersburg and Moscow, but from the start of his rule as Viceroy his analysis of the Russian problem showed remarkable breadth of vision. In a long letter to Argyll from Simla in July 1869 he stated his firm conviction that, whatever noises she might make, Russia would not really move south of the Oxus. It would, he argued, be very difficult for her to do so, as she would have to deal with circumstances 'quite different from ours', which the Russians undoubtedly envied. 'No millions of "mild Hindus", quiet and taxable, inhabiting vast and fertile plains. No such differences of religion and race as enable us to play off Mahomedan, Sikh, Hindu or Buddhist against each other.' Instead, the Russian Empire faced millions of poor, fanatical warlike tribesmen, inhabiting almost inaccessible territories – and correspondingly hard to subdue.[14]

Mayo believed that British relations with Russia were bedevilled by mutual misapprehension, which inevitably led to harmful intrigues. Whether this was a naïve view or a touch of Irish intuition does not matter; the significance lies in what he did. In the course of a spirited correspondence with Sir Andrew Buchanan, our man at St Petersburg, Mayo began to see the advantage of sending his own envoy to assure the Czar of the Raj's peaceful intentions. At about the same time Lord Clarendon, now in his third term at the Foreign Office in London, had been discussing with Brunow, the Russian Ambassador, a proposal that there should, in effect, be a 'neutral zone' in Central Asia between the two empires, for instance in Afghanistan.

Mayo at once objected. He accepted non-interference; he approved of reaching an understanding; but he was opposed to making his relations with the intervening states in Central Asia a treaty condition with a foreign power. To do so would inhibit him from taking his own decisions on the appropriate attitude towards these states. It was, he emphasised, essential that 'we should be responsible to no foreign potentate for any of our dealing with the people who inhabit our frontiers'.[15] It would, however, be in the interests of both countries to have a wide border of independent states between the British frontier and the Russian boundary. Russia, for example, should be asked to adopt the same policy towards Khiva and kindred states as Britain towards Khelat, Afghanistan, and Yarkund (of which more later). The desideratum was that Britain and Russia should proclaim that their objects and civilising missions were the same.

Clarendon, who through Argyll would be made aware of Mayo's views, may well have wondered at the comprehensive, confident opinions voiced by the Viceroy.

Mayo held it to be fundamental that Russia could have no ill-intention against British India if she consulted her own interests. On the other hand, no advance against the Russian Empire was contemplated by the British – although, as he wrote to Buchanan in unusually emotional terms, 'we are determined as long as the sun shines in Heaven to hold India, our national character, our commerce . . .' Mayo concluded: 'We cannot view with any feeling of alarm the advance in Asia of a civilised Christian Power, and the establishment of its influence over wild and savage tribes.'[16]

According to Forsyth, who had been present at Amballa as Commissioner at Jullundur, it was in the aftermath of his successful handling of Sher Ali that Mayo decided to enlarge his foreign policy by making a direct approach to the Russians. Forsyth was then sent to London to obtain permission, and, loyal supporter of Mayo as he was, he was discouraged by Argyll's reaction. The Duke turned a deaf ear to all Forsyth's proposals.[17] Whether Argyll for once thought Mayo might be overreaching himself, or whether he found Forsyth too brash, is not known. But Forsyth was tenacious, and got an introduction to the Russian Ambassador, who in turn suggested to Clarendon that Forsyth should go to Baden-Baden, where he could meet the Russian Foreign Minister. Clarendon agreed; Forsyth set off, and was soon back in London with the news that he had been invited to St Petersburg.

Unhappily, Argyll was still lukewarm and refused to accredit Forsyth, but the latter stuck to his instructions from Mayo and persuaded Clarendon to give him an accreditation, with which he took post for St Petersburg. On 13 October 1869 Forsyth handed Prince Gortschakoff, the Russian Foreign Minister, the letter from Mayo, and in reply the Prince said that Russia had no intention of interfering in Herat, Kabul, etcetera. If Sher Ali stayed within his own dominion he would not be molested by the Russians, and there was no quarrel between Britain and Russia over Asiatic boundaries. The Czar confirmed such admirable peaceful sentiments when he granted Forsyth an audience.

At St Petersburg, Buchanan and Forsyth agreed that they had done enough groundwork to enable them 'at once to settle all future disputes by marking off the boundary of Afghanistan'. Once again Clarendon was in favour but Argyll 'would not take the slightest interest in the matter, and no orders were passed'.[18]

Back in India, Mayo was impatient to press matters to a conclusion but, not wanting to irritate Argyll further, he thought he should now communicate with St Petersburg through London. 'This gave the Russians an opportunity of reconsidering their position,'[19] Forsyth recalled, and nothing positive emerged. But Mayo's bold initiative was not entirely fruitless. He had obtained at least an understanding that the Oxus should be Afghanistan's northern boundary.

In time the Russians played fair. They stopped the Khan of Bokhara from attacking Sher Ali, and persuaded him to deny asylum to the rebel Afghan fugitive Abdur Rahman. Mayo in turn discouraged the Afghan Amir from going to war with Bokhara. In May 1871, however, there were persistent rumours that Russia was about to mount an expedition against Khiva, and Mayo was worried that this might have an unsettling effect on Afghanistan. The Home Government suggested that Mayo should send a mission to Khiva to find out what was happening, but he objected, since the appearance of a British envoy might lead to assumptions that the Raj was prepared to lend support against the Russians. Mayo was learning the wiles of diplomacy. (The Russian expedition did not, at that time, proceed, and Mayo told Alison at Teheran that he had it on good authority that the 'Financial Departments of the Russian Government refused to provide the supplies'.[20])

Eastern Turkestan was another area in which Mayo took his own line. The territory had been part of the Chinese empire since the first half of the eighteenth century, but the natives, mainly Muslims, and most of their rulers, had latterly taken refuge in the neighbouring state of Kokand. After several unsuccessful attempts Yakub Beg (also known as Yakub Kushbegi, or the Atalig Ghazee or Defender of the Faith, as he called himself), a Kokand lieutenant, drove the Chinese out in 1863. In 1864 he took Kashgar and in 1865 captured Yarkund. Then he declared himself independent and set about subduing the rest of the province. An able soldier, Yakub was regarded as a good administrator, according to the crude standards of the day.

In the early nineteenth century the British were largely indifferent to affairs beyond Kashmir, but circumstances changed in 1865 when the Chinese recognised Yakub. A year later Forsyth, from the Jullundur Division, put forward a proposal to open up relations with Eastern Turkestan. He had two main arguments – the trading opportunities for Indian tea and manufactured goods, and the defence implications. The proposition was that if overtures were not made to Yakub the Russians would penetrate into Eastern Turkestan, which provided an easy approach to India. Lawrence was not impressed; he did not believe it was possible to trade with foreign countries without getting involved in internal politics. Nor did he agree that British India was vulnerable to a Russian advance through Eastern Turkestan.

Lawrence had another objection. The route to Yarkund lay through Kashmir, whose ruler the Maharaja levied customs and transit duties. Forsyth knew that the Maharaja would do all he could to stop trade developing beyond his frontier. Lawrence, strongly influenced by the Maharaja's loyal behaviour during the Mutiny, was unwilling to interfere with the conduct of the rapacious Kashmiri officials, but in 1867 he agreed to appoint Dr Henry Cayley as temporary commercial agent at Leh to try to remove some of the trade restrictions. A year later he approved a grant of 5,000 rupees for improvements to the road through the Chang Chemo pass, and allowed trade talks with Yakub Beg to start. The Maharaja objected strongly; Lawrence wavered; but Donald Macleod urged the necessity of stationing a British officer in the Ladakh area. Cayley reported that all the accounts of Kashmiri extortions were true, and the Maharaja was still intriguing against the British presence when Mayo took over.

Mayo, it will come as no surprise, had a much more positive attitude and no vestigial feelings about the Maharaja. In Forsyth's words, with 'Lord Mayo's arrival the prospect of a more generous policy seemed to dawn'.[21] Mayo accepted advice that Yakub was now firmly established and keen to trade. Moreover, Yakub had no great love for the Russians, who were encouraging the Amir of Kokand to unseat him. In keeping with his general policy, Mayo was bound to react favourably to prevent a small power from being overrun by a more powerful neighbour. Unlike Lawrence, he saw no difficulty in promoting friendly relations without threatening independence. He had always believed that the best way to check Russian influence was by 'pushing our commerce northwards'. He had penned this in a letter to Argyll after he had been only a couple of months in India. A year later, thinking back to Lawrence, he added, 'It may be desirable to adopt a Thibetan policy and discourage all communications with the outer Asiatic world. But it is not a policy which is English or commercial and certainly it is impossible if we are to maintain our position in the civilised world.' He hoped that within the year he would have established trading relations with Yakub, 'but we must try and keep what we are doing quiet for the present, as it is not impossible that if it was much discussed in the newspapers others might be there before us.'[22]

Meanwhile the Kashmiri merchants and officials remained unhelpful. The Maharaja had done his best to terrorise the smaller chiefs on his frontier, and was also suspected of having a hand in the murder of a British officer, Robert Thorp, who was found dead at Srinagar. Mayo now set about removing all obstacles to trade with Eastern Turkestan. First, in order to eliminate any possible Russian threat, he instructed Forsyth – while on his mission to St Petersburg – to obtain an undertaking that the Russians had no designs on Yakub's domain. This may well have been a facile agreement, but Mayo had put down a marker.

Next, he started negotiations with Kashmir to allow British engineers to lay out an improved route through the Chang

Chemo valley, and he sent Captain Grey as his personal envoy to signify the importance he attached to successful completion. Back from Russia, Forsyth negotiated a treaty with the Maharaja on lines proposed by Grey, and Mayo ratified it when he met the Maharaja at Sialkot in the spring of 1870. The Viceroy was not at all disposed to allow the Kashmiri ruler to continue his intrigues, and at Sialkot told him bluntly not to interfere in territories beyond his own frontier. The Maharaja reluctantly agreed, but Mayo was well aware that he would have to be carefully watched.

Yakub Beg was naturally delighted at Mayo's approach and sent his envoy, Mirza Shadi, to Calcutta to ask for a British mission to be sent to Yarkund. The ubiquitous Forsyth was selected as the emissary. In theory he was going 'purely on a friendly visit' as requested by Yakub, but as London was far from enthusiastic about the whole exercise, Mayo had to explain that 'the underlings of the Cashmere State' had hindered our trade with Central Asia.[23] To emphasise that this was not a formal diplomatic mission Forsyth was to travel without a military escort, and he was under orders not to take part in politics or internal disputes. He was not to proceed if conditions in Turkestan were disturbed. 'I will run no risk,' Mayo told Forsyth, and he was to be sure to return before snow closed the passes. There was, it must be admitted, a touch of chicanery in these arrangements, since, as Mayo well knew, it was impossible to keep political and commercial in separate compartments.

Forsyth set out in April, and the Kashmiris, as expected, did their best to obstruct him. They even bribed Mirza Shadi to spread false rumours about Forsyth while he was actually escorting him. Eventually poor Forsyth, having been subjected to such humiliations as being given half-starved ponies and inadequate supplies, reached Yarkund. It had been an exhausting journey. Nothing, he recalled, could surpass the desolation of Chang Chemo. Bare and gravelly, with no sign of vegetable life beyond a few tamarisks, the desert hills rose tier on tier in huge plateaux to the height of 19,000 feet. At Yarkund he found that Yakub Beg had gone to fight rebels on his north west frontier. Attempts were made to retain him till Yakub returned, but mindful of his orders and aware that if he lingered he would have to stay throughout the winter, he turned back to Kashmir. This was disappointing, but he brought back a wealth of relevant information, and Mayo, greatly impressed by Forsyth's behaviour, said the only damper to the expedition was 'the behaviour of our own feudatory [the Maharaja]'.[24] There were some tangible results well worth the £1,750 that had been authorised to cover the expedition. Trading conditions steadily improved; Yakub punished Mirza Shadi for his treachery, and sent another mission to Calcutta at the end of 1871. Northbrook, continuing Mayo's efforts, later concluded a commercial treaty with Eastern Turkestan.

This aspect of Mayo's attitude to external states has been discussed at length, although in retrospect it may seem that not a great deal was achieved. Trade with Yakub's territory was not likely to reach an enormous volume, and the suspected Russian encroachment did not materialise. But Mayo, by his forthright dealing with the intransigent Maharaja at Sialkot, and by resolutely pushing into new terrain, had shown the benefits to be derived from his consistent foreign policy.

Mayo's objectives, unchanged from the time of his arrival, were succinctly set out in a minute he wrote at the end of 1871.

> We should establish with our frontier states of Khelat, Afghanistan, Yarkund and Nepal and Burma intimate relations of friendship; we should make them feel that though we are all-powerful, we desire to support their nationality; that when necessity arises we might assist them with money, arms, and perhaps, in certain eventualities with men. We should create in them outworks of our Empire, and assuring them that the days of annexation are passed, make them know that they have everything to gain and nothing to lose by endeavouring to deserve our favour and support. Further, we should strenuously oppose any attempt to neutralise these territories in the European sense, or to sanction or invite the interference of any European power in their affairs.[25]

These were good imperialist aims and, in the temper of the time, not unworthy. In his three years of office Mayo went a long way to see his foreign policy realised.

Burma has not been mentioned at any length because it gave him little trouble. On 11 June 1869 he had warned the Chief Commissioner there not to interfere in the affairs of Upper

Burma, as the annexation of this or any adjacent state was not an event which he contemplated or desired.[26] Elsewhere, he could point with some pride to the *cordon sanitaire*, the ring of friendly states. He had effectively ended the civil war in Afghanistan, and turned a doubtful neighbour into a firm ally. He persuaded the Persians to define their boundaries with Afghanistan through British arbitration. He paved the way for cordial commercial relations with Eastern Turkestan. Lastly, he established an informal agreement with the Russians that they and the British should respect each other's sphere of influence. Mayo would have described the list as being 'not bad for a Paddy'. Historians may agree that, for an amateur diplomat in charge of his own foreign department, it was much more.

As the *Friend of India* put it, 'There will a day come – such days do come – when some sycophant will tell the world that Lord Mayo's foreign policy was not his own. But it *was*. There is not a man in India – not to speak merely of the Foreign Office – who could have dared to think of, still less initiate, the policy that from the Indus to Thibet will be associated with Lord Mayo's name.'[27] It is, however, fair to point out that later Viceroys did not have the same freedom of manoeuvre as ever-improving communications tightened the grasp of the Secretary of State in London. The shape of things to come was already apparent with the completion, in June 1870, of a direct telegraph system between England and India by submarine cable through the Red Sea – an occasion which saw an excited exchange of telegrams between Mayo and the President of the United States to celebrate the line connecting the Eastern and Western Hemispheres.[28]

14
The Fiscal Can of Worms

Mayo inherited a financial mess bad enough to give any British Chancellor of the Exchequer nightmares. There were many contributory reasons, some of them historical, for the deplorable state of Indian finances. The Mutiny had put an enormous strain on the exchequer, and since then the Indian Government had been running at a loss. In 1860 James Wilson, the former Treasury Minister (and founder of *The Economist*) sent out from England to be the Financial Member of the Executive Council, described the condition of the Indian finances as one of chronic deficit, and his successor Samuel Laing saw that deficit as 'a huge bully with whom weary rounds must be fought'.[1] Laing lost his battle, and Charles Trevelyan and William Massey, who came afterwards, did no better.

It was not only costs directly attributable to the Mutiny that imperilled the budget. The East India Company had been primarily a commercial concern, much more interested in profits than in social reform, but when the Company gave way to the Raj a new priority emerged. Security was now the first objective, and security implied a commitment to improve the welfare of the native population. So when order had been reestablished the cry throughout the sixties was for more public works and improvements to roads, bridges, canals, and railways. New barracks with better sanitation had also to be built for the much bigger European army now stationed in India, while the corps of civil servants needed to administer the new programmes multiplied as though by natural growth. To compound the ineluctable increase in the charge to public funds, prices throughout India had risen at a rate that far outstripped government revenue.

The financial structure at Calcutta was ill suited to cope with the changed situation. There was, for example, a most unsatisfactory borrowing system. Not only were works which were intended to yield a return defrayed by loan, non-revenue-earning projects such as barracks and jails were also financed by borrowing, with the result that the public debt mounted steadily. The Indian Exchequer also had to meet growing 'Home Charges', which were applied to meet the interest on the public debt, to purchase stores required in India, and to cover various costs connected with the India Office. In Mayo's last fiscal year (1871) these charges totalled £16.2m. Apart from the size of the sums, as an added difficulty the yearly demand did not arrive from London till after the presentation of the budget, but it had to be accommodated without question or appeal.

Before Wilson arrived there had been no Financial Department worth the name, and even now the accounts and estimates were in a mass of confusion. As the deficits grew the imperfections of the old system, or lack of system, were starkly revealed.

Mayo's fiscal problem is best illustrated by the financial outrun for the period before he took office. Since an attempt was first made to adopt a proper budget system, only two years had shown any appreciable credit balance, and in the last three years there had been deficits of £2.5m, £1m and £2.7m – over £6m in all.[2] Today these would be dismissed as paltry sums in terms of government finance, and no jobbing back, notional comparisons, or inflationary calculations will give much idea of their significance. But all figures are relative, and it was with relativity that Mayo was concerned. In a further quirk of Indian accounting, these figures are for what was termed 'ordinary' expenditure. Adding the outlay on 'extraordinary' or reproductive works, the total deficit in the three years before Mayo's first budget was more than £11m. In the same period the cash balances fell from £13.8m to £10.2m, and the public debt increased by nearly £6.5m.[3]

No sooner had Mayo doffed his official uniform to get down to the balance sheets than he came on the first real horror – the estimates trundled out by the Financial Member had always been falsified by events. The 1867–8 budget *estimates* had shown a surplus of £3.5m, but the actual *results* produced a substantial deficit. So Mayo had to deal with an unsound system and advisers who were merrily racketing on with a formidable gross error, both relatively and absolutely.

According to Strachey, Mayo had immersed himself in past

financial statements at the India Office before he left England, and it was not long before he showed that he had a firm grasp of what was at stake. Temple, who was in charge of the Financial Department during the whole of Mayo's time as Viceroy, records, somewhat ruefully, that although Mayo was an advocate of improvement, impressionable and popular, and a grand and conspicuous man generally, this did not stop him being a meticulous accountant. 'Had his training been in the bureau of an auditor, instead of in the field and the Cabinet, he could hardly have been more punctiliously anxious respecting the public accounts than he actually was.'[4] Temple was unaware that the first thing Mayo did when he took over the Kildare Hunt was to put their precarious funds into shape.

But Mayo was not only concerned with the minutiae of domestic book-keeping. As he soon wrote to Argyll:

> We hold India by a thread. At any moment a serious danger might arise. We now owe 180 millions, more than 85% of which is held in England. Add 100 million to this and an Indian disaster would entail consequences equal to the extinction of half of the national debt. The loss of India or a portion of it would be nothing as compared to the ruin which would occur at home . . . I do declare that with such a revenue as ours, borrowing in time of peace . . . is little short of a crime. [5]

Just as with his foreign policy, Mayo took a far-sighted view of what was required in dealing with finance. His sense of economics might be sketchy, but his horizon stretched well beyond the confines of Government House.

Believing, as he did, that there could be no social progress without a sound financial base, he was determined to stick to the simple point that spending must not exceed revenue. He told Fitzgerald that he hoped to cure some of the 'gross abuses of Indian administration, of which extravagance and contempt of all financial control are the worst'. With this in mind, he instructed Temple to frame a budget which would remove the threat of deficit.

Temple recalled that Lawrence had left him a parting instruction to increase the revenue by reintroducing income tax. (There had been none in India since 1865.) Newly arrived, Mayo agreed that this would have to be done, and the old certificate-tax, which had been brought in by Temple's immediate predecessor Massey at the rate of one per cent on incomes over £50 a year, was revamped as a tax on incomes. The catchment area was enlarged to cover traders and professional men, as before, plus landowners and fundholders.

Temple's budget was designed to yield a nominal surplus, and Mayo was delighted at the prospect – 'spending at the same time 1½ millions on barracks and diminishing none of the items of useful expenditure'.[6] But he was soon disillusioned, as serious errors in the estimates came to light. Mayo knew what he had to do. He had 'to recover the finances from a state of deficit, which, I believe, is quite inexcusable and could easily have been avoided. But unless we have a war, which God forbid, we will do it.'[7]

Mayo was furious at the delay in submitting accounts to the Finance Department. The 'actuals' did not come forward till December, and no quarterly returns of income and expenditure were laid before him in Council. These seemed to him to be very rudimentary requirements. Temple had gone home on leave at the beginning of the hot season, and Mayo soon 'began to suspect that there was something *very* wrong'.[8] He decided to take matters into his own hands, and all Departments were subjected to a programme of severe retrenchment – the Public Works budget suffering most. The salt tax was increased to produce another £185,000. But this was not enough, and Mayo reluctantly doubled the rate of income tax for the second half of the year to raise another £300,000. The result was to produce a small surplus of £118,000.

Today the main interest is not in the actual figures but in the manoeuvring and personalities involved. The revision had been done in Temple's absence, and – without disclosing what was afoot – Mayo had sent him a friendly letter. 'I hope you will gain strength and enjoy yourself at Homburg, and that you will neither lose your heart nor your money.'[9] But, with his austerity measures under way, he wrote to Seymour Fitzgerald, 'What Temple will say then he arrives I cannot think. He will be in a very awkward position.'[10] On 23 October he despatched a brief note to await Temple's arrival at Bombay, saying that his own financial plans had been well received.

What transpired when they met is not known, but on 19 November Temple made an unrepentant speech when introducing the bill 'to enhance the duties leviable under the India Income

Tax', saying blandly that the actuals had exceeded the estimates by £1.3m, chiefly because more had been spent on public works and army matters.[11]

On balance, Mayo was right to be annoyed by Temple's facile optimism with his original estimates, though Bartle Frere commiserated with Temple for the way he had been treated while he was on leave. In his view the Viceroy should not have made spasmodic reductions in the absence of his principal financial adviser.[12] But Stafford Northcote, no longer Secretary of State, who still kept up a friendly correspondence with Temple, told him: 'I must candidly say that I think you are open to the charge of having been over sanguine in your budget speech; but the offence has brought its own punishment with it, and I hope will lead to reformation.'[13]

In the hope of easing his financial troubles, Mayo insisted on much prompter submission of returns from the provinces, and a more efficient collation at Calcutta. But this was only tinkering with the basic problem. The truth was that the financial structure was no longer capable of meeting the demands on it.

Until Mayo introduced his reforms, the local governments ran their several provinces at the expense of the imperial revenues, but had no financial powers of their own. Each year they submitted their estimates for the next twelve months, and the central government, after comparing the totals with the expected revenue from the whole country, then allotted each local government a grant for its services. This method of cutting up the cake was readily open to abuse. The local governments inflated their bids, knowing they would not get all they wanted; the central government had the invidious task of vetting their proposals in detail; and the result was much bad feeling. Calcutta accused the provinces of extravagance, while the local bodies resented their lack of financial independence. Mansfield recalled an Indian metaphor to describe their dislike of being mere revenue collectors. 'They admit that the elephant's trunk can rend the tree, but they deny that it can pick up the pin when the elephant can not see the pin with its own eyes.'

Mayo's remedy was bold. In future, under the Provincial Services Scheme, as it was called, the local governments would get a single grant each year to cover the cost of named services. The internal distribution would be for them to decide; any saving at the end of the year could be carried over; but any excess would have to be met by raising local taxes. The underlying philosophy was that this would restrain the rise in local expenditure, would relieve the strain on central government, both financially and by cutting out detailed scrutiny, and would give more scope for local initiative. (The reader will recognise that these innocent beliefs were advanced at Westminster in the 1950s to justify the introduction of the general grant to British local authorities. The latest variation is rate-capping, but in the whirligig of time no governments – Indian or English – have solved the problem of the relationship between central and local funding.)

The Provincial Services Scheme was not a new idea in India. James Wilson, Laing and Massey had all toyed with something like it, but got nowhere. Lawrence, far from supporting any form of devolution, actually wanted to make supervision of local accounts more rigorous. In 1868 he forwarded a plan to this effect to the Secretary of State, who had no difficulty in rejecting it.

Mayo, not liking what he saw, soon identified the main defect as the complete lack of incentive to local economy, and – as a start – in February 1870 he proposed to transfer all expenditure on roads and communications from imperial to local funds. This would at least relieve Calcutta of much detailed work and go some way towards promoting self-reliance.[14] In August he went further and proposed that local governments should get one grant to cover a whole crop of functions, including jails, police, education and medical services, as well as roads, etcetera.

This was a fundamental change, and the provinces reacted in very different ways. Muir in the North West Provinces, Keatinge the Chief Commissioner of the Central Provinces, Napier at Madras, and Fitzgerald at Bombay all gave their approval. But the real reactionaries stood revealed in their opposition. Durand, now Lieutenant-Governor of the Punjab, said the scheme would merely shift unpopular taxation from the centre to local governments. Grey at Bengal was equally opposed, and declared that he could not raise additional funds by upping taxation. Mayo commented wryly:

In a struggle between the Bureaux most people seem to forget that there is such a thing as an Empire and a People of India, that national bankruptcy is national ruin, and that we hold the purse strings not in the interest one day of the Madras army, at another of the education of Bengalee Baboos, and on a third to build palaces in Bombay, but that our sole object is to work for the good of all.[15]

Mayo was not to be deterred by the sniping of his critics, and went ahead with his famous Resolution of 14 December 1870. According to Chapman this was the Viceroy's own work, much of it drafted in his own hand.[16] He transferred expenditure under all the August headings, pointing out that the items were essentially local, which meant that Calcutta could not control them. The mortmain of the Finance Department could be seen in the restrictions on increased salaries, and on extra appointments, but Mayo hoped, as his Resolution said, to produce greater care and economy, more certainty in the fiscal system and, above all, opportunities for self-government. Argyll thought the plan a step in the right direction, and Mayo put it into effect in the financial year 1871–2. He admitted it had imperfections – 'but it is all I could carry – the principal opponent being the finance minister,' he told Mansfield.[17] For Mayo had not been able to carry Temple with him.

The new system was sometimes called the Decentralisation Scheme, but Mayo did not care for this. As he wrote to Arbuthnot, he had not decentralised finance, or renounced a particle of efficient control. What he had given up was 'the power of meddling and petty interference'. He was confident he had not impaired the public service, but 'the mania for brick and mortar has been checked and a general feeling in favour of economy seems for the moment to prevail'.[18] John Strachey had no doubt that but for Mayo's personal clout the Provincial Scheme could not have been carried through. R. B. Chapman, the Secretary of the Finance Department, summed it up. 'He [Mayo] found serious deficit and left substantial surplus. He found estimates habitually untrustworthy and left them thoroughly worthy of confidence. He left the local governments working with cordiality, harmony and freedom, under the direction of the Governor-General in Council.'[19] In round figures, Mayo inherited a deficit of £2.7m for the year 1868–9; this he transformed into a surplus of £118,000 in 1869–70, and showed further surpluses of £1.4m and £3.1m in the next two years. Bearing in mind the time it normally takes for economies to become effective, the results are an indication of Mayo's firmness of purpose.

One of his political motives associated with the Provincial Scheme remained largely unrealised in his time.

> I hope gradually to commence the establishment of native municipal institutions. We must gradually associate with ourselves in the government of this country more of the native element. We have neglected this too much. Were we to quit India tomorrow we should leave whole Provinces in which would not be found a man capable of administrating the affairs of a small district.[20]

But the climate was not yet propitious.

It would be wrong to imagine that all was sweetness and light in Mayo's financial house. He was, inevitably, subjected to much virulent criticism over the income tax, which became a permanent feature of his rule. We go back again to James Wilson, who first introduced it as a temporary measure. Like all temporary expedients, the tax remained on the statute book longer than intended, but it was allowed to lapse when Charles Trevelyan, who had been notorious for opposing it while Governor of Madras, became Finance Member. Lawrence thought it would have to be restored; Temple included it in his budget proposals for 1869–70; and Mayo, the new Viceroy without any practical experience of Indian finance, had to accept it.

One of the main weaknesses – and one of the reasons that made it necessary to resort to a tax on incomes – in the Indian budget arose from the fluctuating nature of the revenue from opium, chiefly sales to China. Opium was a government monopoly, cultivated under licence, and its contribution to the imperial exchequer varied from £6m to £8m, or about one sixth of total revenue. (In 1868 Northcote advised Temple not to overestimate the opium revenue, but the optimistic Finance Member did not heed the warning.) In Mayo's time there were alarms that China was growing more of its own supply, and some thought was given to changing the monopoly to an excise system or setting up an opium reserve fund. In March 1869 Temple put the opium estimate at over £8m, but in November he had to admit that the price was falling. The estimate was now

£1m less, and in April 1870 there was a further decline of the same amount.

While the moral implications of the trade exercised both the Indian Government and public opinion at home, Temple's view was that 'If the Chinese will have opium, they may as well get it first rate from us, as second rate at home, and they may as well consume it taxed as untaxed.'[21] George Campbell's conscience was equally undisturbed. Whatever the moral aspect, 'economically there was no fault to be found'.[22] John Strachey, writing much later, was even more forthright. In his learned work on *India, Its Administration and Progress* he fulminated: 'If, in deference to ignorant prejudice, India should be deprived of the revenue which she now obtains from opium, an act of folly and injustice would be perpetrated as gross as any that has ever been inflicted by a foreign Government on a subject country.'[23]

Mayo thought opium sales 'one of the deepest blots on our Escutcheon',[24] but two other comments show his perplexity. Writing to Napier at Madras on 20 November 1870, 'I do not think the people overtaxed. On the contrary, if we take land revenue, which is *rent*, and opium, which the *Chinamen* pay, out of our column of our receipts, India is the lightest taxed country in the world.'[25] Again to Napier on 4 January 1871, he was still arguing with himself. 'As long as opium is what it is all Imperial Taxation should be kept down, for if opium goes we must come heavily on the people in some way or other. The noxious drug, however, appears most particularly strong just now, and we have every hope of high prices for some time.'[26] The moral, social and financial aspects of the opium crop were to exercise the rulers of India for long enough. Mayo, for his part, was unhappy about it, but was reluctantly prepared to take a pragmatic view.

Mayo, as we have seen, accepted the imposition of income tax for the year 1869–70, but he insisted that it should be at the low rate of one per cent of incomes over £50 per annum, adding that 'the country should be saddled with it quietly'. This of course was a forlorn hope, and the revival of the tax was widely denounced, especially by the Bengal zemindars, now for the first time brought within its scope. The opposition might have become less vocal with the passage of time, but as one of his emergency measures Mayo doubled the rate for the second half of 1869–70, and much to his distress had to endorse a still higher rate of $3\frac{1}{8}$% in the 1870–71 budget. Mayo did not like the latest budget and said so in the Legislative Council. Temple, who saw the income tax as the panacea for India's financial problems, had wanted an even higher rate of 4%, but by this time relations between the Viceroy and the Finance Member were so bad that Mayo wanted Argyll to replace him. 'I need not tell you that Sir Richard Temple's financial administration does not command in any way the confidence of the country.'[27]

There was now a widespread clamour against the tax, both in principle and as levied. Public protest meetings were common, and there were many reports of corruption by local officials who had to collect the tax. Often the official would agree to a lower assessment, in return for payment which he pocketed. Mayo eventually came round to the view that no direct tax could be raised through local native collectors without causing oppression.[28] The Governors and Lieutenant-Governors unanimously bore witness to the unrest provoked by the higher rate. Part of the trouble, as Mayo realised, was that the decision on the incidence of the tax was an arbitrary one. There was no question of an elected government representing the taxpayers being consulted. The very existence of the tax brought into sharp relief the Raj as conqueror, imposing his will on a subject race.

Mayo took the news from the provinces very seriously. 'I own the events of this year have shaken my confidence in it considerably. I am inclined to think its outrun will be less than we expected. I cannot disagree with the reports which come from all parts of the country of the oppression with which its levy is accompanied. A tax which is unpopular as well as unfruitful, is a mistake.'[29] He accordingly reduced the rate from $3\frac{1}{8}$% to 1% in the 1871–2 budget, and by raising the threshold he also reduced by half the total number of taxpayers. But the outcry continued, and Mayo decided that the tax simply was not appropriate to Indian conditions. To Temple he wrote, expressing his frustration: 'I think it is unsuited to India and consider Mr Wilson made a great mistake in touching it at all.'[30] He made up his mind to drop the tax at the end of the current financial year.

Unhappily, he did not live long enough to do this. After his death Temple continued to argue in favour of the tax, and in his memoirs he describes it lovingly as an engine of finance, created during times of ease and quiet, which could effectively be used to meet national difficulties. Without the tax the budget would produce only a slender balance, and once dropped its renewal would be impossible. But, good Treasury arguments though these might be, Temple did not eventually get his way. Mayo's successor, Northbrook, abolished the tax in March 1873, and Argyll writing to Temple regretted that it had not been retained at a low rate, but added acidly, 'In such matters the Viceroy must have a predominant voice, and I suspect that Lord Mayo would have taken the same course, had he lived.'[31]

Mayo and Temple were antipathetic. Temple did not openly criticise the Viceroy, and in his memoirs loyally stated that Mayo died having reached 'the rare height occupied by those regarding whom all men speak well'.[32] But Temple, a close friend of Lawrence, was accustomed to getting his own way, and it came as a shock to him that Mayo, an ebullient extrovert, should have such a meticulous approach to accounting.

Mayo, who was much closer to the Stracheys, was inclined to mock Temple's pomposity and interminable speeches in Council. On one occasion, when Temple was explaining at length why the export duty had been taken off shawls but not off rice, he passed the Stracheys a mischievous doodle.

> Sir Richard's the white-haired laddie
> Who always takes care of the girls:
> He keeps on the burden on paddy;
> But takes off the duty on shawls.[33]

The Members of Council took this as harmless badinage and do not seem to have realised how deep was the rift between Mayo and Temple. Durand, wrongly, thought that Temple would get the Lieutenant-Governorship of the Punjab – a possibility that Mayo did not even consider. Writing to Argyll, he damned Temple with faint praise. 'If he wants originality, he possesses courage and determination. He is not an accomplished financier, but he is watchful and prudent.'[34] Lest it be thought that this was simply a case of incompatibility, there were others who shared Mayo's doubts. Stafford Northcote wrote regretfully to Mayo in March 1869, 'The Duke of Argyll told me the other day that he feared Temple was not strong enough for his post.'[35] The veteran Lord Halifax, with his wealth of experience at the India Office, commented, 'I hear that Sir R. Temple is famous for his tint of "couleur de rose", but it is too serious a matter to trifle with.'[36]

Nevertheless in the matter of appointments Temple had the last word. After he had finished his stint as Finance Member he was successively to head the governments of Bengal and Bombay.

Two final thoughts on the relationship between Mayo and Temple. In his memoirs Temple recalls that Mayo told him that the most important quality was '*enthusiasm* which makes a man believe in the possibility of improvement and strive to attain it'.[37] Temple may have thought such gusto vaguely improper; he belonged to the class of civil servants who resent having to work under a strong, active chief. Lastly, Owen Burne, normally the most discreet of private secretaries, had this to say:

As for Sir Richard Temple, I can only say that he never in reality gave Lord Mayo much support. This is perhaps a grave, but none the less a true charge. Lord Mayo saw through his superficial qualities, although he admired his pluck under many difficulties. The real reductions in expenditure were made in Sir Richard Temple's absence . . . he resisted the Provincial Services Scheme, while to him was due the one unpopular measure – the continuance of the Income Tax.[38]

15
A Bubble in the Native Mind

One reason for Mayo's doubts regarding the income tax was his conviction that permanent discontent with any form of taxation imposed on a subject race could become the core of a political danger that could not be overestimated. He was also concerned to see that hatred of the tax was compounding signs of unrest that had already appeared in the North West Provinces – and which were confirmed by events at Roorkee and Allahabad in the summer of 1870.

The Roorkee incident, a minor scare in itself, was magnified as being symptomatic of something deeper. On 2 July 1870 a native called Yakoob made a deposition before the magistrate at Roorkee that on 19 June several students at the local college had told him that 'this time they were going to kill every European and Christian', and that a fakir was preaching in the bazaar that there was about to be a general massacre. Alarming rumours began to circulate. It was alleged that the military were going to church with their rifles loaded (which was untrue), that a European soldier had been shot by a Sikh at Moradabad, and that Moradabad itself had risen. Before it was ascertained that there was no truth in these reports the college soldiers had been issued with extra ammunition, and it was clear that, a bare thirteen years since the rising at Meerut signalled the start of the Sepoy Mutiny, public opinion was still hypersensitive to anything that might hint at a renewed rebellion.

A more serious disturbance soon followed, this time at Allahabad. A few days after Yakoob had started his Roorkee hare the native Sappers at Allahabad were mustered in the middle of the night for a roll call to check if there were any absentees. The young officer on duty had, however, ordered 'Assembly' to be blown without first sounding the 'Sapper' call. As a result, the 103rd Native Infantry turned out as well, and in view of the unusual time of night assumed that they had been called to disarm the Sappers. Embarrassed explanations restored order, but in the aftermath there was an undercurrent of suspicion that all was not well.

On 25 August a Mrs Paxton, the wife of a tradesman in Allahabad, told Major-General Vaughan that she had overheard two servants talking. The burden of their conversation was that the 4th Native Infantry were coming at midnight; that the jail inmates would be freed; and that they – the two servants – would murder the Paxtons. About 3 a.m. she heard another voice saying it was 'just off' till the next night. Other, unspecified, rumours were current in the bazaar.

On the 26th Vaughan ordered the Field Battery and the 11th Bengal Calvalry to make a show. But the artillerymen went too far, loading their guns, sleeping in their clothes, and fixing a rendezvous for women and children. This did not have the reassuring effect that Vaughan wanted; panic spread rapidly, and people began to stream out of the city. Vaughan then called up two European companies from Cawnpore, and Mr Robertson, the magistrate, sent round a letter urging everyone to keep calm. On 30 August Vaughan became alarmed that the police, already heavily armed, had managed to get hold of a large quantity of ammunition. (Mayo was later angry that 26,000 cartridges, unguarded, were available in the police lines.)

The Allahabad panic had subsided by 2 September, but unrest seemed to have spread to Benares, where there were reports that the 5th Native Infantry and the city people were going to rebel. Sentries were strengthened, though no further evidence came to light.

Mayo, in the minute he later circulated to Council, concluded that Vaughan's orders had been too loosely defined, and were 'an act of great carelessness'. Robertson's circular, he thought, was imprudent, and it was not surprising that Reuter should have sent a telegram to *The Times* that 'a portion of the Native Army is in a mutinous state'.[1] Writing privately to Argyll, Mayo said that, on reflection, there was 'a somewhat unusual Bubble in the Native Mind', which he ascribed to three causes. First, the Franco-Prussian war had raised doubts about British strength as a world power – native princes were studying press reports of events in Europe and poring over their maps with unusual care. Second, the Wahabi movement (discussed later in this chapter) was having an unsettling effect, and lastly – and inevitably – there was the discontent over the income tax.[2]

The Allahabad panic had no immediate sequels, but in 1871 there were communal riots at Bareilly on a day when Hindu and Muslim festivals coincided. The Government stopped the rival processions – it may be thought with good reason – but the Indian press denounced this interference with religious observances.[3] In the course of a prison outbreak, again at Bareilly, seven were killed and over twenty seriously injured. Superstitions were giving rise to the wildest rumours. As in 1857, it was said that *chupattees* were being handed round as a signal; there had been a miraculous birth at Jhansi; Muslims believed that the Qiyamat (day of resurrection) was at hand. The Lieutenant-Governor of the North West Provinces was warned by his officers to expect trouble, and from as far away as Burma Major-General Fytche reported pagoda gossip that the end of the Raj was at hand, and that articles had been published suggesting that the British intended to annex further territory.

Individually, these happenings, imagined or real, and suppositions might be discounted, but for most of his last two years Mayo had to deal with unrest fomented by two different sects – the Kukas and the Wahabis. Fortunately they did not combine in their subversive activities, and from their origins and history it seemed impossible that they would do so. But there was always the possibility that they might both lend fuel to a conflagration to spread throughout the whole country.

Unrest in the Punjab was primarily due to the Kukas, a Sikh sect formed at Rawalpindi in the 1840s. The Kukas, originally concerned with demolishing tombs and idols and preaching a life of abstinence, became more highly organised after 1863, when Guru Ram Singh emerged as their leader. Their creed required them to carry on their persons a knife and an axe, and they regarded it as righteous to give their lives in order to stop the slaughter of cattle. This meant that they were encouraged to kill Muhamadan butchers and those who purchased beef, with the incipient danger that the opposition to killing cows was bound to appeal to the Hindu population as a whole. Since the British annexation of the Punjab in 1849 the Kukas had been committed to overthrowing the Raj and restoring Sikh supremacy, and from 1867 onwards the movement started to make converts in large numbers. Unsubstantiated reports – statistics were never a strong feature of British administration – suggested that there were between three and four hundred Kukas in the Punjab.

On 14 June 1871 Kukas raided a slaughterhouse near the Golden Temple at Amritsar, killing four butchers and three others; and the next day there was another attack at Raikote.[4] The Kukas were caught and executed, but their confessions revealed that far from being an isolated attack, this was the outcome of careful planning. Mayo, unrealistically for once, thought that with the executions the Kuka disturbances would now subside.[5] He was heartened when the Maharaja of Kashmir, who had even permitted the recruitment of a Kuka contingent in his militia, disbanded it, and he also told the Punjab Government not to prosecute Ram Singh.[6]

In January 1872, however, the Kukas were again active. A force of 200 Kukas attacked the Malodh Fort, and the next day started fighting in the small native state of Malerkotla. The local Nawab with some timely help from his neighbours, the Maharajas of Patiala, Nabha, and Jind, then dispersed the Kukas and inflicted heavy casualties. But the veneer of tranquillity had been torn aside. Cowan, the officiating Deputy Commissioner at Ludhiana, hurried to Malerkotla and summarily tried some seventy Kukas who had surrendered. Next day, despite orders from Forsyth, now Commissioner of the Amballa Division, to hold them for further proceedings, he ordered forty-nine of them to be blown from guns. To make matters worse, Forsyth, on arrival, tried and hanged another sixteen. Mayo was horrified; his indignant telegram to the Lieutenant-Governor read 'Clear the Line – stop any summary executions without your express orders'; and in rejecting the halting explanation that was offered he added that 'During the whole of the Mutiny (Norman tells me) no such event took place'. Writing to Argyll, Mayo said that the Deputy Commissioner had, of course, been suspended, but he regretted that elements in Calcutta society thought that Cowan was really a good fellow for taking such exemplary action.[7]

Forsyth remained of the view that Mayo had overreacted. In his autobiography he recalled:

I knew the crisis was most important. If I repudiated his [Cowan's]

> action and showed that there was a division amongst rulers, the natives would take advantage of it, and as reports were hourly coming in of further disturbances threatening Jullundur and Amritsar, promptitude, and united action, was absolutely necessary. I recollected how, at the outbreak of the Mutiny, the prompt execution of a Sikh at Amballa had checked a threatened rising of the nation. I therefore decided to take upon myself the responsibility for Cowan's act. I wrote a letter approving of what he had done in the circumstances.[8]

As well as hanging the Kukas, Forsyth was clear that their leader Ram Singh could no longer be left at large. So he arrested him and sent him to Delhi. (Later, Northbrook, seeing Ram Singh as a focus of discontent, deported him to Rangoon without trial.) Cowan was turned out of the service and Forsyth was relieved of his post and sent to Oudh, feeling that, in view of his past association with Mayo, he had been hard done by. A year later, however, Northbrook entrusted him with a second mission to Eastern Turkestan, and he was officially rehabilitated. Cowan and Forsyth were penalised, not so much for their grave error of judgement as for revealing by their action how fragile was the British hold.

Mayo's letter about Cowan's misdemeanour was one of the last he wrote before he left for Burma and the Andamans, and during his voyage he was still exercised about the possibility of renewed Kuka activity. Before then the assassination of Chief Justice Norman gave him more immediate cause for anxiety, but to understand the significance of the murder it is necessary to look more closely at the history of the Wahabi movement.

The original Wahabis were an Islamic sect founded by Abdul Wahabi in the early eighteenth century in the Nejed district of Arabia. Like most revivalists, they preached the extirpation of worldly practices and a return to the original faith. After Abdul Wahabi's death in 1792 his followers spread throughout the Turkish empire, but latterly lost their political significance and remained as a purely religious movement.

The Wahabis in India had the same broad doctrinal objectives as their Arabian counterparts, but had no direct connection with them other than their name. The Father of Indian Wahabism was one Sayyid Ahmad Shahid, born in 1786, whose principal tenets were the purging of religious innovations and the creation of an ideal Muslim state by a *jehad*. From the start Patna, where most converts were made, was the centre of Wahabism, but there was also a sizeable colony at Sittana. Their first campaigns were aimed at the Sikhs, because the Muslims were worse off under the Sikhs than elsewhere in India under British rule – and the chances of success were greater. Fighting with the Sikhs continued from 1826 to 1831, and the British were not particularly distressed to see the Wahabis keeping Runjeet Singh occupied, but the situation changed when the British annexed the Punjab. Between 1850 and 1857 no fewer than sixteen expeditions, employing a total of 33,000 regular troops in all, had to be mounted against the Wahabis in the north west. During the Mutiny they tried to stimulate rebellion along the frontier, and some of the leading mutineers captured at Delhi were apostles of Wahabism. Sittana remained a trouble spot, and further expeditions were necessary under Sir Sydney Cotton and Neville Chamberlain, the latter in 1863 resulting in no more than a Pyrrhic victory with over 800 European and native losses.

In 1864, following trials at Amballa, Sir Herbert Edwardes, the sessions judge, sentenced eight Wahabis, three of them to death, although their penalty was commuted to transportation for life. A further trial in 1865 implicated a much larger number and disclosed the extent of their organisation and seditious activities. There was little sign of Wahabism in Madras or Bombay, but their missionaries were active throughout Bengal. Recruits were taken to Patna and thence, by Amballa, across the frontier. Meanwhile Muslims generally were urged to provide funds, either by a percentage of their daily earnings – the usual form for religious exactions – or in the case of the very poor by providing handfuls of grain. Before Mayo arrived, Grey at Bengal had commissioned a lengthy police enquiry which confirmed that the widespread Wahabi plot still contemplated a full-scale *jehad*.

Against this background, Mayo, with memories of conspiracies by secret societies in Ireland fresh in his mind, was determined to suppress centres of Wahabism, and for a time he allowed the widespread arrest of Muslims suspected of belonging to the sect. In August 1870 it became apparent that many of the arrests had been made on insufficient evidence, and that the suspects were being detained for lengthy periods without trial. Fitzjames Stephen, doubting the legality of this procedure, opined that the Government's action had been 'muddled and mismanaged'.[10] The Bengal Government wanted to set up a special tribunal to speed up the trials, but Mayo disagreed. But he was fully aware that Government prestige was suffering and he told Grey in Bengal and Durand in the Punjab to release most of the small fry, and bring to trial only the ringleaders.[11] He also told Muir in the North West that he objected to witnesses being brought to court in chains.[12]

While most of the Wahabis were poor, two respectable merchants, Amir Khan and Hushmadad Khan, had been arrested in July 1869 and kept in custody. On 1 August 1870 Chisholm Anstey, a barrister of some notoriety in Bombay, applied for a writ of habeas corpus in the Calcutta High Court. It was refused because the Governor-General had powers to detain people suspected of treasonable practices. But embarrassment followed when it was realised that most of the warrants, under Regulation of 1818, had been wrongly issued. Mayo gave instructions for those detained under the Regulation to be released, except for the most dangerous cases.

Reacting to Anstey's intemperate speeches in court, Mayo must have cast his mind back to another eloquent barrister, Isaac Butt, during his term as Chief Secretary for Ireland. Butt, a former Conservative MP, had defended the Fenian sympathisers, becoming somewhat attracted by their grievances. In 1868 he founded the Amnesty Association, and in November 1869 published in the *Nation* proposals for the formation of a nationalist party of all classes – not just Fenian revolutionaries. It was not the happiest precedent for Mayo.

Meanwhile, fully conscious that the Wahabis would spare no pains to gain a prestige victory, and might 'even embark in a very expensive legal contest, both here and in England',[13] he fixed a deadline for the completion of the trials – 'in great hopes that before the 1st of February there will be no untried Wahabee prisoner in Bengal'.[14] Inevitably it took longer, but by the end of July the trials were over. The principal offenders were convicted, and though there might be appeals, no Wahabi was now confined awaiting trial. At the end of August Mayo told Burne that the Wahabi problem had been 'vigorously grappled with'.[15]

Eventually it was not till the end of December 1871 that the final appeals were disposed of. Hushmadad Khan had been freed without evidence being called, and three others had their sentences quashed, but the convictions of Amir Khan, who had been the Wahabis' banker, and one other were confirmed. The Calcutta press were inclined to think that the Viceroy could now afford to be merciful to the aged Amir Khan, who, it might be supposed, had learned his lesson.

Mayo was optimistic. He had, he believed, put the Wahabi menace to rest; he was reducing the income tax, with its latent danger of uniting opposition to the Government; and he did not, of course, know that the Kukas – as we have already noted – would soon be active again. But it was always dangerous to conclude, as the Viceroy did in one of his periodic letters to the Queen, that tranquillity generally prevailed.[16] (In 1842, just before the Afghans in Kabul rose to put the British to the sword, Sir William Macnaghten wrote that all was peace 'from Dan to Beersheba'.)

An insight into Mayo's thinking is seen in his request to William Hunter, then a member of the Bengal Civil Service and latterly Director of Statistics, to write a treatise on 'Our Indian Musulmans: Are They Bound in Conscience to Rebel against the Queen?' This was in May 1871, and Hunter, nothing if not productive, rushed his manuscript home to reach the printers in Edinburgh by the end of August. In it he had no difficulty in tracing the Wahabis' ancestry and in exemplifying the extent of their conspiracy. The answer to the basic question posed by his title depended on whether Muslims were entitled to regard India as still a country of Islam – in which case rebellion against the British intruder would be justified – or whether it was now a country of the enemy, in which case Muslims were not, doctrinally, entitled to rebel. Hunter quoted with approval the opinion of the Calcutta Muhammadan Society that 'if any misguided wretch, owing to his perverse fortune, were to wage war against the Ruling Powers of this Country, British India, such war would be rightly pronounced rebellion; and rebellion is strictly forbidden by the Muhammadan Law.'[17] He also referred to other, more qualified, opinions by Muslim law doctors, which were less favourable to the British cause.

So far this might be seen as a propaganda exercise, designed to allay criticism at home about the Wahabi trials as much as to influence Indian sentiment. But in his final section Hunter dealt with the causes of Muslim discontent. He quoted O'Kinealy, the officer in charge of the Wahabi prosecutions: 'I attribute the great hold which Wahabi doctrines have on the mass of the Muhammadan peasantry to our neglect of their education.'[18] A well-supported charge, and there were others relating to interference with Muslim beliefs, and more pragmatic matters. 'No Muhammadan gentleman of birth can enter our regiments.' In Bengal, the Permanent Settlement of 1793 had elevated the Hindu collectors and allowed them to accumulate wealth that would have gone to the Muslims under their own rule. Figures showed that of over 2,000 civil jobs in Bengal 681 were held by Hindus, but only 92 by Muslims. 'In fact, there is now scarcely a Government office in Calcutta in which a Muhammadan can hope for any post above the rank of porter, messenger, filler of inkpots, and mender of pens.'[19] It was a formidable list, and Hunter concluded with proposals for extensive improvements to Muslim education.

As Mayo commissioned this book, and as Hunter was an extremely loyal official, and later the author of an admiring biography of the Viceroy, it must be assumed that these views echoed Mayo's. They may have been meant to open the way for reforms more far-reaching than those which he had already introduced (chapter 8). But it was too late. Hunter's book was available in London in August 1871, and a few weeks later in India. But Mayo's optimism was soon shattered by the first political murder since 1857.

On 20 September 1871, J. P. Norman, the officiating Chief Justice of the Calcutta High Court, was assassinated. The *Englishman* reported that about eleven o'clock in the morning Norman was stabbed while going up the steps of the Town Hall. He was at once carried to the nearby shop of Messrs Thacker, Spink & Co. Dr Fayer, the government physician, soon arrived, but poor Norman did not recover and died during the night.

The assassin was identified as a fanatical Muslim called

Abdoolah. According to Clive Bailey, the Secretary of the Home Department, he was a man of some education. He had studied at the Mirzapur Madrassa near Delhi (one of the schools where Persian and Arabic were taught as well as English). He was well read in the narrow theological learning of his creed, and had been the Imam of a mosque in Calcutta. Other details that emerged were that at the Madrassa he had announced that he would kill an English judge and become a martyr, and that he claimed to be related to the ruler of Swat. He was known to have Wahabi views; he sympathised with Amir Khan and Hushmadad Khan and attended their trials. On arrest he claimed to be insane, but he later abandoned this pretence and denied all knowledge of the murder.

Abdoolah, who had narrowly escaped lynching at the scene of the crime, was tried on 28 September before Mr Justice Paul. He was calm and collected and questioned several witnesses. He said he had presented a petition to Norman, who refused to accept it. This made him angry, and after that he did not know what occurred. He was convicted and his execution fixed for 12 October.

The Viceroy was at Simla when he heard of the murder. His first reaction was of profound regret that the assassin should have singled out Norman, who 'was so amiable and kind. He was a regular Philo-Native and always went out of his way to be civil and good to them.'[20] Mayo was not alone in thinking that the imprudent hurrying of the trial might be interpreted as a sign of panic, and on 8 October he telegraphed to order a fortnight's stay of execution. His reasoning was cogent. Nothing had yet been discovered about the assassin's antecedents or associates. If the murder was part of a conspiracy the respite might lead to the belief that Abdoolah had 'split' on his fellow conspirators, who might then try to save themselves by disclosure. Mayo added that the photographs, said to have been widely circulated, had only just reached Simla, and there had been no time for a reaction. Then followed Mayo's real motivation. He recalled that he had used the respite stratagem in Ireland, and it had led to the arrest of a notorious Fenian who Mayo knew was in London, but whom the Metropolitan Police could not trace at the time.[21]

On 11 October an extraordinary edition of the *Gazette* offered

10,000 rupees for information leading to the discovery of accomplices in the crime. The murderer's supposed name was given as Moulvie Abdoolah Wilaytee; he was said to be about forty years of age and apparently a native of Peshawar or that neighbourhood. No one came forward to claim the reward, and he was executed on 4 November. On the scaffold he reiterated that he had killed Norman in a fit of anger. His body was burned within the walls of the jail.

The question remains – was this an isolated crime, or was it part of a Wahabi conspiracy? The official view was that 'So far nothing has come to light which would induce the belief that Abdoolah was in combination with any party, or acted otherwise than as a zealot on his own fanatical and heated fancy.'[22] The Indian press, such as the *Friend of India*, the *Daily Examiner* and the *Times of India*, were far from convinced, and supported the conspiracy theory. The perceptive Bailey pointed out that Justice Norman had refused to fix a date for the Wahabi appeal; this decision was conveyed to counsel for Amir Khan and Hushmadad Khan on 19 September – the day before the murder.[23] Temple and Burne both thought the assassin was connected with the Wahabis and that the murder was intended to be a warning to the Government of India.[24]

What did Mayo, surveying these events from the heights of Simla, make of the official reports, the press comments, and the analysis of the many anonymous letters, all investigated to no avail? He went no further than saying he was disposed to agree there was some connection with Wahabism.[25] At the back of his mind was the Fenian history of his Irish days, and he always tended to equate Fenianism and Wahabism. He may also have recalled a past event which now escaped notice. The Duke of Edinburgh, whom Mayo entertained so royally, was shot by a would-be assassin on an earlier visit to Australia in 1868. Luckily His Royal Highness was only slightly wounded, but the man who fired the shot, Henry James O'Farrell, declared – and then denied – that he was a Fenian selected by lot to kill the Duke. It would be easy to envisage other attempts on the lives of prominent people being inspired by subversive organisations, whether Fenian or Wahabi. The irony is that before long a third, and successful, attempt was to be made, this time on Mayo himself.

16
The Convict Settlement

During 1871 Mayo had often said he intended to visit British Burma, the Andaman Islands, and Orissa, and in August he asked Rear-Admiral Cockburn, the naval Commander-in-Chief on the Indian seas, to place a man-of-war at his disposal, as he wished to conduct his tour with some ceremony. He said he would probably start about the end of January 1872, and invited the Admiral to accompany him. Cockburn replied that he would come up to Calcutta with the flagship *Glasgow*, but, not being in good health, asked to be excused from taking part in the tour. (A peevish letter from the good Admiral's secretary rejected a suggestion that a special consignment of food and wine should be sent on board for His Excellency. This would be contrary to the etiquette followed in HM ships; the Navy would provide.)

On 24 January 1872 the Viceroy and Lady Mayo, accompanied by the Marquess and Marchioness of Drogheda, Burne and his wife, Miss Milman, Miss Norman and Captain De Robeck ADC, embarked on the *Sir William Peel* at Prinsep's Ghat and sailed down river to join the *Glasgow*, then at anchor off Saugor. The steamship *Dacca*, which had been placed at the Viceroy's disposal by the British India Steam Navigation Company, followed the next day with the rest of the party, which included the Earl of Donoughmore, Count Waldstein, and a merry gathering of friends from Kildare. Barrow Ellis and Charles Aitchison were among the officials in attendance.

Up to the last moment Mayo had been in two minds about leaving Calcutta at this particular time as he was concerned about affairs in Khelat, Colonel Pollock's safety in his journey to Seistan, and other matters, and said he would return at once from Rangoon should he receive any unfavourable telegrams of importance. But as the curtain rose on this ill-fated expedition all the news that came in was good. Pollock had made a safe journey through the disturbed districts of Khelat, the Looshai campaign was going better than expected, and elsewhere there was no evident cause for anxiety. With a light heart Mayo disembarked at Rangoon.

His reception there was enthusiastic and he carried out a strenuous programme, visiting public institutions, receiving deputations, conferring rewards, holding durbars, and attending native games and entertainments, all the formal duties of his office. He held a Levee and Ball on 30 January, an afternoon party on board ship on 1 February, and a Grand Public Ball on 2 February, the day before he left Rangoon. The mercantile community had a full schedule of optimistic demands, and their address urged a standard measure for rice, more immigration of coolies to provide additional labour, a larger grant for roads and canals, the introduction of a bankruptcy law, and the construction of a railway to Prome. The merchants had been quick to congratulate Mayo on being the first Governor-General since Dalhousie to visit Burma, and they were not going to miss the chance of getting something out of the occasion. Mayo, however, had done his homework, along with Ellis and Aitchison, and his speech in reply – amended in his own handwriting – gave them as much grounds for hope as they could expect.

Other addresses followed from bodies down to St Paul's Institution and the Convent School, and from the native communities, the Karens, the Sooratee, and the Hindus. The Karens, expressing their thanks for the protection of British rule, added a colourful touch. 'Formerly your servants were a wild people and our rulers were very arbitrary and cruel, so that we were very degraded and little better than slaves. But our Elders had a tradition that the Karens would be made free and enlightened by people coming in ships from the West.'[1]

At Moulmein it was the same story. 'We the inhabitants of Moulmein are filled with unutterable joy at having this opportunity, which occurs once in a lifetime of beholding Your Excellency's face which is like the polished glass or the face of the lovely moon.'[2] They spoke more truly than they knew when they referred to the uniqueness of the occasion.

The *Glasgow* sailed at daylight on the 5th, as Mayo wanted to gain a few hours for the inspection of the settlement at Port Blair in the Andamans.

The Andaman Islands lie on the east side of the Bay of Bengal, on a latitude just south of Madras. Surrounded by coral reefs, they are covered to the water's edge with dense jungle and enclose some of the most picturesque harbours to be found. In 1857 the Government of India sent a Committee to visit the islands and select a place for a settlement, initially for mutineers and rebels undergoing penal servitude, and eventually for all convicts from India under sentence of transportation. Port Blair, a harbour on the east coast of the Great Andaman, was chosen as the best site. (A penal colony had been established there in 1789 by Lieutenant Blair, but it was abandoned in 1796, mainly because of the prevalence of malaria and the hostility of the natives.) A new batch of convicts arrived in January 1858, and when Mayo paid his visit the complement of prisoners had increased to about 7,000.

Port Blair was under the charge of a Superintendent assisted by a Deputy and several subordinate officers and overseers. A detachment of British infantry, a wing of native infantry, and about 200 police were stationed in this grim outpost. As early as March 1869, in a letter to John Strachey, Mayo had referred to a possible inspection of the Andamans and expressed the naive hope that he would find not only a thriving but also a completely self-supporting settlement.[3] Burne, in his official report, said that 'Crime is comparatively small considering the character of life prisoners convicted of the worst offences'.[4] But other correspondence gives a less reassuring picture of life on this devil's island. In June 1871 Captain Rogers, the Assistant Superintendent at Port Blair, wrote itemising the dreadful conditions. 'Want of good feeling and sociability between officials. Every man for himself having his ideas eternally on how to save money and get out of the place.' One could scarcely imagine that it was a popular station, but jail discipline did not exist; opium, bhang and other drugs were freely available to prisoners; marriage was allowed, but wives were hired out to fellow convicts. 'At any moment the convicts could arm themselves, crush our small force and escape, and as we have no ship or vessel of any kind, nothing would be known of it until the mail, which comes once in six weeks . . .'[5] In December 1871 Major-General (later Field-Marshal Sir Donald) Stewart, who had been despatched as Superintendent, reported that some progress had been made, but there were still a good many escapes.

Mayo's party landed at Ross Island – Stewart's headquarters – at 11 a.m. on 8 February to visit the convict establishments there, consisting of some 2,000 men, and in the afternoon they were to move to Viper and Chatham Islands, where the worst convicts were kept. During the preliminary discussion Burne checked the security arrangements that had been made with Stewart. Guards had been posted at each locality, and an armed body of police and of chuprassies was to accompany the Viceroy. At first all went well. Mayo made a thorough inspection of Ross Island and seemed almost annoyed with the precautions taken, at one time ordering his escort to keep back. He was always unconcerned about his own safety, but after the murder of Chief Justice Norman the members of the Executive Council, together with his brother and Burne, had prevailed on him to carry a loaded stick. At Burne's personal request, he had it with him on the 8th. There were, however, no particular grounds for supposing that his life was in danger at Port Blair. 'Indeed', Burne recorded, 'the feeling of the convicts was said to be one of self-interested satisfaction at his visit, in expectation of pardons and indulgences.'[6]

The Viceroy was impatient to see Mount Harriet, a hill about a thousand feet high and a mile and a half from the landing pier at Hopetown, since he had heard it suggested as a possible site for a sanitorium. On the morning of the 8th there was some casual discussion about visiting the hill during the afternoon, but nothing was decided and – in painful innocence of what was to happen – it was eventually settled that Lady Mayo and some of her friends should climb it on the following morning, and that the Viceroy should do so as occasion offered during the day.

At 2.30 in the afternoon Mayo took off in the *Glasgow*'s steam launch to go to Viper and Chatham Islands, and as the inspection of Chatham was finished sooner than expected he said he would go over to Hopetown, which was only a short distance across the harbour, and make his ascent of the Mount. It was then about 5 p.m., and as daylight lasted till about half past six, it was thought there would be sufficient time to do the climb before dark. At Hopetown Mayo's party met the Earl of Donoughmore and some of the others, whom Mayo asked to accompany him, but they thought better of it and the Viceroy's small contingent went on alone.

Mayo at first rode on a pony, but soon dismounted and did not reach the top of the hill till near sunset. He sat down for about ten minutes to rest, drink some water, and exclaim on the beauty of the view. On their return, as they approached the landing pier – some three hundred yards or so away – it was already getting very dark. Bearers with torches were sent to light the road, but Mayo ordered them to keep well in front, as he disliked the smell and smoke from the flames. On reaching the huts near the landing-stage they found a line of men drawn up under convict overseers, and Stewart explained, in one of the last ironies, that they were *jampan* bearers fetched over from Ross Island to carry Lady Mayo's party up the hill next day. Mayo had now reached the pier, a narrow one with steep stone sides.

About twenty-five yards from the boat, Stewart, with permission, turned aside to have a last word with one of the overseers about the morning's arrangements. It was now quite dark, and Mayo was still protected by his escort – his personal *jemadar* and two British officers. The sailors from the *Glasgow* were sitting in a group at the end of the pier. Mayo lengthened his stride to reach the boat when, in Burne's words, 'all in an instant, we heard a rushing noise, and saw a man fastened like a tiger on the Viceroy's back'. They rushed on the assassin and secured him, but he had inflicted two mortal wounds.

Mayo stumbled a few paces forward and fell over the pier into the shallow water. With some help he raised himself, still with his senses fully about him. He said 'Burne, they have hit me.' He walked a few paces and said 'I don't think I am much hurt.' They laid him on a cart on the pier, but blood began to flow rapidly as they tried to staunch his wounds. In a faint voice Mayo said 'Take me to the ship.' As they carried him to the boat he twice said 'Lift up my head.'[7] These were his last words.

It took twenty minutes to reach the steam launch and then the *Glasgow*, while they supported his head and rubbed his legs in a vain attempt to keep up warmth.

We imagined that the Viceroy had fainted from loss of blood, and would have given our lives for a little brandy to give him. But, alas, during these dreadful moments of nearing the ship, Major-General Stewart turned to me, shook his head, and said, 'I fear the worst'. The Viceroy's face had changed. We none of us thought that he had actually breathed his last. He had not given one sigh or expression of pain from first to last, but he must have expired at the moment of Major-General Stewart's exclamation.[8]

The darkness, the torches, the sudden thrust by the murderer, the wounded man's rise from the water – it was dramatic, as assassinations are. Mayo had died, as he did everything else, with style and dignity. The precautions had been extensive. It seemed, though no one admitted it at the time, that some at least had felt a sense of premonition, but the security had not been enough.

Burne had the unhappy task of breaking the news to Lady Mayo, who had just dressed for dinner after a pleasant day being rowed round the harbour. A post mortem carried out the same night confirmed that Mayo had been struck twice, and that either of the wounds was sufficient to kill him.

The assassin's motives were never satisfactorily explained. He was indentified as Sher Ali, a Pathan aged about twenty-five. He was for some time a sowar in the Peshawar Police, and while acting as Colonel Pollock's orderly in 1867 was accused of a murder in the streets of the city. He denied the crime, but was sentenced to transportation for life and sent in 1869 to the Andamans. There he was regarded as a good conduct prisoner, with only a single minor offence, and was employed as a barber. He had the free run of the Hopetown ground and was one of the few prisoners permitted to receive letters from India.

On the morning of 9 February Stewart was handed a message from a European convict with the intriguing name of Roper Curzon stating that Sher Ali had given out that he had received a letter informing him that his brother had murdered Mr Justice Norman and that he was proud of the deed. Moreover, when he heard of the Viceroy's impending arrival he had drawn his savings, which he used to treat Muslim convicts with cakes and Hindus with sugar. Convicts who were examined confirmed, in effect, the story about the letter and the distribution of gifts, though no reason had been given except that it was 'an offering to god'. He was also heard to say on the same day that the Lord Sahib was coming. Only two facts seem clear. The iron kitchen knife used for the crime had been polished and carefully sharpened, and the assassin had been in recent correspondence with India.

The official conclusion was that the deed was one of private revenge for what the man believed was undeserved transportation, but this was greeted with widespread scepticism. Newspapers from the Indian press to the *New York Times* all attributed the murder to the Wahabis, and James Wilson, the editor of the *Indian Daily News*, felt so convinced that this was the case that he had a pamphlet published in London. In it he argued that there was great dissatisfaction with Mayo's government, though not with him personally, caused mainly by inequities in the assessment and collection of the income tax, and by the persecution, as it was seen, of the Wahabis, particularly Amir Khan and Hushmadad Khan. In Wilson's view the assassination of Mr Justice Norman and Mayo could not be put down to private reasons, because they had no personal enemies. It did not, however, suit the Government to admit that the murders had a political origin, since they were most unwilling to recognise that there were grounds for political discontent.

Wilson went on to discount other theories that had been advanced. Private malice he dismissed because this would have implied a personal relationship with the murderer, which did not exist. Personally, both Norman and Mayo were widely popular. Some had suggested that religious fanaticism, the belief that to kill an infidel opened the gates of paradise was the explanation. But any infidel would do for this purpose. Was it likely that the fanatic would patiently wait till he had the chance of killing the Governor-General or the Chief Justice when he could easily have found an ordinary victim? Lastly, *The Times* had suggested a 'fraternity of hatred' as the root cause. But if such a brotherhood did exist, assassination would have been much more common. In Wilson's macabre mathematics, some 30 million would only have to dispose of one Briton for 300 of their brethren to wipe out the conquering race. Wilson concluded that the murders arose from a general sense of oppression (especially the income tax), and a particular grievance in a part of the nation (the Muhammadans) which felt neglected in one way and persecuted in another. He makes a case, though he does not prove it.

George Campbell, as Lieutenant-Governor of Bengal equally familiar with the background, took a different line, holding that there was no connection between the two murders. He thought that the characters of the assassins and the circumstances could not have been more different. The evidence leading to Sher Ali's earlier conviction, consisting of such matters as footprints corresponding to his boots, was wholly circumstantial. Nothing, Campbell argued, could be more galling to a free tribesman from the hills than transportation to the Andamans for life, especially if he was innocent.[10]

Owen Burne, recollecting emotion in tranquillity in his memoirs, retained the idea that, knowing the feeling against the Viceroy and Norman for the Wahabi prosecutions, and the precautions that had to be taken even in Calcutta for the Viceroy's safety, 'by some mischance Sher Ali had received a letter from the Patna malcontents, inciting him to commit the deed, to accomplish which, we afterwards learned, he had followed us unnoticed throughout the day without being able to get a chance until at the moment we appeared to be in comparative safety'.[11]

The mystery is unsolved, but judging from Mayo's own words when he was lifted from the water – 'They have hit me' – he himself thought the Wahabis were responsible.

The horror aroused by the assassination can be imagined, the *Friend of India*, for example, calling in fury 'Send the scoundrel to perdition in a pig skin to break his caste.'[12] Sher Ali was hanged on Viper Island on 11 March, unrepentant and making no confession. When Stewart informed him that Lady Mayo's children had telegraphed a message from England to their father's murderer, 'May God forgive you', he became enraged. 'He said if they had sent a message ordering him to be cut to pieces he would have been glad, but a prayer for God's forgiveness he could not take from them.'[13]

Mayo's body was brought from the Andamans to the *Glasgow* before being transferred to the *Daphne* at Sandheads, and arrived at Calcutta on 17 February. John Strachey, Acting

Governor-General, had already sent a signal to Burne that the corpse would be received at Prinsep's Ghat by the Lieutenant-Governor of Bengal and Members of Council, and that, most unusually, everyone in the procession would walk on foot following the coffin, 'which would be more solemn and respectful than any other way'.[14] Another telegram emphasised that Dr Fayrer would be responsible for transferring the body to a new coffin, 'which is pronounced absolutely necessary'.[15] On the next day Strachey – realistically – recommended that the landing should be postponed till Saturday, 'Friday being a mail day, a very large number of Europeans will be absolutely unable to attend notwithstanding their anxious desire to do so'.[16] In the event, the coffin was landed from the P & O Company's wharf as it could not be brought by water up to Prinsep's Ghat. The route was lined with British and native regiments so that they faced each other alternately irrespective of race, with arms reversed and muffled in crape. Campbell relates a strange happening. The cortège had to pass over the suspension bridge at Kidderpore. As its stability was doubtful it was first tested with heavy artillery wagons. The procession crossed in safety, but a few nights later the whole edifice collapsed 'in the most unprovoked manner'.

The body lay in state for two days to enable the vast crowds of Europeans and natives to pay their respects. It was then taken back to the *Daphne* (whose commander was inconveniently struck down with cholera) for conveyance to Bombay and thence to Ireland. There was one unpleasant note. *The Times* of 12 March published a dignified letter from Fitzjames Stephen in which he felt it necessary to dispose, convincingly and at length, of malevolent suggestions that the late Viceroy's voyage to Burma and the Andamans had been undertaken 'for the sake of amusement merely'.[17]

Mayo received a public funeral in Dublin on 25 April, and he was buried, by his own wish, at Johnstown, in a place in the churchyard which he had chosen before he went out to India. An imposing equestrian statue was later erected at Calcutta and invested by the Prince of Wales on 3 January 1876. It could still be seen on the Maidan as late as 1969, but has since been removed by the Government of West Bengal. A bust by Boehm was placed in the crypt of St Paul's, where it was unveiled on 26 July 1886 by the Earl of Cranbrook.

Epilogue

An assessment of Mayo's merit as a person, and his achievements as Viceroy, is made more difficult because he died after a bare three years in office. Her Majesty's chief representative normally stayed at Government House for five years, and it was in the last two that full measure could be taken of the success or failure of his administration. It could accordingly be argued that Mayo's untimely death, and the very circumstances of his murder, enhanced his reputation and elevated him to a higher place in the roll of Viceroys than he would have reached if he had served his full term. It could be thus argued, but the argument would be wrong.

Certainly the immediate tributes paid by those close to him were generous, and there is no reason to question their sincerity. John Strachey, acute and never sentimental, said 'He seemed formed by Nature to be a great Indian Governor. His noble bearing, his magnificent liberality, the dignity and courtesy of his demeanour, the unfailing kindness and unselfishness of his frank and genial nature, made everyone proud of him, and made everyone love him.'[1] Fitzjames Stephen, analytical and not given to exaggeration, said that of the many public men he had met in India there was none to whom he felt disposed to give such heartfelt affection and honour.[2] Temple, who had profound disagreements with Mayo over finance, had no doubt that he was widely esteemed, both in the Executive Council and by those who served in the Departments of State.

The Duke of Argyll, whose painful duty it was to inform the House of Lords of the Viceroy's assassination, recalled that Mayo and he had taken up office at the same time. 'I am happy to say that from that time our negotiations have been most friendly and cordial . . .' No Governor-General, Argyll continued, had been more assiduous, or had more at heart the good of the people. 'I believe his death will be a calamity to India and that it will be sincerely mourned not only in India and in his native country, Ireland, but by the well-affected millions of Her Majesty's subjects in India.'[3]

It is to be noted that these words about a Conservative peer, a former Conservative Mininster and the colleague of Disraeli, came from the Liberal Secretary of State. Not the least of Mayo's achievements had been, first, to stay in Viceregal office when his own party fell from power just after he was appointed, and secondly to retain the full confidence of the Liberal Government and the support of their Minister in charge of Indian affairs. This last relationship was made more poignant by Argyll having himself been more than once tipped to be Viceroy.

The next Viceroy to go out to India, Lord Northbrook, was not so happy in his dealings with Westminster, and by looking briefly at his rule it is possible to find some pointers to Mayo's stature.

Northbrook was a Liberal, appointed by a Liberal Government, with whom he had already held minor office, including that of Under-Secretary of State under Sir Charles Wood (Viscount Halifax). Northbrook's initial policies as Viceroy naturally met with the approval of his former colleagues in the administration at home, but with the Tories back in power in 1874 it was not long before he was at odds with the Marquess of Salisbury as Secretary of State. Ultimately, Northbrook did not serve his full five years, resigning after four. Although he kept a dignified silence about his quarrels with Salisbury, saying that his resignation was due to private reasons and his duty to his family, there can be no doubt that protracted disagreement with the Secretary of State was a strong factor. The point for us is that Mayo succeeded in insulating the Viceroy's conduct of affairs from the hubbub of party conflict at home, something that Northbrook could not do.

Ironically, Argyll was not among those who favoured Northbrook's appointment. He told Gladstone that he considered Northbrook was 'somewhat deficient in the popular elements of character which go so very far in such a post as that of Viceroy'. Doubtless harking back to Mayo's personal qualities, Argyll would have preferred another Irish peer, Lord Dufferin. But Gladstone overruled him; Northbrook got the job; and when Dufferin, much later, became Viceroy he was something of a flop.

There was no disguising the fact that Mayo and Northbrook were very different persons. Mayo was a romantic, an imperialist. 'Teach your subordinates', he told Durand, 'that we are all British gentlemen engaged in the magnificent work of governing an inferior race.'[4] Temple thought that Mayo regarded India as an imperial estate, upon which capital was to be beneficially laid out to the utmost limit compatible with financial safety.[5]

Northbrook did not see it in quite that light. A member of the banking family, the Barings, his approach was cool, methodical, and 'full of the business-like habits which he had inherited'. Argyll thought there was a 'dryness and hardness' in his manner, and today he would have made a good Treasury Minister, preferably the one (now styled Chief Secretary) whose job it is to apply the jeweller's glass to the programmes put forward by other Ministers. Unlike Mayo, who thought India the opportunity of a lifetime, Northbrook did not want to be Viceroy. He had no high political ambitions. A widower, he was reluctant to expose his young daughter to the rigours of the climate, but he believed it was his duty to accept the offer to fill the vacancy. Just as Mayo had prepared himself by intensive scrutiny of the papers in the India Office, Northbrook, required to take post without delay, applied his mind to learning Hindustani on the voyage out.

Whatever Northbrook's merits or demerits, he was a kindly man, with nothing vindictive in his nature. He was not anxious to score marks over his predecessor, but he must have taken very seriously the warning he received from A. O. Hume, the Secretary of the Department of Revenue, Agriculture, and Commerce. Hume, who was much closer to Indian opinion than most officials, stated categorically that

> A studied and invariable disregard, if not actually contempt, for the opinions and feelings of our subjects, is at the present day the leading characteristic of our Government in every branch of the administration . . . we hurry on from change to change, seeking to force in a lifetime growth that to be healthy must be the product of ages . . . we are building a palace on the sand and great will be the fall thereof.[6]

These remarks, criticising 'our Government', but not Mayo himself, were probably aimed at the Stracheys, though they come oddly from Hume, who was an 'enthusiast', had worked on intimate terms with the late Governor-General, and greatly admired him personally. Northbrook's general reaction, encouraged by the Indian press, was that the pace of change had been too fast, both for the administrative machine and for public opinion. The autocratic Stracheys were held principally responsible for pushing ahead with their reforms and projects, and, in short, it seemed that Mayo's gallop was about to come to an end.

Yet it would be untrue to say that Mayo, who had been unrepentant about insisting on his innovations – 'we are trying to do in half a century in India a work that in other countries has occupied the life of a nation'[7] – was about to disappear into the forgotten land occupied by the bold pioneers who usually have to be expended. He was too big for that, he had set the tone for his Executive Council, and for a time Northbrook, a colourless figure in comparison, was keenly aware that he was operating in his shadow. Northbrook's abiding preoccupation was finance. It dominated his letters and his administration, giving some credence to the comment that he saw India 'not so much as an Empire as a budget to be balanced'.[8]

Lord Napier and Ettrick, from his seniority as Governor of the Madras Presidency acting as Viceroy in the interval till Northbrook arrived, approved Temple's budget proposals for 1872–3. This involved the retention of the hated income tax – required once more because of the expected fall in opium receipts – but he raised the threshold from £75 to £100 per annum. Northbrook, when he had time to take stock, was convinced that high taxation, caused by the income tax and the zeal with which local governments exercised their levying powers under Mayo's Provincial Services Scheme, was more of a danger to the security of the Raj than the threat of foreign invasion, and in March 1873 he discontinued income tax altogether. (He had earlier exclaimed in a moment of irritation that 'the only people who really like it, why I can't say, are Temple and Strachey'.)[9]

Mayo, in Argyll's view, would probably have done the same. But had it been a mistake ever to impose it? Mayo, at the time, had little alternative, thanks to the chaotic state of Indian finances; he wanted to keep it at as low a rate as possible, and discontent was greatly inflamed when he had to raise it to over 3%. But it would be hindsight to say that he was in error initially.

Certainly Mayo might have tried to increase his revenue from other sources, such as the salt tax with which he only tinkered. The salt rates varied throughout the country, being much higher in Bengal and Central and Upper India than in Madras and Bombay. This anomaly required an extraordinary internal customs line, stretching from the Punjab to the Bay of Bengal, and 13,000 officials were kept busy administering it. Smuggling was inevitably widespread, and there were problems with the princely states, since over half the line extended along their borders. Northbrook wanted to equalise the duties, but it was feared that the loss of revenue would be insupportable with no income tax. He did, however, succeed in graduating the duties in Bengal and Madras and in abolishing the southern customs line. But Salisbury would not let him increase the rates, and it was not till 1877 that his successor Lytton managed to raise and standardise them. It is surprising that Mayo, impatient with all forms of bureaucracy, did not make a more resolute attempt to grasp this nettle.

Northbrook had further trouble with the customs duties, which in Mayo's time produced an average revenue of £2.6m a year. The duty on imports was generally 7½% and on exports 3%. In retrospect, the most interesting feature is the constitutional wrangle that followed when Northbrook cut the import duty to 5%. Salisbury, who had promised the Manchester cotton industry to remove the tariff, tried to secure its abolition, but he was strongly opposed in Parliament by, among others, Halifax, Argyll, and Lawrence. After a prolonged exchange of recriminations, and the unprecedented despatch to India of Sir Louis Mallet to try to make peace, Northbrook agreed to reduce the tariff on cotton-piece goods to 3½%. By this time free trade was supported by both Conservatives and Liberals, and Northbrook, who knew by now that he was going home, realised that prolonged resistance was useless.

The manner in which Northbrook's representations, vehemently supported by his Executive Council, were dealt with by Salisbury, is significant. In March 1874 Salisbury had issued instructions requiring the Indian Government to give him advance notice of proposed legislation, and in August 1875 he threatened to disallow Northbrook's act which had merely reduced the tariff.[10] Northbrook argued strongly that

Salisbury's interference would undermine the whole authority of the Indian Government; he did not question the paramountcy of the Secretary of State, but he forwarded the Executive Council's minute contending that Salisbury was acting contrary to the spirit of the acts relating to the government of India.[11] In deference to strong opposition, both in India and at home, Salisbury gave way up to a point – but he still held that prior consultation on financial matters was essential to prevent a recurrence of the tariff dispute. Northbrook, when he returned to England, made a weary but dignified speech in the Lords, accepting Salisbury's amendments.

But the damage had been done, and the tariff row was one of the main reasons why Northbrook resigned a year ahead of time. While not faulting his actions, it is hard to believe that, even in the changed temper at Westminster regarding free trade, Mayo and Argyll would ever have let a dispute like this get out of hand, which argues strongly in favour of their statesmanlike qualities.

Relations with the princely states provided a field where Mayo had been highly successful – witness his speech at Ajmere and his friendship with some of the more powerful chiefs who were impressed by his 'genial and robust vigour'. Northbrook was less confident, quoting the 1858 Proclamation which promised to respect 'the rights, dignity, and honour' of the princes so frequently that he seemed to be sheltering behind it as a shield. He managed to maintain at least a semblance of cordiality with Holkar and Scindia, and survived minor squabbles with the Maharaja of Kashmir and the Nizam of Hyderabad (and his able vizier Sir Salar Jung). With Baroda, however, he was much less successful. There had already been plenty of dissatisfaction with the Gaekwar's conduct before matters came to a head when he was accused of conspiring to poison the British Resident. Northbrook took the exceptional step of appointing a commission of inquiry made up of three Europeans (including the Chief Justice of the Calcutta High Court), and three Indians (including Scindia). Ad hoc inquiries seldom convince anyone, and this was no exception. The Commission could not agree; the European members could not find the Gaekwar 'not guilty', while their Indian colleagues could not find him guilty. Northbrook and his Executive Council unanimously decided that he was, in fact, guilty, and recommended that he should be deposed. At home, the India Council sided with Northbrook, but Salisbury did not. In deference to Northbrook's urgent pleas, Salisbury authorised the deposition of the Gaekwar – not because he was guilty of the attempted poisoning, but as an 'act of political necessity, on the ground of his unfitness to govern and the bad moral effect of restoring him'. This decision was probably inconsistent; it was certainly not as expedient as Salisbury hoped; and Northbrook felt he had been let down. But remembering how Mayo had dealt with the wretched ruler of Alwar, would he not have handled the Baroda affair with a surer touch?

It is in foreign affairs that the difference between Mayo and Northbrook becomes most apparent, though Northbrook arrived in India determined to carry on Mayo's policy of good relations with a ring of friendly frontier states, and in his dealings with two of these – Burma and Khelat – behaved much as Mayo would have done.

In Burma, King Mindon had been a thorn in the flesh of the Raj for some time before reports were received that the Burmese were planning to invade the strategically important territory of Western Karenni. There was also disagreement about the passage of British missions through Burmese territory on their way to Western China, and Northbrook was under some pressure to mount an expedition. But our old friend Douglas Forsyth was sent as an emissary to the Burmese court, and in June 1875 signed an agreement with the Burmese Foreign Minister to observe the independence of Western Karenni. Northbrook also inherited from Mayo the internal dispute between the Khan of Khelat and his Sirdars, and proved equally convinced that it would be a mistake to intervene by force of arms. (Lytton later cashed in on Northbrook's patient tolerance by concluding a new treaty with the Khan which ensured that British influence would prevail.)

In Eastern Turkestan Northbrook was content to exploit Mayo's initiative and sent Forsyth back to Yarkund to develop the tentative agreements that had been reached. Early in 1873 an envoy came to Calcutta from Yakub Beg and proposed that a British mission should visit his country to draw up a full-scale commercial treaty. This was done, and a British representative stationed in Yarkund.

Northbrook tried to maintain Mayo's benevolent, vigilant policy towards Afghanistan, but in the end he did not succeed. The reasons were twofold. First, Northbrook did not enjoy the confidence of the Afghan Amir, who had a great admiration for Mayo, so that the relationship, insofar as it depended on personalities, steadily deteriorated. Northbrook got off on a bad foot when Sher Ali was disappointed with the result of the Seistan arbitration and indignantly refused the offer of compensation. Thereafter the grounds for friction were familiar, as Sher Ali wanted an unconditional guarantee of British support against an invader, recognition of Abdulla Jan as his heir (Yakub Khan the rival contestant, was languishing in jail in Kabul despite Northbrook's remonstration), and material assistance in arms and cash. Northbrook offered only a qualified guarantee of assistance, expressed no opinion on the succession to the throne, but helped him with rupees and rifles. In practical terms, the result of Northbrook's reception of the chief Afghan Minister, Nur Muhammad Shah, at Simla in June 1873 were not so different from the outcome of Mayo's meeting with Sher Ali at Amballa, but there was not the same rapport between the parties.

Second, Northbrook's troubles were exacerbated when the Conservatives returned to power and Salisbury was keen to adopt a more aggressive policy towards Afghanistan. The sticking point came when Salisbury ordered Northbrook to send a British mission to Kabul, Sher Ali having obstinately refused to accept a British envoy, or agents, there or elsewhere in Afghanistan. Northbrook, who strongly disapproved of this approach, played for time till he went home in 1876.

Admittedly these difficulties were not all of Northbrook's making. Sher Ali was greatly alarmed when in 1872 the Russians began a campaign against Khiva, and none of the Russians' later activities, or disclaimers, did anything to relieve his anxiety that the Great Bear would eventually stretch his paw across the Oxus. At home, Salisbury too feared that the Russians might acquire a dominant influence in Afghanistan,[12] and he had some support as the Conservative Government viewed the possibility of Russian expansion in Europe as well as in Central Asia with growing apprehension. The revolts in the Balkans in 1875, bringing nearer the spectre of Russo-British conflict there, also whetted British resolve to strengthen Britain's position in the East, and, as a start, to force Sher Ali to receive at least a temporary embassy in his capital.

While it is impossible not to sympathise with Northbrook, who throughout had strong support from the Executive Council, it is also arguable that Mayo would have coped better with the changing circumstances. Two factors can be prayed in aid of this proposition. Northbrook was incensed when, in the spring of 1875, Sir Henry Rawlinson published his *England and Russia in the East*, which made surprising use of official documents and called in trenchant terms for a more resolute policy towards Afghanistan. Rawlinson had earlier warned Mayo of his doubts regarding the Viceroy's conciliatory policy towards the Russians and the value to be placed on Russian assurances; to his mind supping with the Muscovites needed an exceptionally long spoon. Mayo replied that he thought more of the Russian undertakings than Rawlinson did, 'for everything that is spoken in that sense makes the carrying out of an opposite policy (if it is desired) more difficult';[13] and Rawlinson did not persist with his criticism. It was widely believed that Rawlinson, whose intimate knowledge of the country beyond the Indus dated from his service in Kandahar during the First Afghan War, and who now enjoyed great authority in the India Council, had a decisive influence on the change in the British disposition towards Sher Ali's kingdom. It is a moot question whether he would have listened again to Mayo before launching his attack on the policy that had been followed since the historic meeting at Amballa.

Even more important, Salisbury's instruction to insist on a British presence in Afghanistan, which he knew very well was an anathema to Northbrook, was sent with the explicit consent of Disraeli as Prime Minister. Would Disraeli have agreed so readily to go against his old friend Mayo, in whom he had complete trust, and who had always proclaimed the folly of exposing a British agent to the danger of residence in Kabul?

It would be easy to conclude that events marched against Northbrook, and that Mayo had an easier ride. (Lytton, sent out to implement Salisbury's plan, invaded Afghanistan and installed his agent in Kabul, only to have him massacred and be provoked into another, unnecessary, war.) But Northbrook was always too much on the defensive. Unlike him, Mayo as part of his conception of the role of Viceroy, formed and executed his own foreign policy, and in so doing he carried both the Afghan Amir and the Home Government with him. No one could have done more.

Notes

CHAPTER 1

1 Hallam, *Constitutional History of England*, 1854 ed., vol. iii, p. 350.
2 Mayo to Mr Speaker Denison, 26 March 1870, Mayo 38/94.
3 Cited Hunter, *Life of the Earl of Mayo*, vol. I p. 40.

CHAPTER 2

1 Bourke, *St Petersburg and Moscow: A Visit to the Court of the Czar*, Preface.
2 *Op.cit.* vol. II, p. 240.
3 Custine, *Journey for Our Time* (*'La Russie en 1839'*), English edition, trans, Kohler, p. 12.
4 Bourke, *op. cit.*, vol. I, p. 83.
5 *Op. cit.*, vol. II, p. 88.
6 *Op. cit.*, vol. II, p. 54.
7 *Op. cit.*, vol. I, p. 66.
8 Custine, *op. cit.*, p. 110.
9 Bourke, *op. cit.*, vol. II, p. 111.
10 Custine, *op. cit.*, p. 174.
11 Bourke, *op. cit.*, vol. II, p. 126.
12 *Op. cit.*, vol. II, p. 143.
13 *Op. cit.*, vol. I, p. 197.
14 *Op. cit.*, vol. I, p. 196.
15 Custine, *op. cit.*, p. 164.
16 *Op. cit.*, p. 235.
17 Bourke, *op. cit.*, vol. II, p. 37.
18 *Op. cit.*, vol. I, p. 202.
19 *Op. cit.*, vol. II, p. 187.
20 Hunter to Mrs Hunter, 1 October 1869, F. H. Skrine, *Life of Sir William Wilson Hunter*, p. 175.
21 Bourke, *op. cit.*, vol. II, p. 57.
22 *Op. cit.*, vol. II, p. 164.

CHAPTER 3

1 Beckett, *The Making of Modern Ireland*, p. 338.
2 Seventh Earl of Mayo and W. B. Boulton, *A History of the Kildare Hunt*, p. 238.
3 R. Monckton Milnes, *The Years of Promise*, p. 238.
4 Lord John Russell to Clarendon, 7 September 1847, Clarendon Papers, IA.
5 *Hansard*, vol. 102, 6 February 1849, col. 352.
6 *The Times*, 30 August 1848.
7 Mayo to Lady Mayo, 1870, quoted Hunter, *Life* vol. I, p. 67.
8 *Hansard*, vol. 111, 11 June 1850, col. 1068.
9 *Hansard*, vol. 116, 12 February 1852, col. 764.
10 Mayo and Boulton, *op. cit.*, p. 244.
11 *Op. cit.*, p. 277.
12 *Op. cit.*, p. 296.
13 Ranelagh, *Short History of Ireland*, p. 116.
14 Beckett, *op. cit.*, p. 350.
15 *Hansard*, vol. 185, 21 February 1867, col. 738.
16 *Hansard*, vol. 181, 2 August 1866, col. 1910.
17 *Hansard*, vol. 185, 21 February 1867, col. 727.
18 *Hansard*, vol. 185, 6 March 1867, col. 1419.
19 *Hansard*, vol. 187, 23 May 1867, col. 961.
20 *Hansard*, vol. 190, 14 February 1868, col. 775.
21 *Hansard*, vol. 190, 10 March 1868, col. 1353.
22 Beckett, *op. cit.*, p. 366.
23 Burne, MSS EUR D951/7 p. 2.

CHAPTER 4

1 Campbell, *Memoirs of My Indian Career*, vol. II, p. 205.
2 Mayo to Northcote, 12 August 1868, Mayo 33/1.
3 Burne, MSS EUR D/951/17.
4 *The Times*, 12 November 1868.
5 Mayo, Diary for 6 November 1868, quoted Hunter, *Life of the Earl of Mayo*, vol. I, p. 126.
6 Woodham Smith, *Florence Nightingale*, p. 301.
7 Mayo to Northcote, 15 September 1868, Mayo 33/7.
8 Burne, *Memories*, p. 29.
9 *Ibid.*, p. 86.
10 Mayo, Diary for 14 November 1868, Hunter, *op. cit.*, p. 130.
11 Mayo, Diary for 30 November, 1868, Hunter, *op. cit.*, p. 155.

12 Burne, MSS EUR D/951/17.
13 Mayo to Frere, 14 December 1868, Mayo 33/21.
14 *The Times*, 28 September 1868.
15 Argyll to Mayo, 18 December 1868, Mayo 47/1.
16 Mayo to Argyll, 18 January 1869, Mayo 34/3.
17 Mayo to Arbuthnot, 13 September 1868, Mayo 33/6.
18 Mayo, Diary for 29 December 1868, Hunter, *op. cit.*, p. 170.
19 Mayo, Diary for 4 January 1869, Hunter, *op. cit.*, p. 173.
20 Mayo, Diary for 8 January 1869, Hunter, *op. cit.*, p. 176.

CHAPTER 5

1 Emily Eden, 17 July 1840, *Letters*, ed. V. Dickinson, 1919, p. 327.
2 Campbell, *Memoirs of My Indian Career*, vol. I, p. 16.
3 *Ibid.*, p. 206.
4 Emily Eden, 28 April 1836, *Letters*, ed. by her niece, 1872, vol. I, p. 148.
5 Quoted, Virginia Surtees, *Charlotte Canning*, 1975.
6 *The Times*, 13 February 1872.
7 *Ibid.*
8 Burne, *Memories*, p. 60.

CHAPTER 6

1 James Morris, *Heaven's Command*, p. 268.
2 Hunter, *Life of the Earl of Mayo*, vol. I, p. 178.
3 Temple, *Men and Events of My Time in India*, p. 366.
4 *Ibid.*
5 Mayo to Argyll, 18 January 1869, Mayo 34/3.
6 Burne, *Memories*, p. 99.
7 Governor-General, Foreign Department Note, 10 May 1871, MSS EUR D951/17.
8 Burne to Mayo, 16 January 1869, Mayo vol. 15/II.
9 Durand, minute, 27 February 1868, *Life of Sir H. M. Durand*, vol. II, p. 377.
10 Mayo to Temple. 4 October 1870, MSS EUR F86/10.
11 Buckland, *Sketches of Social Life in India*, p. 28.
12 Burne, *op. cit.*, p. 122.
13 J. Strachey, minute 20 January 1871, Mayo 1/III.
14 Mayo to Arbuthnot, 8 May 1869, Mayo 35/58.
15 Mayo to Campbell, 26 November 1871, Mayo 46/258.
16 Argyll to Mayo, 18 March 1870, Mayo 48/7.

17 Burne, *op. cit.*, p. 115.
18 Napier, *Field Marshal Lord Napier of Magdala*, p. 264.
19 *Op. cit.*, p. 266.
20 Mayo to Disraeli, 2 May 1869, Mayo 35/53.
21 Hunter to Mrs Hunter, Skrine, *Life of Sir W. W. Hunter*, p. 175.
22 Salisbury to Temple, 23 February 1877, Temple papers 16/151.
23 *Friend of India*, 5 January 1872.
24 Mayo to Muir, 8 June 1870, Mayo 39/163.
25 Mayo to Argyll, 20 July 1871, Mayo 44/165.

CHAPTER 7

1 Mayo to Argyll, 1 September 1871, Mayo 44/199.
2 Mayo to Argyll, 18 January 1869, Mayo 34/3.
3 Mayo's diary, cited Burne MSS EUR 951/17.
4 *Friend of India*, 29 November 1871.
5 Burne, MSS EUR D951/17.
6 *Ibid.*
7 Mayo to Arbuthnot, 9 May 1869, Mayo 35/58.
8 Mayo, pp. 24/V.
9 Mayo, quoted Hunter, *Life of the Earl of Mayo*, vol. II, p. 282.
10 Parliamentary papers, vol. 47, (1868–69), no. 351.
11 Argyll, *Autobiography and Memoirs*, p. 274.
12 Argyll to Mayo, 12 February 1869, Mayo 47/4.
13 Parliamentary papers, vol. 44 (1872–3).
14 J. H. Rivett-Carnac, *Many Memories*, p. 200.
15 *The Englishman*, 4 April 1870.
16 Mayo to Fowler, 24 January 1870, Mayo 42/30.
17 Mayo to Argyll, 7 July 1869, Mayo 36/151.
18 Argyll to Mayo, 12 November 1869, Mayo 46/37.
19 Richard Strachey to Mayo, 30 June 1870, Mayo 60b/11.
20 Fowler to Mayo, 28 October 1870, Mayo 25/II.
21 Governor-General, minute of 30 December 1870, Mayo 25/II.
22 Mayo to Fowler, 3 January 1871, Mayo 42/2.
23 Mayo to Richard Strachey, 8 February 1872, Mayo 47/24.
24 Rivett-Carnac, *op. cit.*, p. 190.
25 *Ibid.*, p. 202.

CHAPTER 8

1 Mayo to Napier and Ettrick, 18 April 1869, Mayo 35/36.
2 Hume, *Agricultural Reform in India, 1879*, p. 30.

3 Secretary of State to Governor-General, 3 August 1871, no. 27.
4 Mayo to Argyll, 9 June 1871, Mayo 43/132.
5 Mayo to Hume, 17 June 1871, Mayo 43/140.
6 Mayo to Argyll, 8 September 1871, Mayo 44/204.
7 Governor-General, Home Dept note 3 August 1871, MSS EUR D951/7.
8 John Strachey, minute of 30 April 1872, MSS EUR D951/15.
9 Governor-General to Secretary of State, 8 February 1870, Mayo, pp. 12/IV.
10 Mayo to Perry, 26 July 1870, Mayo 40/213.
11 Governor-General, note of 26 June 1871, Mayo 12/III.
12 Hunter, *Life*, p. 226.
13 Mayo to Duke of Cambridge, 2 March 1869, Mayo 34/62.
14 Mayo to Duke of Edinburgh, 17 May 1869, Mayo 34/68.
15 Mayo to Duke of Cambridge, 26 August 1869, Mayo 36/218.
16 Mayo to Prince of Wales, 7 November 1869, Mayo 37/297.
17 Mayo to Fitzgerald, 16 November 1869, Mayo 37/313.
18 Mayo to Bloomfield, 18 May 1869, Mayo 35/70.
19 Bloomfield to Mayo, 22 July, 1869, Mayo 61/XLVII.
20 Mayo to Bloomfield, November 1869, Mayo 37/307.
21 Mayo to Rous, 2 September 1869, Mayo 36/226.
22 Rous to Mayo, 12 January 1871, Mayo 20/I.
23 *Oriental Sporting Magazine*, April 1872, p. 182.
24. Mayo to Calthorpe, 27 October, 1871, Mayo 46/252.

CHAPTER 9

1 *Punch*, 8 August 1900.
2 Mayo to Fitzgerald, 19 October 1869, Mayo 33/12.
3 Argyll to Mayo, 16 July 1869, Mayo 47/20.
4 Mayo to Argyll, 12 August 1869, Mayo 36/194.
5 Foreign Dept to Secretary of State, 30 November 1869, Mayo 10/III.
6 Argyll to Mayo, 28 December 1869, Mayo 47/46.
7 Duke of Edinburgh to Viceroy, 2 January 1870, Mayo 10/III.
8 Mayo to Argyll, 12 August 1869, Mayo 36/194.
9 Viceroy to Queen Victoria, 2 October 1869, Mayo 37/264.
10 *The Times*, 24 January 1870.
11 *The Times*, 7 February 1870.
12 Kaye and Malleson, *History of the Indian Mutiny*, 2nd ed. 1892, vol. II, p. 4.
13 Quoted Maclagan, *'Clemency Canning'* p. 282.
14 Aitchison to Thornton, 8 December 1869, Mayo, 10/II.

15 Viceroy to Queen Victoria, 1 January 1870, Mayo pp. 38/1.
16 Durand to Lady Durand, 25 December 1869, *Life* vol. I, p. 404.
17 Trotter, *India under Queen Victoria*, vol. I, p. 274.
18 Capt W. Birch, Deputy Commissioner of Police, Calcutta, Report of 10 February 1870.
19 Mayo to Argyll, 27 May 1870, Mayo 39/144.
20 *The Times*, 7 February 1870.
21 Maharaja of Benares to Viceroy, 18 September 1869, Mayo 10/II.
22 Mayo to Chamberlain, 6 February 1870, Mayo 38/51.
23 Viceroy, speech at Jubbulpore, 8 March 1870, Mayo 11/5.
24 L. B. Bowring, *Memoirs*, pp. 173–5.
25 *Madras Times*, 18 May 1870, Mayo 11/VII.
26 *The Pioneer*, 18 May 1870, *ibid.*
27 Governor-General to G. N. Taylor, 24 December 1869. MSS EUR D951/17.
28 Mayo to Leslie, 18 May 1871, Mayo 43/101.

CHAPTER 10

1 Mayo to Napier of Magdala, 30 November 1870, Mayo 41/343.
2 Fortescue, *History of the British Army*, vol. XIII, pp. 346 & 399.
3 *Friend of India*, 1 February 1871.
4 Secretary of State to Governor-General, 26 January 1869.
5 Governor-General to Secretary of State, 4 October 1869.
6 Governor-General, minute of 3 October 1870.
7 Mayo to Argyll, 24 August 1869, Mayo 36/216.
8 Durand to Ellenborough, 9 June 1865 *Life*, vol. II, p. 337.
9 Durand to Vivian, 19 August 1869, *op. cit.*, p. 395.
10 Durand, 30 August 1869, *op. cit.*, p. 453.
11 Mansfield, memorandum 3 November 1869, Mayo 21/VI.
12 Napier and Ettrick, minute 15 February 1868, cited Hunter, *Life*, vol. II, p. 129.
13 Argyll to Mayo, 27 April 1870, Mayo 48/13.
14 Durand, minute 30 August 1869, *op. cit.*, p. 445.
15 Mayo to Argyll, 22 November 1871, Mayo 46/263.
16 Mayo to Argyll, 24 August 1869, Mayo 36/216, and 22 November 1871, Mayo 46/263.
17 Mayo to Frere, 17 April 1869, Mayo 35/33.
18 Napier and Ettrick, minute 24 September 1871, Mayo 57/XXXII (a).
19 Governor-General, minute 7 February 1869, Mayo 20/IV.
20 Florence Nightingale to Mayo, 1868, MS 11,223, Nat. Library of Ireland.

21 Florence Nightingale to Mayo, 24 March, 1870, Mayo 58/6.
22 Mayo to Argyll, 25 January 1869, Mayo 34/9.
23 Governor-General, minute 25 August 1869, Mayo 22/VII.
24 Durand, 6 October 1869, *op. cit.*, p. 462.
25 Mayo to Argyll, 1 September 1871, Mayo 44/199.
26 Viceroy to Queen Victoria, 24 January 1872, Mayo 47/16.

CHAPTER 11

1 John Strachey, minute, 30 April 1872, MSS EUR D951/1.
2 Mayo to Grey, 18 September 1869, Mayo 36/243.
3 Mayo to Argyll, 27 September 1869, Mayo 36/256.
4 Governor-General, Foreign Department Note, 28 January 1870, Mayo 4/IV.
5 Mayo to Argyll, 21 July 1871, Mayo 44/166.
6 Bourchier, 11 March 1872, cited Trotter, *India under Queen Victoria*, vol. II, p. 257.
7 Campbell, *Memoirs of My Indian Career*, vol. II, p. 217.
8 Cited Lee-Warner, *Native States of India*, p. 163.
9 Strachey, *op. cit.*
10 Mayo to Argyll, 23 November 1870, Burne MSS EUR D951/17.
11 Mayo to Argyll, 23 February 1869, Mayo 34/55.
12 Secretary of State to Nawab Nazim, 23 December 1870, Parliamentary Papers 1871, vol. 51.
13 Mayo to Argyll, 9 November 1870, Mayo 41/301.
14 Hunter, *Life*, vol. I, p. 229.
15 Governor-General, Foreign Department Note, 11 May 1870, cited Burne MSS EUR D951/17.
16 Mayo to Strachey, 10 October 1870, cited Burne, *op. cit.*
17 Napier of Magdala to Baker, 26 September 1871, H. D. Napier, *Lord Napier*, p. 262.
18 *The Pioneer*, 24 December 1870.
19 Mayo to Chamberlain, 16 December 1871, Mayo 46/290.
20 Mayo, speech at Ajmere, 21 October 1870, *The Times*, 5 December 1870.
21 Lytton to Disraeli, 11 May 1876, quoted Lady Betty Balfour, *Lytton Letters*, 1906 vol. II, p. 21.
22 Major H. Daly, *Memoirs of General Sir H. D. Daly*, 1905, p. 298.

CHAPTER 12

1 Argyll to Mayo, 26 November 1869, Mayo 47/41.

2 Treaty between Marquess of Dalhousie and Amir Dost Mahomed, 30 March 1855, quoted Hunter, *Life* vol. I, p. 249.
3 Governor-General to Afzul Khan, 11 July 1866, quoted Hunter *op. cit.*, p. 251.
4 Durand to Stanley, 8 February 1867, *Life*, vol. I, p. 360.
5 Hunter, *op. cit.*, p. 254.
6 Wyllie, Précis no. 2, para 153, cited Burne, MSS EUR D951/17.
7 Wyllie, *Fortnightly Review*, December 1869.
8 Lawrence to Northcote, 6 March 1868, Lawrence papers, vol. 33.
9 Rawlinson, minute of 20 July 1868, cited Hunter, *The Earl of Mayo*, p. 123.
10 Lawrence to De Grey, 20 April 1866, Lawrence papers, vol. 31.
11 Mayo to Macleod, 25 January 1869, Mayo 34/7.
12 Mayo to Argyll, 26 January 1869, Mayo 34/8.
13 Argyll to Mayo, 19 February 1869, Mayo 47/7.
14 Mayo to Argyll, 4 April 1869, Mayo 35/22.
15 Burne, *Memories*, p. 102.
16 *Gazette of India*, 31 March 1869.
17 *Friend of India*, 1 February 1871.
18 Daly to Seton-Kerr, 23 March 1869, Mayo 4/1 (h).
19 Chamberlain to Burne, 26 March 1869, *ibid.*
20 Burne, *Memories*, p. 103.
21 Durand to Lady Durand, March 1869, *Life* vol. I, p. 385.
22 Parliamentary papers 1879, vol. 56, no. 466.
23 Mayo to Argyll, 4 April 1869, Mayo 35/22.
24 Parliamentary papers 1879, vol. 56, no. 464.
25 Mayo to Fitzgerald, 17 April 1869, Mayo 35/31.
26 Mayo to Lawrence, 3 June 1869, Mayo 35/97.

CHAPTER 13

1 Mayo to Durand, 27 July 1870, cited Burne, MSS EUR D951/17.
2 Mayo to Disraeli, 2 May 1869, Mayo 35/53.
3 Mayo to Derby, 30 January 1870, Mayo 38/40.
4 Mayo to Disraeli, 30 May 1870, Mayo 39/152.
5 Mayo to Alison, 29 October 1871, Mayo 46/256.
6 Goldsmid, *Eastern Persia 1870–72*, p. liii.
7 Burne, MSS EUR D951/17.
8 Mayo to Argyll, 24 January 1872, Mayo 47/17.
9 Hunter, *Life* vol.I, p. 295.
10 Mayo to Argyll, 9 September 1870, Mayo 40/265.
11 Mayo to Argyll, 9 June 1871, Mayo 43/132.

12 Mayo to Argyll, 7 July 1871, Mayo 44/155.
13 Mayo to Argyll, 26 September 1871, Mayo 44/219.
14 Mayo to Argyll, 7 July 1869, Mayo 36/138.
15 Political and Secret Department Memoranda, vol. I, no. c41, part I.
16 Mayo to Buchanan, 26 September 1869, Mayo 36/254.
17 Forsyth, *Autobiography and Reminiscences*, p. 47.
18 *Ibid.*, p. 51.
19 *Ibid.*, p. 52.
20 Mayo to Alison 29 October 1871, Mayo 46/256.
21 Forsyth, *op. cit.*, p. 46.
22 Mayo to Argyll, 2 June 1869, Mayo 39/153.
23 Mayo to Argyll, 7 July, 1870, Mayo 40/191.
24 Burne to Forsyth, 14 January 1871, Mayo 9/VI (b).
25 Governor-General, Foreign Department minute, 29 December 1871, Mayo 7/IV.
26 Mayo to Chief Commissioner, Burma, 11 June 1869, Mayo 35/106.
27 *Friend of India*, 18 February 1872.
28 Viceroy, telegram, June 1870, Mayo 17/II.

CHAPTER 14

1 Quoted Temple, speech on Income Tax Bill, 6 March 1869. MSS EUR F86/89.
2 Chapman, no. 2848, 17 August 1870. Financial Letters and Enclosures Received from India, vol. 87.
3 Viceroy, speech in Legislative Council, March 1871, Mayo 13/II.
4 Temple, *Men and Events of My Time in India*, 1882, p. 374.
5 Mayo to Argyll, 17 May 1869, Mayo 35/64.
6 Mayo to Argyll, 9 March 1869, Mayo 34/76.
7 Mayo to Argyll, 24 August 1869, Mayo 36/216.
8 Mayo to Arbuthnot, 18 September 1869, Mayo 36/245.
9 Mayo to Temple, 5 August 1869, Mayo 36/183.
10 Mayo to Fitzgerald, 28 September 1869, Mayo 36/261.
11 Temple, speech in Legislative Council, 19 November 1869, MSS EUR F86/89.
12 Frere to Temple, 3 December 1869, MSS EUR F86/85.
13 Northcote to Temple, 25 February 1870. MSS EUR F86/85.
14 Mayo, minute of 16 July 1870, Mayo 13/II
15 Mayo to Napier, Madras, 20 November 1870, Mayo 41/325.
16 Resolution of Government of India. Financial Letters and Enclosures Received from India, vol. 90.
17 Mayo to Mansfield, 19 August 1870, Mayo 40/236.

18 Mayo to Arbuthnot, 15 March 1871, Mayo 13/II.
19 Chapman to Hunter, quoted Hunter, *Life of the Earl of Mayo*, vol. II, p. 297.
20 Mayo to Durand, 29 April 1870, Mayo 39/107.
21 Temple, speech on Income Tax Bill, 6 March 1869, MSS EUR F86/89.
22 Campbell, *Memoirs of My Indian Career*, vol. II, p. 297.
23 Strachey, *India, Its Administration and Progress*, 3rd ed. p. 166.
24 Mayo to Frere, 3 June 1870, Mayo 39/156.
25 Mayo to Napier, Madras, 20 November 1870, quoted Burne, *Letters*, etc. p. 157. MSS EUR D951/17.
26 Mayo to Napier, Madras, 4 January 1871, Mayo 42/7.
27 Mayo to Argyll, 14 July 1870, Mayo 40/202.
28 Mayo to Argyll, 4 August 1870, Mayo 40/233.
29 Viceroy, minute, 16 July 1870, Mayo 13/II.
30 Mayo to Temple, 24 March, 1871, Mayo 42/82.
31 Argyll to Temple, 9 May 1873. MSS EUR F86/85.
32 Temple, *op. cit.*, p. 389.
33 Richard Strachey, 2 April 1870, to Mrs Strachey, enclosing the original doodle, MSS EUR F127/319.
34 Mayo to Argyll, 4 December 1871, Mayo 46/283.
35 Northcote to Mayo, 14 March 1869, Mayo 59/xxxvi 87.
36 Halifax to Mayo, 4 November 1869, Mayo 54/93.
37 Temple, *op. cit.*, p. 384.
38 Burne, *Letters*, etc. MSS EUR D951/157.

CHAPTER 15

1 Governor-General, memorandum 18 September 1870, Mayo 2/II.
2 Mayo to Argyll, 9 September 1870, Mayo 40/265.
3 *The Pioneer*, 3 April 1871.
4 Gopal, *British Policy in India 1858–1905*, p. 99.
5 Mayo to Argyll, 28 July 1871, Mayo 44/173.
6 Mayo to Davies, 6 August 1871, Mayo 44/179.
7 Mayo to Argyll, 24 January 1872, Mayo 47/17.
8 Forsyth, *Autobiography*, p. 36.
9 Secretary of State to Government of India, 18 July 1872, Parliamentary papers vol. 45, 1872.
10 Stephen to Mayo, 31 May 1870, Mayo 29/II.
11 Mayo to Grey, 9 August 1870, and to Durand, 14 August 1870, Mayo 40/220 & 231.
12 Mayo to Muir, 14 November 1870, Mayo 41/312.

13 Mayo to Argyll, 12 August 1870, Mayo 40/229.
14 Mayo to Argyll, 10 January 1871, Mayo 42/24.
15 Mayo to Burne, 30 August 1871, Mayo 28/I.
16 Viceroy to Queen Victoria, 8 August 1871, Mayo 44/181.
17 Calcutta Muhammadan Society, quoted Hunter, *Our Indian Musulmans*, Appendix, p. 215.
18 O'Kinealy, quoted Hunter, *op. cit.*, p. 147.
19 Hunter, *op. cit.*, p. 167.
20 Mayo to Campbell, 22 September 1871, Mayo 44/216.
21 Mayo to Campbell, 8 October 1871, Mayo 45/235.
22 Secretary N. W. Govt, minute 28 October 1871, Mayo 28/I.
23 Bayley to Mayo, 23 September 1871, Mayo 28/I.
24 Temple, *Memoirs*, pp. 386–7, and Burne, *Memories*, pp. 123–4.
25 Mayo to Argyll, 26 September 1871, Mayo 44/219.

CHAPTER 16

1 Karens' Address, January 1872, Mayo 19/VII.
2 Address at Moulmein, February 1872, Mayo 19/VII.
3 Mayo to Strachey 21 March 1869, Mayo 35/205.
4 Burne, undated memorandum, Mayo 18/V.
5 Rogers, report no. 2064, 7 June 1871, Mayo 19/VI.
6 Burne, *op. cit.*
7 *Ibid.*
8 *Ibid.*
9 Wilson, *Why Was Lord Mayo Assassinated?* 1872.
10 Campbell, *Memories*, vol. II, p. 223.
11 Burne, *Memories*, p. 134.
12 *Friend of India*, 16 February 1872.
13 Stewart to Burne, 14 March 1872, quoted Burne, *Memories*, p. 135.
14 Strachey to Burne, 14 February 1872. Telegram 4005, Mayo 18/IV.
15 Strachey to Burne, 14 February 1872, Telegram 3909, Mayo 18/IV.
16 Strachey to Burne, 15 February 1872, Telegram 4019, Mayo 18/IV.
17 Stephen, 16 February 1872, letter to *The Times*, 12 March 1872.

EPILOGUE

1 Strachey, minute on Mayo's administration, 30 April 1872, Home Dept Public Proceedings, May 1872, nos 188 & 189.
2 Quoted Hunter, *Life* vol. II, p. 226.
3 Argyll, February 1872, *Autobiography and Memoirs*, p. 279.
4 Mayo to Durand, 20 April 1870, Mayo 39/107.

5 Temple, *Memoirs* p. 378.
6 Hume to Northbrook, 1 August 1872, Northbrook papers, vol. 13.
7 Mayo to Argyll, 19 April 1869, Mayo 35/37.
8 Bence-Jones, *The Viceroys of India*, p. 79.
9 Northbrook to Grant Duff, 9 September 1872, Northbrook papers, vol. 20, part 2.
10 Secretary of State to Governor-General, 6 August 1875, Northbrook papers, vol. 12.
11 Executive Council minute 30 March 1876, Parliamentary papers, vol. 4, (1878–79), no. 240.
12 Salisbury to Northbrook, 19 November 1875, Northbrook papers, vol. 12.
13 Mayo to Lawrence, 19 May 1870, Mayo 39/132.

Bibliography

MANUSCRIPT SOURCES

(i) *Mayo papers (Richard Southwell Bourke, sixth Earl of Mayo)*

The Mayo collection referring to his time as Viceroy (referred to in the Notes as 'Mayo') is in the Cambridge University Library (Add 7490). Papers referring mainly to his time as Chief Secretary for Ireland are in the National Library of Ireland, Dublin (MSS 11,043–11,953) and in the Public Record Office of Northern Ireland, Belfast (MIC 337/1).

(ii) *Viceroys and Governors-General*

Lawrence papers (Sir John Lawrence, first Baron Lawrence) MSS EUR F90.

Northbrook papers (Thomas George, first Earl of Northbrook) MSS EUR C144.

Both of these collections are in the India Office Library.

(iii) *Secretaries of State for India*

Halifax papers (Sir Charles Wood, first Viscount Halifax) MSS EUR F78, India Office Library.

Iddesleigh papers (Sir Stafford Northcote, first Earl of Iddesleigh), British Library, Iddesleigh papers.

Argyll papers (George Douglas Campbell, eighth Duke of Argyll) India Office Records.

(iv) *Contemporaries of Lord Mayo in India*

Papers from the collections of:

Sir Charles Umpherston Aitchison MSS EUR F166.

Sir Owen Tudor Burne MSS EUR D951.

Sir George Campbell MSS EUR E349.

Sir Robert Napier, first Baron Napier of Magdala MSS EUR F114.

Sir Richard Strachey MSS EUR F127.

Sir Richard Temple MSS EUR F86.

All of these collections are in the India Office Library.

OFFICIAL RECORDS

Collections to Financial Despatches to India, vols. 64–78, 1869–72.
Collections to Indian Political Despatches, vols. 101–137, 1869–73.
Political and Secret Despatches to India, vol. 5, 1858–72.
Secret Letters and Enclosures Received from India, vols. 4–11, 1869–72.
All of these are in the India Office Library.

PARLIAMENTARY PAPERS

Parliamentary papers, vols. 46 and 47, 1868–9; vols. 51 and 53, 1870; vols. 50 and 51, 1871; vols. 44 and 45, 1872; and vol. 63, 1877.
Hansard

NEWSPAPERS AND PERIODICALS

The Times.
The Times of India.
The Friend of India.
The Pioneer.
The Madras Times.
Blackwood's Magazine, 1872.
Punch.

PUBLICATIONS

Marquis de Custine, *La Russie en 1839*, Paris, 1843; English edition, translated Kohler, 1953.
R. S. Bourke (later sixth Earl of Mayo), *St Petersburg and Moscow*, 1846.
W. W. Hunter, *Our Indian Mussulmans*, 1871.
J. Wilson, 'Was Lord Mayo Assassinated?', pamphlet, 1872.
Sir Douglas Forsyth, *Report of a Mission to Yarkund*, 1875.
W. W. Hunter, *Life of the Earl of Mayo*, 1875.
O. T. Burne, *Letters on the Indian Administration of the Earl of Mayo*; printed 'for private research' at the Private Secretary's Office Press, Simla, 1877. A copy in the India Office Library, MSS EUR D951/17.
Sir Frederick Goldsmid, *Eastern Persia*, 1876.
General Albert Fytche, *Burma Past and Present*, 1878.
A. O. Hume, *Agricultural Reform*, pamphlet, 1879.
Sir John and R. Strachey, *Finances and Public Works of India*, 1882.

H. M. Durand, *Life of Sir H. M. Durand*, 1883.
Sir R. Temple, *Men and Events of My Time in India*, 1882.
C. T. Buckland, *Sketches of Social Life in India*, 1884.
R. Bosworth Smith, *Life of Lord Lawrence*, 1885.
L. J. Trotter, *India under Queen Victoria*, 1886.
Sir Douglas Forsyth, *Autobiography and Reminiscences*, 1887.
Sir John Strachey, *India, Its Administration and Progress*, 1888; 4th edition, 1911.
W. W. Hunter, *Earl of Mayo* (Rulers of India series), 1891.
Sir Charles Aitchison, *Lord Lawrence*, (Rulers of India series), 1892.
Sir George Campbell, *Memoirs of My Indian Career*, 1893.
D. Martineau, *Life and Correspondence of Sir Bartle Frere*, 1895.
F. H. Skrine, *Life of Sir W. W. Hunter*, 1901.
Duchess of Argyll, *Autobiography and Memoirs of the 8th Duke of Argyll*, 1906.
Sir Owen Burne, *Memories*, 1907.
Sir W. Lee-Warner, *Memoir of Field Marshal Norman*, 1908.
Sir W. Lee-Warner, *The Native States of India*, 1910.
J. H. Rivett-Carnac, *Many Memories*, 1910.
Sir W. Wedderburn, *Allan Octavian Hume*, 1913.
7th Earl of Mayo, *History of the Kildare Hunt*, 1913.
H. H. Dodwell, ed., *Cambridge History of India*, vol. VI, 1922.
Sir Courtenay Ilbert, *The Government of India*, 1922.
V. A. Smith, ed., *Oxford History of India*, 1923.
Hon. J. W. Fortescue, *History of the British Army*, vol. XIII, 1930.
H. D. Napier, *Letters of Lord Napier of Magdala Concerning Abyssinia, India etc.*, 1936.
D. Kincaid, *British Social Life in India 1608–1937*, 1938.
Viscount Mersey, *The Viceroys*, 1949.
C. Woodham-Smith, *Florence Nightingale*, 1950.
P. Woodruff, *The Men Who Ruled India*, 1954.
Amba Prasad, *Indian Railways*, 1960.
Michael Maclagan, *'Clemency Canning'*, 1962.
C. Woodham-Smith, *The Great Hunger*, 1962.
G. J. Alder, *British India's Northern Frontier Policy 1865–95*, 1963.
S. Gopal, *British Policy in India 1858–1905*, 1965.
J. C. Beckett, *The Making of Modern Ireland 1603–1923*, 1966.
L. Dupree, *Afghanistan*, 1973.
J. Morris, *Heaven's Command*, 1973.
T. Desmond Williams, ed., *Secret Societies in Ireland*, 1973.
T. W. Moody, ed., *A New History of Ireland*, 1976.
Ian Copland, *The British Raj and the Indian Princes*, Bombay, 1982.

Mark Bence-Jones, *The Viceroys of India*, 1982.
E. Hobsbawn, ed., *The Invention of Tradition*, 1983.
G. Pottinger, *The Afghan Connection*, 1983.
J. O. Ranelagh, *A Short History of Ireland*, 1983.

Index

(Titles and ranks are the highest eventually reached)

Abdulla Jan, son of Sher Ali, 140, 149, 197
Abdur Rahman, Afghan chief, 144, 152
Aberdare, Lord, *see* Henry Austin Bruce
A'Court, William, 1st Baron Heytesbury, 48, 57
Adolphus Frederick, Duke of Cambridge, 43, 99, 114, 117
Afghanistan, first Afghan war, 57, 60, 70, 113
Afghanistan, Mayo's policy towards, 136–45, 149–50, 198
Afzul Khan, brother of Sher Ali, 137–8
Ajmere College, 131, 195
Aitchison, Sir Charles Umpherston, 132, 135, 181–2
Alfred Ernest Albert, Duke of Edinburgh, 48, 87, 98, 130; invited to be King of Hellenes, 100; 1867 world tour, 102, 180; Calcutta, arrival and festivities, 104–9; Star of India investiture, 107–8; opens railway at Jubbulpore, 109; big-game hunting, 109; press comments on Indian tour, 110–11; marries Grand Duchess Marie Alexandrovna, 100
Allahabad, disturbance at, 170
Allen, William, 37
Alwar, State of, 128–9, 196
Amballa, Durbar at, 85, 139, 140–5, 198
Amherst, Earl, *see* William Pitt
Amir Khan, Wahabi, 176–7, 179, 187
Andaman Islands: penal settlement, history, 183; Mayo's visit, 181–6
Anstey, Thomas Chisholm, 176
Arbuthnot, Sir Alexander John, 49, 82
Argyll, Duke of, *see* George Douglas Campbell
Auckland, Earl of, *see* George Eden
Azim Khan, brother of Sher Ali, 137–9

Bahadur Shah, 61, 125
Bareilly, riots at, 172
Baring, Thomas George, 1st Earl of Northbrook, 44, 49, 76, 94, 148, 168, 174; appointed Viceroy, 191–2; resignation, 191, 195; comparison with Mayo, 195–9
Barlow, Sir George Hilaro, 55
Baroda, Gaekwar of, 107; deposition of, 195–6
Barrackpore, Residence at, 59–60, 69
Barrett, Michael, 37
Bayley, Sir Edward Clive, 44, 179–80
Beaconsfield, Earl of, *see* Disraeli
Bence-Jones, Mark, 9
Bengal, Nazim, Nawab of, 127
Bentinck, Lord George, 28
Bentinck, Lord William Cavendish, 56
Bentine, Mr, 108–9
Bessborough, Earl of, *see* John William Ponsonby
Bhopal, Begum of, 107, 130
Bhopal, Sikander Begum of, 130
Blackwood, Frederick Temple Hamilton-Temple, 1st Marquess of Dufferin and Ava, 71, 191–2
Bloomfield, John Arthur Douglas, 2nd Baron Bloomfield, 99
Boehm, Sir Joseph Edgar, 189
Bokhara, Khan of, 152

Bourchier, Major-General, 124
Bourke, Anne Charlotte Jocelyn, wife of 5th Earl of Mayo, 11
Bourke, Blanche Julia Wyndham, wife of 6th Earl of Mayo, 32, 69, 82, 104, 184, 186, 188
Bourke, Charles, Inspector General of Irish Prisons, 14
Bourke, Dermot Robert Wyndham, son of 6th Earl of Mayo, 33, 98–9
Bourke, Edward Roden, 14, 45, 184
Bourke, Revd George Winfield, 14
Bourke, John, 4th Earl of Mayo, 12; Colonel, Kildare Militia, 13; subject of poem by W. M. Praed, 13
Bourke, John Jocelyn, 14, 34
Bourke, John of Kill and Monycrower, 1st Earl of Mayo, 12; Member of Parliament, 12; Irish Privy Councillor, 12; Baron Naas, 12; Viscount Mayo of Monycrower, 12; promoted Earl of Mayo, 12
Bourke, Joseph, 3rd Earl of Mayo and Bishop of Tuam, 12
Bourke, Richard, Bishop of Waterford and Lismore, 13
Bourke, Richard Southwell, 6th Earl of Mayo: early years at Hayes, 13–15; religious upbringing, 15; family visits to Europe, 15–16; 'an old fox hunter', 16; captain, Kildare Militia, 16; Trinity College, Dublin, 16; expedition to Russia, 18–26; *St Petersburg and Moscow* published, comments therein, 18–26; relief work during Irish famine, 29; MP for Kildare, 30–1; maiden speech in Parliament, 31; marriage, 32; becomes Lord Naas, as father becomes 5th Earl of Mayo, 32; Chief Secretary for Ireland, 9, 33, 34, 36–41; MP for Coleraine, 33; MP for Cockermouth, 33, 42; Master, Kildare Hunt, 9, 34; succeeds as 6th Earl of Mayo, 38; attitude to Fenian movement, 38–9, 41; important speech on state of Ireland, 39; appointed Viceroy of India, 41; preliminary work in London, 43–4; appoints Burne to be Private Secretary, 45; voyage to India, 46; meets Lesseps at Suez, 46; arrives Bombay, 49; arrives Calcutta; ceremonies, 51, 65–7
As Viceroy: Viceregal authority, 52–3; initial energy and extensive travels, 73, 76, 81
Policy on: railways, 84–7; agriculture, 90–2; education, 92–5; legislation, 97–8; military expenditure, 112–19; feudatory states, 133, 195; finance, 160
Individual financial questions: Alteration of Temple's budget, 161; Provincial Services Scheme, 162–5, 193; 1870 Financial Resolution, 164; Income Tax, 160–1, 165–8, 170; opium revenue, 166
Foreign policy towards: Afghanistan, 136–45, 149–50, 198; external states, 135–6, 146, 156; Persia, 147–8; Russia, 150–2; Turkestan, 153–6; Burma, 156–7, 182
Opens Chandah coal mine, 88; seeks commission for son, 98–9; keeps racing stable, 99–100; organises Star of India investiture, 105; as an orator, 110; meets expenses of Duke of Edinburgh's visit, 110; considers position of C-in-C, 118; attends 1872 Delhi manoeuvres, 121; opposed to punitive expeditions, 122; authorises Looshai expedition, 124; vigilance over Kathiawar, 128; intervention at Alwar, 128, 196; founds Ajmere College, 131, 195; attitude to Wahabis, 175–80; Wahabi trials, 175–7; assassination of Chief Justice Norman, 178–80; mentioned, 191–3; comparison with Northbrook, 195–9
Assassination: arrives Andaman Islands, 184; assassinated,

185–6; reasons for assassination, theories, 186–8; body brought to Calcutta, 188–9; funeral and burial, 189; tributes, 190–1
Bourke, Robert, MP, 14
Bourke, Robert, 5th Earl of Mayo, 11, 13, 16, 32
British Relief Association, 29
Brownlow, Major-General, 124
Bruce, Henry Austin, 1st Baron Aberdare, 45
Bruce, James, 8th Earl of Elgin, 41, 61, 63, 67, 85, 126, 129
Buchanan, Sir Andrew, 150, 152
de Burgh, Hubert, 11
de Burgh, Richard, 11
de Burgh, William Fitzadalm, 11
Burke, Edmund, 54
Burma, 156–7; Mayo's visit, 182; Northbrook sends mission, 196
Burne, Evelyne, wife of Sir O. T. Burne, 45, 104–5
Burne, Sir Owen Tudor, 64, 69, 71, 74, 81, 88, 103–5, 110, 129, 169; early service in India, etc., 45; appointed Mayo's Private Secretary, 44–5; with Mayo in Andamans, 181–6; account of assassination, 185–8
Butt, Isaac, Irish lawyer, 176

Cadell, Major, Political Agent, 129
Calcutta, ambience in 1869, 65–6
Calcutta, Government House, 66, 68–9
Calcutta University, 93
Cambridge, Duke of, *see* Adolphus, Frederick
Campbell, General Sir Archibald, 56
Campbell, Field-Marshal Sir Colin, Baron Clyde, 61, 107, 113
Campbell, Sir George, Lt-Governor Bengal, 42, 57, 59, 74, 77–8, 94, 124–5, 165, 185
Campbell, George Douglas, 8th Duke of Argyll, Secretary of State for India, 10, 48–9, 75, 80, 84–6, 91, 104, 114–15, 127–9, 136–44, 149–50, 160, 168, 173, 190, 194
Canning, Charles John, Earl Canning, 41, 45, 59, 63–4, 67–9, 72, 83, 106, 129, 139; policy during and after the Mutiny, 60–2; July 1857 Resolution, 62; Queen's Proclamation, November 1858, 62
Canning, Charlotte, wife of Charles John, Earl Canning, 59–60, 68–9
Cayley, Dr Henry, 153
Cecil, Robert Arthur Talbot Gascoyne, 3rd Marquess of Salisbury, 48, 77, 87, 191, 194–7
Chamberlain, Field-Marshal Sir Neville Bowles, 103, 109, 131, 175
Chandah coal mine, 88
Chapman, R. B., 164
Chevalier, Nicholas, 111
Chillianwalla, 13, 58
Clarendon, Earl of, *see* George William Frederick Villiers
Clerk, Sir George Russell, 44
Clive, Robert, Baron Clive, 53–4, 65
Clifford, Lady de, 17
Clyde, Lord, *see* Field-Marshal Sir Colin Campbell
Cockburn, Rear-Admiral, Naval C-in-C, India, 181
Combermere, Viscount, *see* Field-Marshal Sir Stapleton Cotton
Corn Laws, repeal of, 27–8
Cooper's Hill, College at, 83
Cornwallis, Charles, 1st Marquess, 54–5, 67
Cotton, Sir Arthur Thomas, 43
Cotton, Field-Marshal Sir Stapleton, Viscount Combermere, 107
Cotton, Lt-General Sir Sydney, 175
Cranbrook, Earl of, *see* Gathorne-Hardy, Gathorne
Cullen, Archbishop, 37
Curzon, George Nathaniel, Marquess Curzon, 9, 118
Curzon, Roper, Andamans prisoner, 186
Custine, Astolphe, Marquis de, 18, 22–5

Dalhousie, Marquess of, *see* James Andrew Broun Ramsay
Daly, General Sir Henry Dermot, 133
Daunt, O'Neill, candidate at Kildare election, 30
Davies, Sir Robert, 78
Deasy, Timothy, 37
Derby, Earl of, *see* Edward George Geoffrey Smith Stanley
Dewan Sorai, boar hunt at, 109
Dharmsala, Lord Elgin's tomb at, 82
Disraeli, Benjamin, 1st Earl of Beaconsfield, 9, 28, 40–1, 47–8, 76, 146, 191, 198
Dufferin and Ava, Marquess of, *see* Frederick Temple Hamilton-Temple Blackwood
Durand, Major-General Sir Henry Marion, military member of Executive Council, 10, 16, 44, 64, 70, 75, 108, 113–18, 134, 137, 142, 192; Lt-Governor Punjab, 76, 163, 176; death, 78
Durbar, history and significance, 105–6

East India Company, 53–4, 105, 126, 133, 135, 158
Eden, Emily, sister of George Eden, 57, 59–60, 140
Eden, George, 1st Earl of Auckland, 57, 70, 140, 149
Edinburgh, Duke of, *see* Alfred Ernest Albert
Edwardes, Sir Herbert Benjamin, 175
Elgin, Earl of, *see* James Bruce
Ellenborough, Earl of, *see* Edward Law
Ellenborough, Jane Elisabeth Digby, Countess of, 57–8
Elliot, Sir Gilbert, 1st Earl of Minto, 55
Ellis, Sir Barrow Helbert, 74, 181–2

Fayrer, Sir Joseph, Surgeon-General, 189
Fenian Brotherhood, *see* Ireland, political organisations
Fitzgeorge, Lieutenant, 108
Fitzgerald, Sir William Robert Seymour Vesey, Governor Bombay, 49, 77, 160, 163
Forsyth, Sir Thomas Douglas, 86, 153, 173–4; mission to St Petersburg, 151–2; missions to Turkestan, 155–6, 196; mission to Burma, 196
Fowler, Sir John, 85–7
Francis, Sir Philip, 54
Frere, Sir Henry Bartle Edward, 43, 47, 85, 119, 148, 162
Fytche, Major-General, 172

Gathorne-Hardy, Gathorne, 1st Earl of Cranbrook, 189
Gholam Mahomed, Prince, 130
Gladstone, William Ewart, 40, 47–8, 191
Goldsmid, Major-General Sir Frederick John, 147
Gortschakoff, Prince, 152
Gough, Field-Marshal, Sir Hugh, 1st Viscount Gough, 58, 107
Government of India: Executive Council, 72, 194–5; individual departments, 72–3; Legislative Council, 73; legislative process, 73, 95–7; Presidencies and Provinces, 77
Graine-ni-Mhaile, Granny O'Malley, 12
Grant, General Sir James Hope, 45
Grey, Sir William, Lt-Governor Bengal, 77, 79, 124, 175–6
Gwalior, Maharaja Scindia of, 106, 129–30, 142, 195

Halifax, Viscount, *see* Charles Wood
Hardinge, Field-Marshal Sir Henry, 1st Viscount Hardinge, 58, 67
Harris, George Francis Robert, 3rd Baron Harris, 107
Hastings, Francis Rawdon, 2nd Earl of Moira and 1st Marquess of Hastings, 9, 56, 69
Hastings, Warren, 54–5
Havelock, Major-General Sir Henry, 61
Hayes estate, Meath, 13–14, 29, 34

Heytesbury, Lord, *see* William A'Court
Houghton, Lord, *see* Richard Monckton Milnes
Hume, Allan Octavian, 91–2, 192–3
Hunter, Sir William Wilson, 77; biography of Mayo, 9, 19, 26, 30, 96, 148; treatise on Muslims, 177
Hushmadad Khan, alleged Wahabi, 176–7, 179, 187
Hyderabad, Nazim of, 106, 195

Iddesleigh, Earl of, *see* Stafford Henry Northcote
India Act, 1784, 154
India Council (at Westminster), 85, 196
India, Government of, *see* Government of India
Indore, Maharaja Holkar of, 106, 129, 142, 195
Ireland: 1845–51 famine, 27, 32; British Relief Association, 29; comments by Trevelyan, 36; Corn Laws repealed, 27–8; Mayo's relief work, 29;
Political organisations: Fenian Brotherhood, 36–41; Irish Confederation, 31; Irish Republican Brotherhood, 36; Young Ireland Party, 31, 36
Individuals, *see under* W. Allen, M. Barrett, T. Deasy, T. J. Kelly, M. Larkin, W. Smith O'Brian, J. O'Mahony, E. O'Meagher, J. Stephen
Ishaq Khan, Afghan chief, 144

Jaipur, Maharaja of, 104, 128, 130
Jascote, tribal raid at, 122
Jhansi, Rani of, 125
Jind, Maharaja of, 139, 173
Jodhpur, Maharaja of, 127, 132
Johnstown, Mayo buried at, 189
Jung Bahadur, 82
Jung, Sir Salar, Hyderabad Minister, 87

Kashmir, Maharaja of, 81, 106, 153–6, 173, 195
Kathiawar, 128, 131
Kaye, Sir John, historian, 69
Keatinge, Colonel, Political Agent, 128; Chief Commissioner, Central Provinces, 163
Kelly, Thomas J., 37
Kennedy, Robert, Secretary, Kildare Hunt, 35
Khamgaon railway line, 85
Khelat, Khan of, 148, 182, 196
Kildare Hunt, 9, 16; Mayo appointed Master, 34; Laragh run, 35
Kildare, Marquess of, candidate at Kildare election, 30–1
Kohat, durbar at, 81
Kukas, Sikh sect, 172; early history, 172; leader, Guru Ram Singh, 172–4; Amritsar and Raikote raids, 173; attack on Malerkotha, 173

Laing, Samuel, 158, 163
Larkin, Michael, 37
Law, Edward, 1st Baron Ellenborough, 57, 62, 108, 113, 142
Lawrence, John Laird Mair, 1st Baron Lawrence, 41, 43–4, 48, 58, 66–8, 76, 83, 97, 102, 107, 112, 126, 137–45, 194; early career and service during Mutiny, 63; annexation of Bhutan, 64; 'masterly inactivity', 64; Afghan policy, defects, 137–8; negative attitude to Turkestan, 153–4; financial policy, 163–5
Lawrence, Major-General Stringer, 53
Lesseps, Ferdinand de, 46–7
Looshai expedition, 124, 182
Lucie Smith, General, 88
Lytton, Edward Robert Bulwer, 1st Earl of Lytton, 194, 196, 198

Macaulay, Thomas Babington, 1st Baron Macaulay, 56
MacLeod, Sir Donald Friell, Lt-Governor Punjab, 66, 78, 139, 142, 153
MacNaghten, Sir William Hay, 177
Macnaughton, Chester, 131
Macpherson, Sir John, 54

Mahomed, Dost, Afghan ruler, 57, 136–7, 141
Maine, Sir Henry James Sumner, 75, 95
Mallet, Sir Louis, 194
Mansfield, General Sir William Rose, 1st Baron Sandhurst, 10, 16, 66, 75–6, 113–19, 164
Martini Henry rifle, 119
Massey, William Nathaniel, 43, 158, 161, 163
Mayo, Countess of (wife of 6th Earl), *see* Bourke, Blanche Julia Wyndham
Mayo, 1st, 3rd, 4th, 5th and 6th Earls of, *see* Bourke, John of Kill and Monycrower, Joseph, John, Robert, and Richard Southwell
Mekram boundary dispute, 147
Metcalfe, Charles Theophilus, 1st Baron Metcalfe, 56–7
Merewether, Sir William Lockyer, 148
Milnes, Richard Monckton, 1st Baron Houghton, 30
Minto, Earl of, *see* Elliot, Sir Gilbert
Mirza Shadir, Turkestan envoy, 155–6
Moira, Earl of, *see* Francis Rawdon Hastings
Moradabad, reported rebellion at, 171
Moriarty, Bishop of Kerry, 37
Morris, Jan, writer, 70–1
Moulvie Abdoolah Wilyatee, assassin of Chief Justice Norman, 179–80
Muir, Sir William, Lt-Governor North West Provinces, 66, 78–9, 94, 163
Mutiny, Indian, 52; causes, 59–60; course of, 61; military strength before and after, 112

Nabha, Maharaja of, 139, 173
Nadir Shah, 53
Nana Sahib, 125
Napier, Field-Marshal Robert Cornelis, 1st Baron Napier of Magdala, 10, 16, 46–50, 112, 114–19, 129; relationship with Mayo, 76
Napier and Ettrick, Sir Francis, 9th Baron Napier (Scottish) and 1st Baron Ettrick, Governor of Madras, 50, 77, 90, 94, 97, 119, 163; Acting Viceroy, 193
Nicholas, Czar of Russia, 9, 21–2, 152
Nicholson, Brigadier-General John, 61
Nightingale, Florence, 30, 44, 120
Norman, J.P., Chief Justice, assassinated, 174–80, 186–7
Norman, Field-Marshal Sir Henry Wylie, 75–6, 114, 184
Northbrook, Earl of, *see* Thomas George Baring
Northcote, Sir Stafford Henry, 1st Earl of Iddesleigh, Secretary of State for India, 41–2, 84, 138, 162, 165, 169
Nur Muhammad Shah, Afghan Minister, 143, 197

O'Brien, William Smith, 31–2
Ochterlony, Major-General Sir David, 56
O'Connell, Daniel, 27–8
O'Connell, John, candidate at Kildare election, 30
O'Farrell, Henry James, would-be assassin, 102, 180
O'Mahony, John, 36
O'Meagher, Edward, 37
opium revenue, 165
Outram, Lt-General Sir James, 61, 107

Palmerston estate, 16, 29, 34
Palmerston, Viscount, *see* Henry John Temple
Palumpore, durbar at, 81
Patiala, Maharaja of, 87, 107, 130, 139–40, 173
Paul, Mr Justice, 179
Paxton, Mrs, witness at Allahabad, 171
Peel, Sir Robert, 27–9, 80
Pitt, William, Earl Amherst, 56, 70
Pollock, Field-Marshal Sir George, 57, 107
Ponsonby, John William, 4th Earl of Bessborough, 30